DIVINATIONS: REREADING LATE ANCIENT RELIGION

Series Editors: Daniel Boyarin, Virginia Burrus, Derek Krueger

A complete list of books in the series is available from the publisher.

Sefer Yeṣirah and Its Contexts

Other Jewish Voices

Tzahi Weiss

PENN

UNIVERSITY OF PENNSYLVANIA PRESS

PHILADELPHIA

Published by
University of Pennsylvania Press
Philadelphia, Pennsylvania 19104-4112
www.upenn.edu/pennpress

Printed in the United States of America on acid-free paper

1 3 5 7 9 10 8 6 4 2

Library of Congress Cataloging-in-Publication Data

Names: Weiss, Tzahi, author.

Title: Sefer Yeṣirah and its contexts : other Jewish voices / Tzahi Weiss.

Other titles: Divinations.

Description: 1st edition. | Philadelphia : University of Pennsylvania Press, [2018] | Series: Divinations: rereading late ancient religion | Includes bibliographical references and index.

Identifiers: LCCN 2017034900 | ISBN 9780812249903 (hardcover : alk. paper)

Subjects: LCSH: Sefer Yezirah. | Cabala—Early works to 1800. | Jewish cosmology.

Classification: LCC BM525.A419 W45 2018 | DDC 296.1/6—dc23

LC record available at https://lccn.loc.gov/2017034900

To Judith, Miriam, Sarah, and Rachel
"Who hew out great columns from intangible air"

Contents

A Note on Transliteration of the Hebrew Alphabet

	Name of the letter	*Transliteration within a word*	*Transliteration of a sole letter*
א	*alef*	*ʾ, a*	*a*
ב	*bet*	*b, v*	*b, v*
ג	*gimel*	*g*	*g*
ד	*dalet*	*d*	*d*
ה	*he*	*h*	*h*
ו	*waw*	*w*	*w*
ז	*zayin*	*z*	*z*
ח	*ḥet*	*ḥ*	*ḥ*
ט	*ṭet*	*ṭ*	*ṭ*
י	*yod*	*y*	*y*
כ	*kaf*	*k, kh*	*k, ḵ*
ל	*lamed*	*l*	*l*
מ	*mem*	*m*	*m*
נ	*nun*	*n*	*n*
ס	*samek*	*s*	*s*
ע	*ʿayin*	*ʿ*	*ʿ*
פ	*pe*	*p, f*	*p, f*
צ	*ṣade*	*ṣ*	*ṣ*
ק	*qof*	*q*	*q*
ר	*resh*	*r*	*r*
ש	*shin*	*sh*	*š*
ת	*taw*	*t*	*t*

Introduction

Sefer Yeṣirah is one of the most enigmatic, yet influential, texts in the history of Jewish thought. The text is striking for its rhythmic phrasing and evocative language; it connects the essence of language with the foundations of the world. This short treatise has fascinated Jewish thinkers and kabbalists, as well as Western thinkers and writers, from Gottfried Wilhelm Leibniz to Umberto Eco and Jorge Luis Borges.

Because of its unique style as well as the fact that it does not explicitly refer to other Jewish sources and was not quoted by other Jewish sources in late antiquity, it is difficult, if not impossible, to contextualize. When I present *Sefer Yeṣirah* for the first time to my students, I joke that after about 150 years of scholarship on *Sefer Yeṣirah*, we know almost everything about this book except for four minor issues: Who wrote it? Where and when was it written? What does it mean? And what was its "original" version? Scholars disagree about the time and context of the book, proposing first-century CE Hellenism,[1] the rabbinic sphere of the second to sixth centuries CE,[2] Neoplatonism of the fourth or fifth centuries CE,[3] fifth to the sixth century CE Palestine,[4] the Syriac-Christian milieu of the sixth to seventh century,[5] or the ninth-century Islamic world.[6] This diversity reflects what seems to be an inherent and radical inability to contextualize *Sefer Yeṣirah*.

Sefer Yeṣirah appeared in the Jewish world at the beginning of the tenth century. In this period, it was already interpreted as a canonical treatise by leading rabbinic figures living on three continents, and it had many different versions. The surprising appearance of *Sefer Yeṣirah*, as if out of the blue, is the result of its absence from the Jewish world before the tenth century, along with its immediate acceptance. Furthermore, *Sefer Yeṣirah* had a remarkable reception in Jewish milieus from the tenth century on. Joseph Dan describes the two main stages of its impact on the Jewish world—stages with little in common:[7] in the first, between the tenth and the twelfth centuries, it was read by at least five commentators as a sort of philosophical or scientific text.[8] In the second, from the end of the twelfth century on, it was interpreted by mystics and kabbalists as a mystical, mythical, and magical treatise. These facts about *Sefer Yeṣirah*'s reception raise essential questions: Where was *Sefer Yeṣirah* before its canonization in the tenth-century rabbinic world? Why was *Sefer Yeṣirah* initially understood as a philosophical and scientific treatise, and later viewed as the canonical composition of Jewish mysticism?

My main goal in this book is to demonstrate that the evolution of *Sefer Yeṣirah* and its reception have something in common: they point us to an alternative picture of the history of Jewish thought in late antiquity and the early Middle Ages. I claim that *Sefer Yeṣirah* is a rare surviving Jewish treatise written and edited around the seventh century by Jews who were familiar with Syriac Christianity and were far from the main circles of rabbinic learning.[9] *Sefer Yeṣirah* does not show strong awareness of the articulations, insights, or even the existence of the rabbinic world. *Sefer Yeṣirah*, to put it slightly differently, conveys much information about its intellectual world in terms of language, physiology, astrology, and cosmology. We have no reason to assume that the text tries to conceal its context; it is more reasonable to assume that our information about its world is limited. *Sefer Yeṣirah* is a unique, fascinating, and information-packed trace of another and unknown Jewish environment.[10] Similarly, in the second part of the book, when we follow the mystical, magical, or mythical ways in which *Sefer Yeṣirah* was understood before the end of the twelfth century, a trace of another Jewish milieu beyond the scope of the medieval canon of familiar rabbinic figures comes into view. An investigative integration of the above hypotheses can help us outline the "margins of Jewish mysticism," a Jewish mystical thought that was not included in the classical canon of Jewish thought, for various historical reasons, but that was very important for the development of a Jewish horizon of thought.

My conclusions, as with any scholarly work, are based on the work of other scholars, and references to their works are to be found throughout the book. I want to mention the works of four authors who particularly helped me reach my conclusions. Shlomo Pines's paper on the similarities between the first chapter of *Sefer Yeṣirah* and the Pseudo-Clementine homilies brings important evidence to bear in support of the possibility of a Christian-Syriac context for *Sefer Yeṣirah*.[11] Guy Stroumsa, in his article about a possible Zoroastrian origin to the perception of the *sefirot in Sefer Yeṣirah*, referred to the importance of the sixth-century treatise *The Mysteries of the Greek Letters*, which, as I will demonstrate, can be of much help in contextualizing *Sefer Yeṣirah*.[12] Haggai Ben-Shammai's article on the reception of *Sefer Yeṣirah* claims convincingly that Saadya's aims in interpreting *Sefer Yeṣirah* were apologetic and probably a reaction to other *Sefer Yeṣirah* commentaries concerned with myth, mysticism, and magic.[13] And in two articles, Klaus Herrmann discusses fragments of commentaries to *Sefer Yeṣirah* preserved in the Cairo Geniza, written between the end of the tenth century or the beginning of the eleventh, in the spirit of Hekhalot literature. These fragments clearly demonstrate that there were other Jewish approaches to *Sefer Yeṣirah* before the end of the twelfth century, of which we know very little today.[14] My work begins where these important studies leave off.

Sefer Yeṣirah: A Short Introduction

Sefer Yeṣirah opens with the following depiction of the creation of the world, from what it calls "thirty-two wondrous paths of wisdom":

> [With] thirty-two wondrous paths of wisdom, YH, the Lord of hosts, the God of Israel, the Living God, God Almighty, high and exalted, dwelling forever, and holy is his name (Isa. 57:15), created his universe with three books (*sefarim*): with a book (s.p/f.r) and a book (s.p/f.r) and a book (s.p/f.r).
>
> Ten *sefirot belimah* and twenty-two foundation letters.

> Ten *sefirot belimah*, the number of ten fingers, five opposite five, and the covenant of unity is exactly in the middle, by the word of tongue and mouth and the circumcision of the flesh.
>
> Ten *sefirot belimah*, ten and not nine, ten and not eleven. Understand with wisdom, and be wise with understanding. Test them and investigate them. Know and ponder and form. Get the thing clearly worked out and restore the Creator to his place. And their measure is ten, for they have no limit.
>
> Ten *sefirot belimah*, restrain your heart from thinking and restrain your mouth from speaking, and if your heart races, return to where you began, and remember that thus it is written: *And the living creatures ran to and fro* (Ezek. 1:14) and concerning this matter the covenant was made.[15]

Accordingly, the number thirty-two, constituting the paths of wisdom, comprises the twenty-two letters of the Hebrew alphabet—the foundation letters—and the "ten *sefirot belimah*." The meaning of *belimah* is unclear,[16] and I think that the most reasonable meaning of the word *sefirot* is, as Yehuda Liebes suggests, "counting" (ספירה); therefore, the phrase refers to the decimal counting system.[17] In the paragraphs that we have just quoted, the ten *sefirot* are joined to the twenty-two letters of the Hebrew alphabet to constitute a new numerical formula of thirty-two, which it calls the "thirty-two wondrous paths of wisdom."[18]

Scrutinizing these passages, which discuss the role of the ten *sefirot*, it seems at first glance that *Sefer Yeṣirah* demands precision. The numbers are not to be read differently: "Ten *sefirot belimah*, ten and not nine, ten and not eleven." It would seem that the numbers, in their precision, specify some kind of scientific or magical quality. Because of the numbers' ontological and epistemological qualities, a reader of *Sefer Yeṣirah* is obliged to understand their role in the creation of the world and in the created world: "Understand with wisdom, and be wise with understanding. Test them and investigate them. Know and ponder and form. Get the thing clearly worked out."

Along with its enthusiastic pathos about the obligation to investigate the world with numbers and letters, *Sefer Yeṣirah* warns readers about the very thing it counsels—thinking!: "Ten *sefirot belimah*, restrain your heart from thinking and restrain your mouth from speaking, and if your heart races, return to where you began."

Regarding this gap between the obligation to investigate and the restriction on inquiry, Liebes has noted that it should be understood not only as a contradiction but also as an essential part of the dialectical path charted by *Sefer Yeṣirah*. According to Liebes, *Sefer Yeṣirah* is not merely a cosmogonic treatise; it would be more accurate to read it as a treatise about heavenly creativity and the human creativity inspired by the creation of the world. He says that *Sefer Yeṣirah* is actually a treatise of *ars poetica* that argues creativity's need of both terms: one should understand the world and articulate one's insights, while also making room for astonishment, for prediscursive and unarticulated phenomena—without investigating them.[19]

Poetic and surprising ideas, like the dual obligation/restriction of investigating the world, occur throughout *Sefer Yeṣirah*. Another example from the same chapter concerning the *sefirot* describes two unexpected dimensions alongside the familiar three spatial dimensions of the world: the moral dimension and the dimension of time: "Ten *sefirot belimah*, and their measure is ten, for they have no limit: dimension of beginning and dimension of end, dimension of good and dimension of evil, dimension of above and dimension of below, dimension of east and dimension of west, dimension of north and dimension of south. And the unique lord, a trustworthy divine king, rules over them all from his holy abode forever and ever."[20]

Thus the treatise asserts that, as with the ten *sefirot*, there are ten, not six, directions in the world. In addition to the familiar six directions—north, south, west, east, above, and below—there are four other directions: the moral dimension, which comprises the directions of good and evil; and a dimension formed by the directions of the beginning and the end. Such an approach demonstrates why so many people were inspired by *Sefer Yeṣirah*.

The Letters

Following the first chapter, which is dedicated to discussions about the role of the ten *sefirot*, *Sefer Yeṣirah* discusses the role of the twenty-two letters of the Hebrew alphabet in the creation of the world and in the created world. It divides the letters into three groups: the first group, comprising the letters *alef*, *mem*, and *shin*, is named *immot*, *ummot*, or *ammot*, a designation with no clear meaning in Hebrew. The second group, called the "double letters," contains the six letters that can be pronounced doubly: *bet*, *gimel*, *dalet*, *kaf*, *pe*, and *taw*, as well as the letter *resh*. The third group, called the "simple letters," comprises the remaining twelve letters of the Hebrew alphabet: "The twenty-two letters are the foundations: three *immot* letters, seven double (letters), and twelve simple (letters) . . . three *immot* A, M, Š . . . seven double letters B, G, D, K, P, R, T . . . twelve simple letters H, W, Z, Ḥ, Ṭ, Y, L, N, S, ʿ, Ṣ, Q."[21]

Notably, the criteria for this division are not clear-cut; we are left wondering about the basis for the division of the letters into these three groups. According to *Sefer Yeṣirah*, the triad of *alef*, *mem*, and *shin* represents initials of three of the four foundations: *alef* stands for air (אויר), *mem* for water (מים), and *shin* for fire (אש).[22]

The next set of letters, the double letters, comprises the six Hebrew letters that can grammatically be pronounced in two ways—plosive and fricative, B, G, D; and K, P, T, as well as the letter *resh*. For example, the letter *bet* can be pronounced both as *b* and *v*; and the letter *pe* can be pronounced as *p* or as *f*. But to these six, rightfully identified as double letters, *Sefer Yeṣirah* adds the *resh*, which does not have a double pronunciation in regular Hebrew grammar. A few scholars have presented important accounts of the role of the *resh*, indicating contexts in which it could have had a double pronunciation.[23] These observations explain why *resh*, and not other letters of the alphabet, had this attribute; I agree with Joseph Dan that grammatical determinants are not the only reason for this anomaly.[24] As we saw at the beginning of this introduction, *Sefer Yeṣirah* argues that the world has ten dimensions and not six, in order to demonstrate that the number ten can be found in the foundation of the universe. Similarly, in the paragraphs dealing with the triad A-M-Š, *Sefer Yeṣirah* states that there are only three, not four, elements: air, water, and fire; it does not mention earth.[25] As several scholars have stressed, *Sefer Yeṣirah* subjects the facts to its ends where necessary and, in the case before us, alters received wisdom so that the given will correlate with the preordained numbers in the three groups of letters, not the other way around.[26] It seems that here, too, *Sefer Yeṣirah* wants to demonstrate that a classical typological number such as seven stands at the heart of the created world; therefore, the *resh* was added to the group.

The third group of letters, "simple letters," appear, in all probability, to be designated as such, insofar as they are devoid of any specific shared characteristics. Along with the grouping of the letters, the discussions in *Sefer Yeṣirah* devoted to the letters reveal a singular, if not innovative, attitude. The letters are described as units that can be combined with one another and thus create the world in its ontological and epistemological pathways. Combinations of letters demarcate, according to the book, the limits of human knowledge and allow for the creation of everything: "Twenty-two letters: he carved them out, he hewed them, he weighed them and exchanged them, he combined them and formed with them the life of all creation and the life of all that will form.[27] How did he weigh and exchange them? *Alef* with them all, and them all with *alef*; *bet* with them all, and them all with *bet*. And they all rotate in turn. The result is that [they go out] by 221 (231) gates. The result is that all creation and all speech go out by one name."[28]

In this description, we find that, despite a limited number of letters in the alphabet, amounting to one name, everything can be created: "the result is that all creation and all speech go out by one name." A similar approach to the letters, their infinite combinations, and creation that derives from them can be found later on in *Sefer Yeṣirah*: "How did he combine them?[29] Two stones[30] build two houses: three build six houses: four build twenty-four houses: five build 120 houses; six build 720 houses; seven build 5,040 houses. From here on, go out and ponder what the mouth cannot speak and what the eye cannot see and what the ear cannot hear."[31]

This articulation that a limited number of basic signifiers, the letters or the stones, enable unlimited creativity within language, the houses, is interesting from a modern linguistic perspective. Since the basic components of the language expounded by *Sefer Yeṣirah* are not the phonemes but rather the written letters, the linguistic approach of *Sefer Yeṣirah* presents a clear preference for written language over speech. And consider the linguistic structure advanced by *Sefer Yeṣirah*: the limited number of signifiers and unlimited creativity within language looks like a raw model of the Saussurian differentiation between *parole* and *langue*: "From here on, go out and ponder what the mouth cannot speak and what the eye cannot see and what the ear cannot hear."

The Structure of Discussion About the Letters

Sefer Yeṣirah's discussions about the ten *sefirot* and the twenty-two letters contain interesting insights as well as an exposition of the enduring structures involved in sustaining the created world. An example of such a structure is the three parallel levels of the created world. According to *Sefer Yeṣirah*, each letter functions and signifies on three levels: the celestial world or the universe (עולם), mankind or the human body (נפש), and the year or time (שנה): "Seven double letters: B, G, D, K, P, R, T. He carved and hewed them, he combined them, weighed them and he formed with them the planets in the universe, the days in the year and the apertures in mankind. . . . He made *bet* rule, and bound to it a crown, and combined one with another, and formed with it Saturn in the universe, the Sabbath in the year, and the mouth in mankind."[32] Every letter is responsible for a certain aspect of each level. It seems that a letter governs its aspect, perhaps even creating it. Thus in the last example, the letter *bet* rules: "Saturn in the universe, the Sabbath in the year, and the mouth in mankind." Another structural issue, which is of much interest yet remains abstruse, is the description of the last triple structure, A-M-Š., as divided into male and female. Although assumptions as to the meaning of this division may abound, the laconic language of *Sefer Yeṣirah*, on this issue as well as others, tends to hide more than it reveals. For example, one finds this division described: "He made *alef* rule over wind, and bound to it a crown, and combined them with each other, and formed with them air in the universe, and humidity in the year, and corpse in mankind, male and female—male with *alef*, *mem*, *shin*, and female with *alef*, *shin*, *mem*."[33]

Abraham the Patriarch and Sefer Yeṣirah

Abruptly, at the end of *Sefer Yeṣirah*, the book's laconic discussions are replaced by a new and totally different discourse, which appears in a sole paragraph describing Abraham the patriarch as having investigated and understood the secrets of *Sefer Yeṣirah*: "When Abraham our father came, and looked, and saw, and investigated, and understood, and carved, and combined, and hewed, and pondered, and succeeded, the Lord of all was revealed to him. And he made him sit in his lap, and kissed him upon his head. He called him his friend and named him his son, and made a covenant with him and his seed forever."[34]

The last paragraph is thought to be from a late layer in the evolution of *Sefer Yeṣirah* because of its pronounced developed literary form. Further support for the view that this paragraph is alien to the spirit of *Sefer Yeṣirah* can be seen in the fact that biblical heroes or later Jewish figures had otherwise received no mention in the body of *Sefer Yeṣirah*, as well as in the fact that in this paragraph, Abraham is said to be contemplating an already-extant *Sefer Yeṣirah*. Furthermore, although there are versions of this paragraph in all the recensions of *Sefer Yeṣirah*, its second part, which gives a detailed description of the meeting of God and Abraham—"And he made him sit in his lap, and kissed him upon his head. He called him his friend and named him his son, and made a covenant with him and his seed forever"—is absent from the earliest recension of *Sefer Yeṣirah*, from the tenth-century manuscript found in the Cairo Geniza.

Gershom Scholem and Moshe Idel give divergent readings of Abraham's contemplative relationship to *Sefer Yeṣirah*. Scholem argued that when Abraham studied *Sefer Yeṣirah*, he achieved a mystical revelation. In this mystical vision, God "made him sit in his lap, and kissed him upon his head. He called him his friend and named him his son."[35] Idel argues that the key word in this paragraph is "succeeded," demonstrating that after Abraham "came, and looked and saw and investigated, and understood, and carved and combined, and hewed, and pondered," he was equal to God: he could create the world and had the highest magical abilities.[36]

It is difficult to decide whether this paragraph belongs to the early version of *Sefer Yeṣirah*. Nevertheless, throughout the centuries, in the eyes of most readers of *Sefer Yeṣirah*, this paragraph was not just taken to be integral to *Sefer Yeṣirah* but was considered its most important paragraph. From a very early stage, because of this paragraph, *Sefer Yeṣirah* was attributed to Abraham.

How to Place *Sefer Yeṣirah* in Context

Most of *Sefer Yeṣirah* concerns the role, status, and function of the twenty-two letters of the Hebrew alphabet in the creation of the world and in the created world. Although *Sefer Yeṣirah* begins by declaring that the world was created by "thirty-two wondrous paths of wisdom," Ithamar Gruenwald has shown that its main interest is in the twenty-two letters of the alphabet and therefore does not mention the ten *sefirot* after the first chapter.[37] The common assumption in *Sefer Yeṣirah* scholarship has nevertheless been that *Sefer Yeṣirah*'s approach to the alphabet and its role in the creation of the world is similar to the normative Jewish perception of the Hebrew letters—in other words, the approach of the rabbinic and Hekhalot literatures. Most scholars who have tried to find a context for *Sefer Yeṣirah* have consequently not given much attention to the issue of the letters and have preferred to focus on two other matters: the origins of the notion of the ten *sefirot*; and the equivalents between more specific notions or terms in *Sefer Yeṣirah* and those found in other Jewish and non-Jewish texts of late antiquity and the early Middle Ages.

This book takes a step back to examine the context of *Sefer Yeṣirah* by considering its approach to the letters, which are, after all, its main interest. I argue that the attitude taken by *Sefer Yeṣirah* to the role of the Hebrew alphabet is substantially different from that of other Jewish sources. Paying close attention to how *Sefer Yeṣirah* talks about the letters can open new horizons and can assist in suggesting a context for the book.

In Chapter 1, I will present a panoramic picture of relevant approaches from non-Jewish sources to alphabetic letters in texts from late antiquity to the early Middle Ages. Those sources will later help us contextualize *Sefer Yeṣirah*.

Chapters 2 and 3 focus on the main role of the alphabet in *Sefer Yeṣirah*: the creation of the world based on letters. These chapters identify two traditions known to late antiquity that give this sort of account of the creation of the world. One describes the creation of the world from the ineffable name or its letters; the other holds that the world was created by all twenty-two letters of the alphabet. Close scrutiny of these two traditions shows that in rabbinic sources, the dominant notion was that the world was created with the letters of the ineffable name, while in non-Jewish and, especially, in Christian sources, we can find the account of the creation of the world from the twenty-two letters of the alphabet. As the final step of the inquiry in these chapters, I will strengthen the case for *Sefer Yeṣirah*'s connection to the Christian-Syriac world. There are many good reasons to assume that *Sefer Yeṣirah*'s writers or editors lived sometime around the seventh century and were deeply familiar with Syriac notions. This conclusion, which relies on concrete and contextual resemblances, should be seen in light of the apparent near-absence of engagement between Syriac Christianity and the rabbinic culture in Babylonia: we have very few examples showing a possible influence of Syriac texts on rabbinic ones.[38]

How Was *Sefer Yeṣirah* Understood by Its Early Readers?

Sefer Yeṣirah was accepted into the rabbinic canon in the tenth century. Before the second half of the twelfth century, it had spawned at least four commentaries that can be roughly defined as scientific-philosophical in nature. Nevertheless, in the last three decades, a number of studies dealing with different issues in the history of the reception of *Sefer Yeṣirah* have all taken the view that even before the last part of the twelfth century, *Sefer Yeṣirah* was understood as a mystical, mythical, or magical treatise.[39]

In Chapter 4, I will look at an early and enigmatic time in the history of *Sefer Yeṣirah*, the unknown period beginning when it was conceived up until the tenth century. I will examine two traces of how *Sefer Yeṣirah* was understood in the Jewish world. The first is a short gloss inserted into some recensions of *Sefer Yeṣirah* before the tenth century. A careful reading of this gloss reveals that its author was influenced by the Hekhalot literature and other Jewish myths and read *Sefer Yeṣirah* in that context. The second trace of a Jewish reception of *Sefer Yeṣirah* is the well-known ninth-century epistle of Agobard of Lyon, which describes the insolence of the Jews. I suggest that the ninth-century French Jews whom Agobard describes were probably acquainted with the cosmogony of *Sefer Yeṣirah*, though not necessarily with *Sefer Yeṣirah* itself, and saw that cosmogony as part of a wider mythical and mystical realm.

Chapter 5 examines sources testifying to how *Sefer Yeṣirah* was understood between the tenth century and the end of the twelfth century. Central to this chapter is a discussion of a medieval midrash about *Sefer Yeṣirah* and Ben Sira, preserved in an eleventh-century manuscript and composed between the ninth and the eleventh centuries. This midrash has been discussed in the scholarly literature, but inaccurate dating and insufficient analysis of its contents have prevented scholars from fully understanding its importance in the history of the reception of *Sefer Yeṣirah*. *Sefer Yeṣirah* is here described in an unambiguously mythical and magical manner that reflects a common understanding of this treatise at the time. In addition to investigating this lengthy midrash, I will reexamine Rashi's treatment of *Sefer Yeṣirah* and argue that he was influenced by this midrash about *Sefer Yeṣirah* and Ben Sira. Last, I will discuss a short, very popular, and boldly mystical statement that was included in most recensions of *Sefer Yeṣirah* before the eleventh century.

Should *Sefer Yeṣirah* Be Considered a Book?

In the first comprehensive commentary on *Sefer Yeṣirah*, R. Saadya Gaon states that there are several versions of the text and consequently that one of the purposes of his commentary is to determine the correct one.[40] Saadya was not alone in noting the textual problems of *Sefer Yeṣirah*, which were, in fact, discussed by most of its early commentators.[41] Indeed, the first three commentaries that were written on *Sefer Yeṣirah*—by Saadya, Dunash Ibn Tamim, and Shabbetai Donnolo—were written on the basis of different versions of *Sefer Yeṣirah*. The fact that there are three (or possibly more) main recensions of *Sefer Yeṣirah*[42] raises fundamental issues: What is it exactly that we intend to date when discussing *Sefer Yeṣirah*? Is it viable to assume that there is one urtext written by a single author whose date needs to be determined? How can we establish the date of a treatise when we cannot reconstruct its earliest version and when there is not even scholarly agreement about the very existence of such an original?

Daniel Abrams, in his extensive and comprehensive study about kabbalistic manuscripts and textual theory, suggests an original path to investigate *Sefer Yeṣirah*. According to Abrams, since it is essentially impossible to reconstruct *Sefer Yeṣirah*'s urtext and since there are great differences between the manuscripts of this composition, *Sefer Yeṣirah* scholarship should focus on more valid evidence: the manuscripts themselves. He says, in other words, that there is no *Sefer Yeṣirah* (Book of Formation) but rather *Sifrei Yeṣirah* (Books of Formation) and therefore instead of trying in vain to establish the "original" *Sefer Yeṣirah*, one should trace the history of *Sefer Yeṣirah*'s acceptance and the ways that this fluid text had been modified over the years by its medieval commentators. Each recension reflects, according to Abrams, a certain moment in *Sefer Yeṣirah*'s history of acceptance, and that moment should be committed to scrutiny.[43]

Abrams did not offer textual evidence to support his argument, and although his theoretical suggestion appeals to me, I did not find much support for it in the manuscripts of *Sefer Yeṣirah*. In my opinion, the textual history of *Sefer Yeṣirah* should be divided into two stages: in the first stage, before the tenth century, there are indeed differences between the recensions of *Sefer Yeṣirah*. During that period, the book was edited and reedited by various redactors, and a few glosses were inserted. That was the reason for the discomfiture of its early commentators with regard to its correct version. Therefore, in analyzing the history of *Sefer Yeṣirah* before the tenth century, I used a similar method to the one that Abrams suggested.[44]

Nevertheless, in the second stage, after the tenth century, the three recensions of *Sefer Yeṣirah* remained the main ones, and it would be rare to find new glosses within *Sefer Yeṣirah*. Therefore, the assumption that the book continues to change during the High Middle Ages has no textual support. From a careful reading of tens of manuscripts of *Sefer Yeṣirah*, I have not found evidence of conspicuous interventions of late medieval commentators in the versions of *Sefer Yeṣirah* but rather, the contrary. New versions that combine the short and the long recensions of *Sefer Yeṣirah* constitute the main modification that can be encountered.

The differences between the versions of *Sefer Yeṣirah*, hence, occurred before the book was interpreted by its early commentators, and it seems that these commentaries framed its versions. Moreover, even if one scrutinizes the three main recensions of *Sefer Yeṣirah*, the differences between them are less crucial than might be assumed. At first glance, they are mainly differences in length and manner of editing that did not influence the structure of the book and its basic arguments. Ithamar Gruenwald, who published the first critical edition of *Sefer Yeṣirah*, has articulated it: "The three recensions differ from one another mainly in the length of the text and in inner organization of the material. The differences of reading between the three recensions are not as many as is generally assumed."[45]

There are, as Gruenwald states, great differences between the image of *Sefer Yeṣirah* in scholarship and the reality of this book according to its manuscripts. We would not be wrong in saying that the textual problem of the version(s) is less complicated than assumed and that those problems were sometimes over-theorized in scholarship. From all the recensions of *Sefer Yeṣirah* known to me, the basic issues of the book remain stable: in all the recensions, twenty-two letters are divided into the same three groups: *immot*, "doubles," and "simples." Each of these groups contains the same letters without variations, and the discussions about the letters use identical terminology and symbolism. Similarly, in all the recensions, the first paragraphs of *Sefer Yeṣirah* deal with the ten *sefirot*, and only minor differences can be found between the recensions. For example, the differences between the long and the short recensions are related to the length of the discussion but are not reflected nor do they have any influence on the meaning or the symbolism of each letter. In the same vein, the great differences between Saadya's recension and other recensions of *Sefer Yeṣirah* are related to the way in which the text is edited, but there are merely a few differences in terms of content and terminology.

A different methodology to analyze the textual labyrinth of *Sefer Yeṣirah* has been suggested by Gruenwald and Ronit Meroz. Forty years ago, Gruenwald suggested that there are thematic and terminological reasons for making a distinction between *Sefer Yeṣirah*'s first chapter and subsequent chapters of the book and that it seems that the first chapter reflects a different treatise, which was integrated into *Sefer Yeṣirah*.[46] Such an approach can help explain, for example, the opening paragraph of the book by determining the odd number: thirty-two, as an editorial addition. This number thirty-two is not discussed throughout *Sefer Yeṣirah*; it was added by an editor of the book who combined together the main chapters of the book discussing the twenty-two alphabetical letters, with the new chapter about the ten *sefirot*. In an alternative suggestion put forth a few years ago, Meroz argues that *Sefer Yeṣirah* comprised three distinct compositions that are described in the opening paragraph as: a book, a book, and a book (ספר, ספר, וספר).[47] If Gruenwald's or Meroz's hypothesis is correct, we must suppose, as Meroz noted,[48] that the three main recensions of *Sefer Yeṣirah* all evolved from one branch—after the book was redacted, and that the sections of *Sefer Yeṣirah* known to us had already been edited at that juncture.[49] It would be a mistake to assume that the early forms of *Sefer Yeṣirah* are merely a result of a redaction of various preexisting compositions. It would be more suitable to perceive it as a combination between original and eclectic materials. In comparison with other late antiquity and medieval compositions, such as the Hekhalot literature, *Sefer haBahir*, and the Zoharic literature, *Sefer Yeṣirah*, despite all the differences between its recensions, seems to have a coherent structure with unique and distinct terminology. Of course, *Sefer Yeṣirah* is a layered text, and preceding the tenth century, its readers edited it, reedited it, and added material. Nevertheless, we have to listen to the manuscripts themselves and observe the great similarities between the three recensions. We should conclude that there was an early composition from which the three main recensions of *Sefer Yeṣirah* developed, a composition that Peter Hayman tried to reconstruct as "the earliest recoverable text of *Sefer Yeṣirah*."[50]

My main goal in this study is not to publish a new edition of the "early" *Sefer Yeṣirah*, so I will not discuss every word in the book with the purpose of determining whether it is part of that early version. My purpose is to date and locate the early version of *Sefer Yeṣirah*; in order to do so, I will determine the *terminus a quo* and the *terminus ad quem* of central themes and basic issues that relate to the core of *Sefer Yeṣirah* and that can be found in all its recensions.

Chapter 1

Discussions About Alphabetical Letters in Non-Jewish Sources of Late Antiquity

Sefer Yeṣirah's assertions about the role of the twenty-two letters of the Hebrew alphabet were not conceived in a vacuum. Some scholars have argued that the engagement with letters in *Sefer Yeṣirah* and in other Jewish sources is a unique phenomenon referring solely to intra-Jewish issues, such as the myth of the creation of the world by speech, the holiness ascribed to the Hebrew language, the holiness of the name of God, or the holiness of the Bible, including the letters it is composed of.[1] However, as early as the beginning of the twentieth century, Franz Dornseiff and other scholars in his wake have, as the result of detailed investigations, found evidence that discussion of alphabetical letters is not only to be found in rabbinic and other Jewish sources but can also be encountered in Greek, Gnostic, Neoplatonic, Neo-Pythagorean, Christian, and Samaritan texts.[2] Examining late antique engagement with alphabetical letters from a wider perspective reveals that Jewish texts were neither more developed nor earlier than non-Jewish sources and that it would be untenable to single out a Judaic origin for this phenomenon. It would be more plausible to assume that Jewish discussions about alphabetical letters were adaptations of earlier non-Jewish ones. Any attempt to contextualize *Sefer Yeṣirah* must therefore not only take into account a wide range of possible sources but also recognize, penetrate, and understand the widespread preoccupation with letters, in order to trace the different channels of its development.

One must consider the disparate attitudes adopted toward letter discussions in late antiquity in order to decipher the genealogy of these discussions. In some contexts in late antiquity, discussions of letters were considered negatively; in other contexts, they were adopted without criticism. For example, some early church fathers and a few Neoplatonic thinkers rejected letter discussions, claiming that they were Gnostic, nonrational, and inappropriate; in the same period, they were considered legitimate in rabbinic sources. Although this can explain why letter discussions are more prevalent in Jewish sources than in Christian or Neoplatonic ones, it does not in any way indicate that the origins of this phenomenon are Jewish.

Even without deciding whether the main sources for the narrative of the creation of the world from letters in *Sefer Yeṣirah* derive from Jewish or non-Jewish traditions, I call attention at least to the possibility of letter discussions having non-Jewish origins and to study the development of these traditions, which continued to evolve in some non-Jewish milieus throughout the first millennium CE.

A prefatory response to the above question is offered by a reading of *Sefer Yeṣirah*. It would be difficult to assume much affiliation between it and other Jewish sources, since most discussions about the letters in *Sefer Yeṣirah* do not employ methods that were known in rabbinic sources and vice versa. For example, *Sefer Yeṣirah* contains neither midrashim on "defective" spelling and *plene* spelling nor *gematria* (calculating and comparing numerical value of letters), nor do we find mention of the graphic shape of the letters or the meanings of the final Hebrew letters *ḵ-m-n-p-ṣ*. *Sefer Yeṣirah* is mainly concerned with the number twenty-two and with the secondary divisions of the letters into the numbers three, seven, and twelve, and pays scant attention to other methods of dealing with the letters of the alphabet, and thereby to a great extent differentiates itself from rabbinic sources.

My main goal in this chapter is to demonstrate that while many church fathers and a few Neoplatonic thinkers rejected letter discussions as Gnostic or irrational, such discussions were still developed in more marginal Christian contexts throughout the first millennium CE. Consequently, my argument in the following chapters is that the myth about the creation of the world from twenty-two letters was not discussed in rabbinic texts but was developed in some Christian circles, especially Syriac ones. *Sefer Yeṣirah*, as I will demonstrate, borrowed this and other motifs from those Christian origins.

Early Roots

There is evidence of extensive preoccupation with alphabetical letters as well as myths about their importance only from the first century CE, although the roots of these phenomena probably go back much further. Ancient wellsprings, such as sources from the ancient Near East,[3] biblical literature,[4] and ancient Greece[5] are possible springboards. An important example of an ancient Greek notion that influenced discussions and myths about the alphabetical letters in late antiquity is the Greek word *stoicheion* (στοιχεῖον), which refers to, among other things, both an alphabetical letter and a physical element. It became a point of convergence for discussing the creation of the world from letters. An early source that can exemplify the double meaning of the word is a paragraph from Plato's *Timaeus*, which explains the primal significance of the four physical elements. Here the letters are seen as similar to physical elements, and, unlike syllables, they constitute indivisible primary units: "But we speak of fire and the rest of them [water, air, and earth], whatever they mean, as though men knew their natures, and we maintain them to be the first principles and letters [στοιχεῖα] or elements of the whole, when they cannot reasonably be compared by a man of any sense even to syllables or first compounds."[6]

In Plato, the alphabetical letters have an atomic character, as they cannot be divided into more basic components. It seems that the fact that letters and physical elements share a word and similar qualities, in conjunction with other biblical and Akkadian perceptions of written signs as independent units, will have a significant role in the crystallization of myths about the creation of the world from alphabetical letters. In this respect, it is worth noting that in *Sefer Yeṣirah*, one finds the interesting phrase *otiot yesod* (אותיות יסוד),[7] which means, literally, "element letters." As Gershom Scholem has noted, there is good reason to assume that *otiot yesod* in *Sefer Yeṣirah* is a Hebrew adaptation of the Greek *stoicheion*.[8]

Another well-known example of an ancient idea that influenced later discussions and speculation about letters is the discussion of the symbolic meaning of the seven Greek vowels. Aristotle's *Metaphysics* is one of the earliest sources to refer to the association between the seven vowels and other collections of seven things. Aristotle takes a critical stand and argues that it is unreasonable to correlate different things in this way:

> If all things must share in number, it must follow that many things are the same. . . . [T]hings that differed might fall under the same number. Therefore if the same number had belonged to certain things, these would have been the same as one another, since they would have had the same form of number; e.g., sun and moon would have been the same. . . . There are seven vowels, the scale has seven strings, the Pleiades are seven . . . and the champions who fought against Thebes were seven. Is it then because the number is what it is, that the champions were seven or the Pleias consist of seven stars? Surely the champions were seven because there were seven gates of for some other reason, and the Pleias *we* count as seven, as we count the Bear as twelve, while other people count more stars in both.[9]

Although Aristotle rejects comparisons between different objects associated with the same number, the example he gives suggests that at least some of the specific correspondences between the vowels and other matters composed of seven parts were well known.

A later example, which connects the seven vowels and the planets, can be found in Plutarch's (ca. 46–125 CE) discussion of the letter E, a capital epsilon, which stood at the entrance to the temple of Delphi.[10] Writing to his friend the poet Sarapion, Plutarch offers seven possible reasons for this letter being placed at the entrance to the temple. One rationale relates to the fact that epsilon is the second in the order of vowels in the Greek alphabet and designates the sun; it is fitting for it to stand at the gates of the temple of Apollo, the god of the sun. Thus the claim: "There are seven vowels in the alphabet and seven stars that have an independent and unconstrained motion; that E is the second in order of the vowels from the beginning, and the Sun the second planet after the moon, and that practically all the Greeks identify Apollo with the Sun."[11]

This explanation in Plutarch refers to a specific issue related to the correspondence between the Greek vowels and the planets. It is important to stress that this correspondence was well known and, moreover, that the vowels symbolized planets. Such a correspondence found its way at a later period into *Sefer Yeṣirah*. Although it seems that *Sefer Yeṣirah* gives little attention to the Hebrew *matres lectionis* (vowels), A, H, W, Y,[12] it defines Hebrew equivalents to the seven Greek vowels, the seven double letters B, G, D, K, P, R, T. These seven letters, according to *Sefer Yeṣirah*, correspond to the seven planets: "Seven double letters: *bet*, *gimel*, *dalet*, *kaf*, *pe*, *resh*, *taw*. He carved and hewed them, he combined them, weighed them and exchanged them, and he formed with them the planets in the universe. . . . These are the seven planets in the universe: Sun, Venus, Mercury, Moon, Saturn, Jupiter, Mars."[13]

I contend that *Sefer Yeṣirah* did not adapt these ideas directly from Greek sources. *Sefer Yeṣirah* represents a case of a Hebrew treatise that took on this Greek tradition after it had been adapted to Semitic languages, as these ideas continued to develop throughout late antiquity and the early Middle Ages along various channels.

Discussion and Rejection of Letter Speculations in Late Antiquity

The use of hermeneutic methods based on letter discussions spawned debates in the writings of the church fathers as well as in Neoplatonic circles. The existence of such debates is of utmost relevance to our discussion, as it reflects on the extent of the concern with letters and the resistance it aroused.

Irenaeus of Lyon's (second century CE) *Against Heresies* provides one of the most detailed testimonies to such a debate.[14] Irenaeus attributes to Marcus, a disciple of Valentinus,[15] a polemical description of the employment of letters as well as homilies on letters. The length, detail, and breadth of the Gnostic discussions about letters that Irenaeus quotes prohibit an all-inclusive and detailed description; I will therefore present only the more relevant ones. One such discussion is the description of the body of truth (ἀλήθεια) in terms of opposed pairs of letters, which look like the Hebrew A-T B-Š letter-exchange method.[16] This source makes a strong connection between the process of creation and alphabetical letters. Truth, the foundation of human discourse, is composed of letters: "[T]he Tetrad explained these things to him as it said: 'I also wish to show you Truth itself. I have brought her down from the dwellings on high that you might look on her unveiled and learn of her beauty and also hear her speak and admire her wisdom. See, then, *alpha* and *omega* are her head on high; *beta* and *psi* are her neck; *gamma* and *chi* are her shoulders with hands; her breast is *delta* and *phi*; *epsilon* and *upsilon* are her diaphragm; *zeta* and *tau* are her stomach; *eta* and *sigma* are her private parts; *theta* and *rho* are her thighs; *iota* and *pi* are her knees; *kappa* and *omicron* are her legs; *lambda* and *xi* are her ankles; *mu* and *nu* are her feet.'"[17]

The role that Marcus gives to the alphabetical letters in their connection to the organs of the body of "Truth" is similar to the role of the letters at the level of the human body (נפש), one of the three levels of the created world in *Sefer Yeṣirah*. At this level, as we saw in the Introduction, each letter represents or is responsible for a certain organ of the human body. *Sefer Yeṣirah* describes the three levels of the three *immot* letters *A-M-Š*: "He made *alef* rule over air [*ruaḥ*], and bound to it a crown, and combined them with each other, and formed with them air [*awir*] in the universe, and humidity in the year, and the chest in mankind male and female. He made *mem* rule over water, and bound to it a crown, and combined them with each other, and formed with it earth in the universe, cold in the year, and the belly in mankind male and female. He made *shin* rule over fire, and bound to it a crown, and combined them with each other, and formed with it heaven in the universe, heat in the year, and the head in mankind male and female."[18]

Of special interest is Irenaeus's account of the similarity in both structure and content of the emanation of the upper worlds from letters as presented by Marcus and the myth of creation widespread in Mandaean sources. In her book on the Mandaeans, Ethel Stefana Drower describes their particular approach to the alphabet and the role of letters in the creation of the world.[19] A reading of Mandaean sources discloses the importance of letters in the divine realm[20]—for example, the use of letters to name various elements in the pleroma and the title given to the great mother in one of the Mandaean creation myths, "Mother of the Twenty-Four Letters of the Alphabet,"[21] which recalls Marcus's "Truth." One can infer from Mandaean texts that, similar to the description of the body of the truth in the Valentinian myth, the body of Adam Kasia, the primordial man, is also composed of letters.[22] The fact that similar depictions can be found in early Valentinian Gnosticism and in later Mandaean sources demonstrates that those beliefs were prevalent over an expanse of time and geographic location. This illustrates and justifies my claim that *Sefer Yeṣirah*, in around the seventh century, represents a variant of these diverse expressions.

Another point relevant to my argument follows from Marcus's contention concerning the hierarchy between different groups of letters. According to him, the consonants are superior to the vowels and semivowels.[23] Marcus believes that since the creator lacks voice or utterance, the vowels, being closer to vocalization, have a lower status: "Know, then, that these your twenty-four letters are symbolical emissions of the three powers which embrace the entire number of characters on high. You are to consider the nine mute letters as belonging to Father and Truth, because these are mute, that is, they are unspeakable and unutterable. The eight semivowels, as belonging to Word and Life, because they are, as it were, intermediate between the mutes and the vowels, they receive the emission from the Aeons above; but an ascent from those below. The vowels too are seven. They belong to Man and Church, because the voice that came forth through Man formed all things; for the sound of the voice clothed them with form. So Word and Life possess eight [of the letters]; Man and Church seven; Father and Truth, nine."[24]

This text is unusual among those from late antiquity that I know of, in attesting to the superiority of the consonants over the vowels. The more prevalent attitude in late antiquity to the letters was opposite; the seven Greek vowels symbolized the seven planets or divine beings and were considered to be superior to the other letters. Long sequences of Greek vowels in many Greek and Coptic amulets testify to the uniqueness and high status of the vowels. Certain texts from the Nag-Hammadi library[25] contain sequences of vowels in this vein, symbolizing the highest realm of human cognition. In a treatise called "The Discourse of the Eighth and the Ninth," for example, combinations of vowels are used to praise God: "Grace! After these things, I give thanks by singing a hymn to you. For I have received life from you, when you made me wise I praise you. I call your name that is hidden with me: a ō ee ō ēēē ōōō iii ōōōō ooooo ōōōōō uuuuuu ōōōōōōōōōōōōōōōōōōōōōō.[26] You are the one who exists with the spirit. I sing a hymn to you reverently."[27]

The vowels, specifically because of their vocalization, are seen here as hidden and exalted and therefore are apt for the praise of God; as Patricia Cox-Miller puts it: "[T]he vowels of the alphabet designate that point at which the human and divine worlds intersect. . . . [T]o speak this language is not only to invoke the God; it is also to sound the depths of one's own primal reality. These strings of vowels are hymnic recitations of praise to the God and to human Godlikeness."[28]

Another well-known example of the symbolic meaning of the vowels can be gleaned from the Pythagorean Nicomachus of Gerasa's (60–120 CE) treatise "Introduction to Arithmetic." Nicomachus writes that the seven vowels are the sounds of the seven celestial spheres. Those sounds are ineffable but can be revealed through other means, such as arithmetic, geometry, and grammar. In terms of hierarchy, the vowels, according to Nicomachus, are like the soul of the material consonants that constitute the body: "For indeed the sounds of each sphere of the seven, each sphere naturally producing one certain kind of sound, are called 'vowels.' They are ineffable in and of themselves, but are recalled by the wise with respect to everything made up of them. Wherefore also here (i.e., on earth) this sound has power, which in arithmetic is a monad, in geometry a point, in grammar a letter (of the alphabet). And combined with the material letters, which are the consonants, as the soul to the body."[29]

The elevation of the vowels over the consonants, on the one hand, and taking the consonant to be superior to the other letters, on the other—this divergence will contribute to our discussion in the following two chapters. It is an opposition reflected in the differences between the two main traditions concerning the creation of the world from letters. As we will see, the main tradition in Jewish sources, in both rabbinic and Hekhalot literature, sees the world as having been created by the letters of the ineffable name: Y, H, W. This is similar to, and probably caused by, the approach that gives higher status to the vowels, compared with the other letters. Similarly, the second approach to the creation of the world from letters, arguing that the world was created by all the letters of the alphabet, being the approach at the heart of *Sefer Yeṣirah*, does not hold the vowels to be superior and, as such, is much closer to Marcus's account.[30]

Irenaeus, however, rejects Marcus's opinions, calling them stupid and unfounded. To illustrate their absurdity, he refers to a historical argument concerning the evolution of Greek writing. According to Irenaeus, the Greeks received an alphabet, comprising only sixteen letters, from the Phoenicians via Cadmus, and the remaining letters were gradually formed only later. Irenaeus employs ridicule to ask whether the "Truth," which, for Marcus, comprises twenty-four letters, did not exist until the Greek alphabet was fully developed:

> Who would not hate the deplorable contriver of such falsehoods, when he sees the Truth made into an idol by Marcus and branded with letters of the Alphabet? The Greeks confess that it is only recently—relative to what was from the beginning, which is expressed by "Yesterday and the day before yesterday" that first they received sixteen letters through Cadmus. Then, as time went on, they themselves invented others; at one time the aspirate, at another the double letters; last of all, Palamedes added the long letters to the rest. By inference, before these letters were made by the Greeks, Truth did not exist! For the body of Truth, according to you, Marcus, was begotten later than Cadmus, and so later than those who existed before him. It is also begotten later than those who added the rest of the characters; later than yourself, because you alone reduced to an idol her whom you call Truth.[31]

Irenaeus rejects another assertion about the importance of the alphabetical letters, contained in a legend common in early Christian circles about the young Jesus, who, in the process of learning the letters of the alphabet, reveals to his teacher the secrets concealed in them. Irenaeus contends that the story is false and should be completely disregarded.[32] It seems that in contesting the tale, he wants to undermine the legitimacy of discussions about alphabetical letters as a realm of mystery.

The debate about the validity of alphabetical speculations was not unique to Christian-Gnostic polemics and can be found also in Neoplatonic milieus.[33] In his commentary on Plato's Timaeus,[34] Proclus (ca. 410–485) reports that Theodorus Asaeus (fourth century) interprets the word "soul" (ψυχή) using *gematria* (*isopsephy*),[35] including what will be defined in medieval Jewish sources as "small *gematria*" (where only the first digit of the numerical value of a certain letter is considered). Theodorus also takes into account the graphic aspect of the letters of ψυχή, based on which he presents various interpretations of the nature of the soul. According to Proclus, Theodorus learned these interpretative methods from the writings of Numenius of Apamea (second century CE) and Amelius (third century). Proclus concludes by noting that Iamblichus (ca. 245–325) strongly objected to these methods and presents three arguments put forth by Iamblichus against letter speculations. First, he asserts that even words possessing opposite meanings may have the same numeric value. Second, he argues that graphic qualities cannot have interpretative value, since the letters have changed their shape over the years. Third, he thinks that the employment of a method such as small *gematria* is futile because using it along with mathematical functions such as multiplication, addition, division, and subtraction will produce the result that all words are equal to one another:[36]

> Theodorus the philosopher, however, of Asine being full of the doctrines of Numenius, speculates the generation of the soul in a more novel manner, from letters, and characters, and numbers. But the divine Iamblichus blames every theory of this kind, in his treatise in confutation of the followers of Amelius, and also of Numenius, whether he includes Numenius among those who adopted this method. . . . The divine Iamblichus therefore says in

> the first place that it is not proper to make the soul every number, or the geometrical number, on account of the multitude of letters. For the words body and non-being itself consist of an equal number of letters. Non-being therefore, will also be every number. You may also find many other things, consisting of an equal number of letters, which are of a vile nature, and most contrary to each other; all which it is not right to confound and mingle together.
>
> In the second place, he observes, that it is not safe to argue from characters. For these subsist by position, and the ancient was different from the present mode of forming them. Thus for instance the letter *Z*, which he makes the subject of discussion, had not the opposite lines entirely parallel, nor the middle line oblique, but at right angles, as is evident from the ancient letters.
>
> In the third place, he adds, that to analyze into the primary ratios of numbers, and to dwell on these, transfers the theory from some numbers to others. For the heptad is not the same which is in units, and tens, and hundreds. This however, existing in the name of the soul, why is it requisite to introduce the disquisition of primary ratios? For thus he may transfer all things to all numbers, by dividing, or compounding, or multiplying. In short, he accuses the whole of this theory as artificial, and containing nothing sane.[37]

Iamblichus, according to this source, objects to letter speculations such as comparison between numerical value of words and interpretations of letters according to their shape. These two methods are well known in rabbinic and later Jewish sources, where they were adapted without critique. The fact that two early and well-known figures such as Irenaeus of Lyon in a Christian context and Iamblichus in the Neoplatonic world strongly objected to letter speculations can explain why they were not prevalent in Christian and Neoplatonic sources. Letter discussions, by nature, look arbitrary and irrational: there is no coherent connection between words whose letters have the same numerical value. Similarly, a historical point of view, well known in ancient times, asserts clearly that the alphabet is a human invention and that the number of the letters of the alphabet as well as their shape has changed throughout the years. These facts, as well as the fact that methods for dealing with letters were developed by Gnostics, among others, gave letter speculation a subversive character in certain contexts. Despite the fact that discussions of the letters were rejected by leading figures as insane, they developed in two main channels: first in Jewish and Samaritan[38] and later in Islamic sources;[39] and then in Christian and Neoplatonic sources, which were unaware of or did not accept the background of hostility to those discussions. Since the Christian sources are more important for our purposes, I will limit my discussion to them.

Letter Speculations in Christian Sources

Reading the early church fathers, it seems that discussions about letters of the alphabet remained marginal and undeveloped as a consequence of the rejection of the Gnostic preoccupation with them, first by Irenaeus of Lyon and then by church fathers such as Hippolytus of Rome (170–235 CE) and Epiphanius of Salamis (ca. 310–403).[40] More marginal Christian circles nevertheless continued to engage with alphabetical speculations, three examples of which follow.

Saint Pachomius (ca. 292–348) is a good example of the use of letter discussions in the monastic literature. He writes about secret writing as well as mystical, contemplative, and perhaps magical uses of Greek letters.[41] The epistles of Saint Pachomius feature tables of letters similar to magic tables,[42] instructions for contemplating certain letters,[43] rules about letters that are not to be written in proximity,[44] sentences ordered according to opposed pairs of letters exchange method,[45] and cryptographs composed of Greek letters. For example, Pachomius instructs his addressees in cryptic letter exchanges: "1. I want you to understand the characters that you wrote to me and that I wrote to you in answer, and how important it is to know all the elements of the spiritual alphabet. Write ν above η and θ; write ζ above χ, μ, λ and ι, when you have finished reading these characters. 2. I wrote to you so that you might understand the mysteries of the characters. Do not write ν above χ, θ and ηι; but rather write ζ above χ, and ν above η and θ."[46]

A second example of this trend emerges in the writing of Barsanuphius of Gaza, who lived in the first half of the sixth century. As Brouria Bitton-Ashkelony and Arieh Kofsky have shown, we can learn from Barsanuphius's correspondence about the use of isolated Greek letters as cryptographs, at times used in a mystical way, and about the interpretation of each letter of the alphabet as a theological instruction.[47]

A third example of the developed and intensive preoccupation with letters in a Christian environment emerges from a detailed treatise, *The Mysteries of the Greek Letters*,[48] which includes many varied discussions on alphabetic letters.[49] It was probably written in the circle of Saint Sabbas in the Judaean desert around the sixth century.[50] It is clear, upon reading this treatise, that its letter speculations were influenced by Jewish and Syriac sources. Within this wide-ranging composition, we find a reference to the number of Greek letters being, according to the author, twenty-two—not twenty-four. From the number of letters, we learn about the creation of the world, composed of twenty-two elements, as well as other matters involving this number, such as the number of books in the Old Testament and the number of miracles performed by Jesus.[51] The secondary division of letters into numbers such as seven,[52] fifteen,[53] and fourteen[54] is extensively discussed, and various fundamental things are taken to have an identical sum in the physical world and in the Holy Scriptures. The interpretative methods employed in the treatise include comparison between the numerical value of the letters of different words (*isopsephy/gematria*),[55] the shape of the letters,[56] and the meanings of their names in Hebrew and Syriac.[57] This composition is of utmost importance insofar as *Sefer Yeṣirah* is concerned because, as we will see in Chapter 3, the traditions that it describes dealing with letters are similar to those in *Sefer Yeṣirah*, and the author claims that their origins are Hebrew and mainly Syriac.[58]

Summary

The various discussions about the letters of the alphabet that took place in non-Jewish sources in late antiquity reveal the wide extent of this kind of usage. In this chapter, I have described the discussions most relevant to the claim for a later contextualization of *Sefer Yeṣirah*. It should be stressed that discussions about the letters of the alphabet can be found in other milieus: they had an important role, for example, in second-century CE Artemidorus's book about the interpretation of dreams,[59] they were extensively discussed in the Samaritan *Memar Marqah* (תיבת מרקה),[60] and one can find discussions about them in such writings as those of the famous Egyptian alchemist Zosimos of Panopolis (end of third–beginning of fourth centuries).[61]

Letter speculations were prevalent in Gnostic sources and were rejected by Christian and Neoplatonic thinkers, but there is nothing Gnostic in these speculations and nothing anti-Christian or anti-Neoplatonic in them. My main argument in this chapter was that although letter speculations were rejected by many Christian writers, they continued to be developed in more marginal Christian circles. In the next two chapters, I will try to demonstrate why it is more reasonable to assume that *Sefer Yeṣirah* was influenced by such an environment.

Although the discussion about alphabetical letters in *Sefer Yeṣirah*—bringing together grammatical arguments and the symbolism of the letters referring to the planets or the organs of the human body—does not have equivalents in rabbinic literature, it was already known about in the first centuries CE in non-Jewish circles. It seems that these views, which were not adopted by mainstream Jewish sources, continued to be developed in other channels and eventually found their way to the core of *Sefer Yeṣirah*.

Debate about the hierarchy of groups of letters, that is, the question of whether the vowels stand highest or lowest among the letters, will be reflected in the difference between the two main traditions of the creation of the world from letters. While the creation of the world from the letters of the ineffable name, as I will show in Chapter 2, is a product of the tradition about the creation of the world from the name of God and the importance of the vowels in Greek and Coptic sources, the creation of the world from twenty-two letters relies on a different hierarchy that does not give symbolic priority to the vowels.

Chapter 2

The Creation of the World from the Letters of the Ineffable Name

Introduction

An extensive survey of the traditions of late antiquity concerning the creation of the world from alphabetical letters suggests that they can be divided into at least two main currents: the first describes the creation of the world from twenty-two letters and can be found in *Sefer Yeṣirah* and, as we shall see, in *The Mysteries of the Greek Letters*; the second concerns the creation of the world from the letters of the ineffable name. This latter tradition, culled from rabbinic sources and the Hekhalot literature, depicts the creation of the world from the letters *he*, *yod*, and, in certain sources, *waw*. Contrary to the definite distinction between the traditions that emerges from the reading of the above-mentioned sources, in Samaritan sources we find the two traditions side by side. To date, most scholars who have discussed the creation of the world from letters have tended to unite the different narratives of the creation of the world from letters without distinguishing between them.[1] The only exception in this matter is Peter Hayman, who does, albeit briefly, address these differences.[2] In this chapter, I will discuss in detail the tradition of the creation of the world from the letters of the ineffable name; in Chapter 3, I will discuss the second tradition, about the creation of the world from twenty-two letters, while trying to demonstrate its Syriac roots. My main argument in these two chapters is that distinguishing between the traditions about the creation of the world from letters will enable us to see that *Sefer Yeṣirah* is not a part of rabbinic literature; it will also enable us to trace the origins of the specific tradition at the heart of *Sefer Yeṣirah*: the creation of the world from twenty-two letters.

As I suggested in Chapter 1, there is a reason behind the differences between the two traditions about the creation of the world from letters. The description of creation from the letters of the ineffable name looks like the result of the confluence of two different, unrelated commitments: the high status of the ineffable name in Jewish sources from the Bible onward;[3] and the hierarchy in Greek and Coptic sources structuring the relationship between vowels and consonants. Although these two issues developed separately and their roots are distinct, the connection between them is natural and requested. It seems that not later than the first century CE, Greek-speaking Jews began to describe the ineffable name as a sequence of four Hebrew vowels (*matres lectionis*). In this vein, Josephus describes the name of God as holy and "consist[ing] of four vowels."[4] It would not be far from the truth to assume that the Greek description of the name of God as a name of four letters, the tetragrammaton, stems from the very same reason.

The development of a belief in the creation of the world from the letters of the ineffable name occurred in the same way. In the first stage, during the last centuries BCE, among other beliefs about how the world was created, there was a tradition about the creation of the world from the ineffable name. Later on, in the second stage, probably from the first or the second century onward, that belief changes its form and instead of the creation of the world from the name of God, one can find depictions of the creation of the world from its letters. Scrutiny of the tradition of creation from the letters of the ineffable name has demonstrated that, in the first place, it has very little, if anything, in common with the second tradition, which depicts the creation of the world from twenty-two letters. It is only an anachronistic point of view that induces medieval Jewish writers as well as modern scholars to discuss these two traditions together, simply because both of them associate the creation of the world with alphabetical letters. To put it slightly differently, I would say that from the Middle Ages onward, the rabbinic midrashim were read through the lenses of *Sefer Yeṣirah*, although there exists a great gap between the two traditions: the first tradition elevates both the name of God and the vowels; the second gives no preference to either.

Mention should be made about the meaning of the creation of the world from the name of God or its letters. In many Jewish sources in late antiquity, from the Apocrypha literature to the rabbinic and Hekhalot literature, as well as in Samaritan sources, there is no real distinction between the narratives of the creation of the world from the name of God or its letters and depictions of the sealing of the abyss with the name of God. There is a reason that sources do not distinguish between the creation of the world and sealing the abyss: the difference between creation and the sealing of the abyss is, for the most part, significant only on the assumption that the creation of the world is ex nihilo.[5] Assuming that there was a primeval matter, the role of the creator was to form it and to overcome its chaotic nature. Therefore, from a more mythical point of view, it is reasonable to say that creation of the world actually means that the cosmos overcame primeval chaos, and hence that there is no real difference between the creation of the world from the letters of the ineffable name and the sealing of the abyss with them.

The Early Roots: The Creation of the World from the Name of God

As mentioned above, the tradition that the world was created with the letters of God's name has early roots:[6] in Jubilees 36, Isaac is leaving his two sons, Jacob and Esau, instructing them to keep to the way of God, by whose name heaven and earth were created:

> And in the sixth year of this week, Isaac called his two sons, Esau and Jacob. And they came to him and he said to them: "My sons, I am going in the way of my fathers to the eternal home where my fathers are. . . . Remember, my sons, the Lord the God of Abraham, your father, and (that) I subsequently worshiped and

> served him in righteousness and joy so that he might multiply you and increase your seed like the stars of heaven with regard to numbers and (so that) he will plant you on the earth as a righteous planting that will not be uprooted for all the eternal generations. And now I will make you swear by the great oath—because there is not an oath that is greater than it, by the glorious and honored and great and splendid and amazing and mighty name that created heavens and earth and everything together—that you will fear him and worship him."[7]

Another source in which God's name is seen as a part of the creation process is the Prayer of Manasseh, which relates that God used "his word" to contain the sea and sealed the abyss with his name: "O Lord, God of our fathers, God of Abraham, and of Isaac, and of Jacob, and of their righteous offspring/ He who made the heaven and the earth, with all their embellishment/ He who bound the sea and established it by the command of his word, he who closed the bottomless pit, and sealed it by his powerful and glorious name."[8]

Rather than the name of God creating the world, here it is a guarantee for its existence. It should be noted that creation through speech, familiar from Genesis, is described in the Prayer of Manasseh as an act of restraining the sea—"who bound the sea and established it by the command of His word," while the name of God is the sealer of the abyss: "who closed the bottomless pit, and sealed it by His powerful and glorious name." As noted above, it seems that there is no real difference between the creation of the world and sealing the primordial chaos.

Another testimonial to the role of the name of God in creation is to be found in a few verses of the Book of Parables in 1 Enoch. In this account, the creation of the world and the sealing of the abyss are indistinguishable: "he spoke to Michael to disclose him his secret name so that he would memorize this secret name of his so that he would call it up in an oath. . . . These are the secrets of this oath—and they are sustained by the oath: The heaven was suspended before the creation of the world; and forever! By it the earth is founded upon the water. . . . By that oath the sea was created."[9] In this text, the mysteries of the ineffable name active in creation include the hanging of the heaven and the creation of the sea.

These three sources offer evidence that the tradition concerning the creation of the world from the name of God, which is not mentioned in the biblical literature, was, in fact, well known in the last centuries BCE. Yet it is only in later sources, from the first or the second century CE onward, that a shift in this tradition can be discerned such that the meaning of the creation of the world by the name of God refers not to the name but to the letters of the name, and thereby to the idea of the creation of the world by the letters of the name of God.

From the Name of God to Its Letters

The Rabbinic Literature

Among a variety of myths about the creation of the world, or *ma'aseh bereishit*,[10] rabbinic literature contains several midrashim about creation from the letters of the name of God[11] or sealing the abyss with them.[12] The aggadic sources, especially Palestinian ones, contain a number of cosmogenic midrashim that discuss the role of the letters *he* or *yod* in the process of creation. From the two midrashim presented by R. Abbahu, one in his own name and the other in the name of R. Yoḥanan, it emerges that the world was created from the letter *he*.[13] So, for example, Genesis Rabbah, as well as other sources, contains a midrash on the word *behibram* (בהבראם), which means "when they were created": "When they were created (בהבראם), R. Abbahu said in R. Yoḥanan's name: 'He created them with the letter *he*.'"[14]

A comparable midrash, also from Genesis Rabbah, arrives at the same conclusion based on the word *hashmaima* (השמימה), which means "toward heaven": "R. Abbahu commented thereon: 'It is not written look at heaven (הבט נא שמים) but toward heaven (השמימה) (Gen 15:5): with this *he*, I created the world.'"[15] Other sources in Genesis Rabbah as well as other rabbinic writings assert a connection between the ineffable name and the letters *he* and *waw*. The sages differ as to how to think about this connection:

> R. Judah ha-Nasi asked R. Shmuel b. Naḥman: As I have heard that you are a master of *haggadah*, tell me the meaning of "lift up a song to him who rides upon the *arabot*, *b-YH* is His name" (סולו לרוכב בערבות ביה שמו) (Ps. 68:5). . . . I asked R. Eleazar, and he did not explain it thus. But the verse *trust ye in the Lord forever, for with YH YHWH created the worlds*[16] (בטחו ביהוה עדי עד כי ביה יהוה צור עולמים) (Isa. 26:4) means: By these two letters did the Lord create His world. Now we do not know whether this world was created with a *he* or the next world with a *yod*, but from what R. Abbahu said in R. Yoḥanan's name, namely, *be-hibbaraam* (בהבראם) means, with a *he* created He them, it follows that this world was created by means of a *he*.[17]

This midrash, whose subject is the word *b-YH* (ביה), claims that this world and the world to come were created from the letters *he* and *yod*, which make up the word in question. The doubling of God's name in the verse—*YH YHWH*—leads R. Eleazar to say that the supposedly abbreviated name *YH* together with the letter *bet* (here an ablative indication) does not refer to God but rather to the letters from which the world was created.

In Midrash Tanḥuma to Leviticus, we find a more explicit claim concerning the connection between the creation of the world, the letters *he* and *yod*, and the ineffable name, which prompts the question: Why did God create the worlds from the abbreviation of His name and not from the whole name?

> *When any of you sin in that you have heard a public adjuration, etc.* (ונפש כי תחטא ושמעה קול אלה וגו') (Lev. 5:1). This text is related: *Never be rash with your mouth, nor let your heart be quick to utter a word before God* (אל תבהל על פיך ולבך אל ימהר להוציא דבר לפני האלהים) (Eccles. 5:1). These [words refer to] human beings who vilify the name of the Holy One, blessed be He. Come and see: when the celestial beings were created, those below were created with half of the name, as stated: *for with YH YHWH created worlds* (כי ביה יהוה צור עולמים) (Isa. 26:4). But why were they not created

> with all of it? So that none of them would repeat the full name of the Holy One, blessed be He. Woe to those creatures who vilify the name of the Holy One, blessed be He, in vain.[18]

This midrash teaches the great importance of the ineffable name; both worlds were created from only two of its letters and not from all four. As a moral lesson, the midrash points to the transgression of invoking the full name of God to no use, the very name, only half of which was employed in the creation of the world.

In a paper dedicated to the sealing of the primeval abyss in texts dating from the first century CE forward, David Sperber points to accounts of this sealing by the engraving of the ineffable name. We learn about the existence of this tradition in an early period from the Prayer of Manasseh, quoted above,[19] and similar elements emerge from a Syriac version of the Psalms of Solomon.[20] Sperber adds to these some early Christian sources giving variants of the legend.[21] The importance of sources is compounded by the light they shed on three rabbinic midrashim concerning the digging of the *shittin* (pits by the side of the altar)[22] by David: the midrashim are in b. Sukkah and Makkot and y. Sanhedrin.[23] According to the Babylonian version, it seems that after David dug the *shittin*, the abyss threatened to wash away the world, to bind it in place, Aḥitophel had to write the ineffable name and throw it inside. Taking into account other Jewish and Christian sources of late antiquity that allude to this matter, we might interpret this midrash as follows: in the process of digging the *shittin*, David struck the ineffable name, which was a seal on the abyss and therefore had to seal it anew with the name that Aḥitophel wrote.

According to the second version of the midrash, in y. Sanhedrin, in the process of digging, David moved a piece of earthenware that had been thrown into the abyss, an act that almost caused the destruction of the world: "When he removed the clay pot, the great deep surged upward to flood the world."[24] It can be assumed, in this case as well, that the presence of the dislodged rock on which the ineffable name had been engraved was a magical way to avert the eruption of the abyss. If this interpretation is correct, it would seem that there are narratives about the sealing of the abyss with the ineffable name in the rabbinic literature as well—and that the story of the digging of the *shittin* by David evokes that story.

Targum Pseudo-Jonathan explicitly connects the ineffable name and the foundation stone. Though this is a relatively late text, it is probable that it preserves early sources. Pseudo-Jonathan recounts that the ineffable name, from which the 310 worlds were created, was engraved on the foundation stone: "And thou shalt put upon the breastplate of judgment the *Uraia*, which illuminate their words, and manifest the hidden things of the house of Israel, and the *Tumaia*, which fulfill their work to the high priest, who seeketh instruction by them before the Lord; because in them is engraved and expressed the Great and Holy Name by which were created the 310 worlds and which was engraved and expressed in the foundation stone wherewith the Lord of the world sealed up the mouth of the great deep at the beginning. Whosoever remembereth that holy name in the hour of necessity shall be delivered."[25] This midrash makes a link between the four elements: the foundation stone, the sealing of the abyss, the ineffable name, and the creation of the world. As such, it shows how different cosmogonic myths became consolidated and how they were understood by certain sages.

The creation of the world from letters was understood by most rabbinic sources as referring to the letters of the ineffable name. A number of midrashim hint at traditions concerning the creation of the world from other letters or from all twenty-two letters of the Hebrew alphabet. It would be, of course, impossible to give an unequivocal clarification to those midrashim, and it could be that along with the main tradition about the creation of the world from the letters of the ineffable name there were, at the margins of the rabbinic literature other attitudes. Nevertheless, a meticulous scrutiny of those midrashim does not support an interpretation of them as referring to letters other than those of the ineffable name, and it suggests that such an interpretation is based on an anachronistic assumption, at odds with the contextual knowledge we actually have.

I will open with a well-known example of such a midrash from b. Berakhot about the magical abilities of Bezalel, the builder of the tabernacle: "R. Judah said in the name of Rav: Bezalel knew to combine letters by which heaven and earth were created."[26] This declaration, which has a few equivalents in the Hekhalot literature, does not evince the specific letters that Bezalel combined,[27] so that we have no indication as to which letters the midrash refers to. Reading the midrash reveals that Rav's main purpose is to stress that Bezalel possessed high magical knowledge and knew how to combine letters by which the world was created. In this respect, Rav compares the created cosmos and the tabernacle as a microcosmos. Rav is not interested in the myth about the creation of the world from letters but rather uses it to underline the role of Bezalel and the symbolic meaning of the tabernacle. The absence in rabbinic literature of any significant assertion that the world was created from all twenty-two letters of the alphabet, as well as the existence of a variety of midrashim regarding the creation of the world from the ineffable name, leads to the reasonable conclusion that, according to this midrash, the world was created by the letters of the ineffable name and not the whole alphabet. Were we not cognizant of the tradition that the world was created from the twenty-two letters of the alphabet described in *Sefer Yeṣrah* and were solely aware of rabbinic sources referring to creation from letters, we would have no doubt that the expression "letters from which heaven and earth were created" refers to the letters *he* and *yod*. Gershom Scholem interpreted Rav in this way: "Bezalel, who built the Tabernacle, 'knew the combinations of letters with which heaven and earth were made'—so we read in the name of a Babylonian scholar of the early third century, the most prominent representative of the esoteric tradition in his generation [Rav T. W.]. The letters in question were unquestionably those of the name of God."[28]

Another midrash connecting the creation of the world from letters other than those of the ineffable name is the famous midrash telling how the world was created from the letter *bet*. The midrash appears in a few places in rabbinic literature[29] as well as in later midrashim that deal extensively with the alphabetic letters: the first appearance, *Letters of R. Akiva*, version A, is a composition of eclectic traditions, most of which are based on the Hekhalot literature;[30] the second, *Letters of R. Akiva*, version B, is based on rabbinic tradition and was probably edited between the sixth and ninth centuries. The midrash focuses on why the world was created from the letter *bet* in particular; so we know that such a tradition existed.[31] However, an examination of this midrash in all its versions reveals that it does not deal with the creation of the world from or by this letter but rather with the word that inaugurates the biblical description of creation: *bereishit*. In this midrash, as in its Samaritan parallel, *bet* signifies the boundary between the chaos that existed before creation, a chaos that is not to be interpreted, and the created cosmos.[32] In this vein, we should also read the version of the midrash from a section of midrash Tanḥuma found in the Cairo Geniza, published by Ephraim E. Urbach: "*Bereishit*: Why did He begin the creation of the world with *bet* and not with *alef*, as *alef* is the head of all the letters of the Torah?"[33] There is a parallel to this midrash as it appears in *Letters of R. Akiva*, version A: "Why did the Holy One, blessed be He, create His world with *bet* in *Bereishit bara* (In the beginning [God] created [Gen. 1:1]) and end the Torah with *lamed* (*leyney kol Israel,* in the sight of all Israel [Deut. 34:12])? When you join them, it becomes *BL*, and when you reverse them, they become *LB* (heart)."[34] In this midrash, too, we observe that creation with the letter *bet* refers to something essentially other than creation from or by letters: the main question is, why did the account of creation begin with this specific letter? The midrash consequently compares the word *bereishit*, with which the Torah begins, with the word *Israel*, with which it ends, such that the role of the letter *bet* in this context is similar to that of the concluding letter *lamed*.

In rabbinic literature, only one source is known to me of a midrash that discloses a definite acquaintance with the tradition about the creation of the world from twenty-two letters. That singular source appears in the same sections of Tanḥuma published by Urbach, and in it, it is written that the Torah that lit up the darkness of the primordial chaos for God also put at his disposal the twenty-two letters: "While He was creating the world, the Torah was, as it were, shedding light before Him, for the world was without form and void, as it is said: 'For the commandment is a lamp and the Torah—light' (כי נר מצוה ותורה אור) (Prov. 6:23). The Holy One, blessed be He, said: I shall ask for laborers. The Torah said to Him: I shall put forth for you twenty-two workers. And these are the twenty-two letters of the Torah."[35]

This midrash, which seems to be expressing a notion similar to the process of creation from the twenty-two letters envisioned in *Sefer Yeṣirah*, belongs to the later strata of rabbinic literature and has, to the best of my knowledge, no parallels. It is reasonable to assume that, at the time of this midrash, a new approach to the creation of the world from letters penetrated the margins of the rabbinic literature. Since this tradition was alien to the rabbinic ones, it was adapted by the midrash according to a more familiar tradition about the creation of the world from the Torah. The claim of the midrash is that the letters from which the world was created were given to God by the Torah, and it is therefore the Torah that is the origin of the alphabetic letters and the world. The midrash mainly focuses on the dialogue between God and the Torah and on the crucial role that the Torah had in the process of creation and does not address the role of the alphabet in creation as an issue of interest. Similarly, yet as a mirror image, as we shall see, *Sefer Yeṣirah* operates in the same manner with regard to the tradition about the creation of the world from the letters of the ineffable name.[36] Throughout *Sefer Yeṣirah*, from its second chapter forward, the ineffable name of God and its letters have no role in the creation of the world and the letters of the ineffable name: *yod*, *he*, and *waw* are neither defined as a distinct group of letters nor do they have any symbolic meaning that connects them to the name of God. In the only instance that *Sefer Yeṣirah* does mention the letters of the ineffable name in relation to the creation of the world, those letters are defined as three letters from the group of the twelve simple letters. In this case, *Sefer Yeṣirah* appropriates the tradition of the creation of the world from the ineffable name and adapts it to its core tradition about the creation of the world from twenty-two letters. It is exactly this manner of adaptation rather than adoption that stresses what can be considered a core percept, as opposed to an appended one in both the rabbinic literature and in *Sefer Yeṣirah* and thereby accentuates the essential disparity between them.

Hekhalot Literature

The dominant attitude toward the creation of the world from letters in the Hekhalot literature, as in the aforementioned rabbinic sources, favors the letters of the ineffable name. The Hekhalot literature is a heterogenous, multilayered corpus of texts created, written, and edited over a long period. Most manuscripts in this literature were edited only during the late Middle Ages, in the circles of *Ḥasidei Ashkenaz*.[37] Consequently, attempting to designate the traditions found in this literary corpus contextually, according to period and location, is problematic. Nevertheless, there are significant differences between the Hekhalot texts and those of *Ḥasidei Ashkenaz*, and there is no reason to doubt the origins of the Hekhalot literature in Babylonia and even earlier in Palestine. The common scholarly assumption is that most of this literature was created between the late tannaitic and geonic periods.[38] I have therefore chosen to adopt an approach to the Hekhalot literature that is based on an inclusive and comprehensive overview rather than a reading of specific isolated paragraphs. This overview allows us to distinguish and extract the predominant approach to the creation of the world from letters in the Hekhalot literature.

The creation of the world from the ineffable name figures in the version of a prayer transmitted by R. Akiva to R. Ishmael at the end of *ma'aseh merkavah*, in which R. Ishmael asks how one can look above the seraphs, to which R. Akiva responds that when he stood in the first celestial palace, he uttered a certain prayer that allowed him to see from the first palace as far as the seventh: "R. Ishmael said: I said to R. Akiva: How can one contemplate above the Seraphs that stand above the head of *ROZYY*[39] *YWY*, God of Israel? He told me: when I ascended to the first palace, I prayed a prayer, and I saw from the first palace to the seventh palace . . . and what was the prayer? Blessed be You, *YY*, Unique God, who created His world with His one name, who makes everything with one utterance."[40]

The special formula in the blessing of R. Akiva enlightens us as to the existence of two traditions of creation that appear side by side: the creation of the world from the ineffable name; and from the speech of God: "who created His world with His one name, who makes everything with one utterance." This is similar to the thought expressed in the above-mentioned Prayer of Manasseh.[41]

In addition to the early narrative of the creation of the world from the name of God, we find in the Hekhalot literature a tradition that is a derivative of it: the creation or sealing of the world from one or more letters of the ineffable name. God created the world and sealed His deeds with one letter of His name: "I call upon you once again in a name greater than all your names, [a name] that is nice and pleasant, in your master's name, since one letter is omitted (from) His name with which He created and founded everything and He sealed with it all his creations."[42]

In this source, we again see that there is no real difference between the creation of the world and the sealing of it: God took a letter from His name, with which He created and sealed the creation. Further sources tying the ineffable name to the creation of the world are contained in a Hekhalot fragment from the Cairo Geniza. The following section, although it is fractured, shows that it deals with the connection between one letter of the ineffable name and the creation of the world: "O[ne] is the world, one (the people of) Israel are, one [i]s the world from [ ] in the earth One is He who creates the world those Israel [among] the nations. One is He who creates the world corresponding to one letter of [His name] before He created the world corresponding one letter of His name [one is?] the world corresponding to one letter of His name."[43]

Although this interesting source is amputated and about a third of the page of this section is defective, its main concern is clear. The source associates the oneness of God, the oneness of the people of Israel, and one letter from God's name from which the world was created. This letter existed before the creation and corresponds to the world, which means that God created the world with it.

The tradition that the world was created from letters was given more detailed articulation in the later layers of the Hekhalot literature. Thus the late Hekhalot composition *Seder Rabbah de Bereishit* includes a midrash about the creation of the world from six letters encompassing the tetragrammaton YHWH (יהוה) and its biblical abbreviation YH (יה):[44]

> *Ma'aseh bereishit*: "In the beginning God created"—do not read *bereishit* [in the beginning] but rather *bara-shit* [created six], and so you find that in [the word] *bereishit* (בראשית), there are six letters with which heaven and earth were created, as it is said: *for with YA YHWH created worlds* (כי ביה יהוה צור עלמים) (Isa. 26:4), YA two (letters), YHWH four (letters), so there are six. Thus you have learned that by these six letters, the Holy One, blessed be He, created heaven and earth. And if you shall say: Were only

> heaven and earth created? Yet this world and the world to come were created by them! As it is said: *for with YA YHWH created worlds* (כי ביה יהוה צור עלמים) (Isa. 26:4). Thus you have learned that with these six letters, the Holy One, blessed be He, created heaven and earth, this world and the world to come. This is why it is said *bereishit*.[45]

This long and detailed midrash addresses two layers of letters: it begins with the six letters of the first word of the Torah, *bereishit* (בראשית) and splits the Hebrew word into two different words, the first in Hebrew the second in Aramaic, which together mean "created—six" (ברא-שית). In its second layer, the midrash says that those six letters correspond to the six letters of the ineffable names: YA YHWH (יה יהוה), the real letters with which the worlds were created.

Of all the Hekhalot material featuring discussions about the creation of the world from the ineffable name or from its letters that I know of, I have found only one case that connects the creation of the world with the number twenty-two. According to the passage at the end of 3 Enoch, the Lord set twenty-two seals on creation: "These are the ninety-two names that are like the explicit name on the chariot, which are graven upon the throne of glory, for the Holy One, blessed be He, took [them] from his explicit name and placed them upon the name of Metatron. He has seventy names with which the King of Kings, blessed be He, and the ministering angels in the high heavens call. And twenty-two seals of his fingerprint in which all the ranks of the *arabot* [heaven] were sealed."[46]

This source connects the creation process and twenty-two seals; according to one, albeit very late, manuscript, the seals refer to the twenty-two letters.[47] The Hekhalot literature is not homogeneous, and one can assume that there were other ways of approaching the creation of the world from letters. Nevertheless, there is good reason to assume that even in this section, the twenty-two seals do not necessarily refer to the twenty-two letters of the alphabet but may refer to a succession of twenty-two letters of the ineffable name. In what follows, I will present the information pertinent to my argument.

In some places in the Hekhalot literature, one can find an original distinction between two layers of the language: on the lower level are the seventy languages designated for everyday discourse; the heavenly language is above this layer and is called the "language of purity." The language of purity is a language of the angels, composed of only three letters: *he*, *yod*, and *waw*. This distinction between ordinary language and the language of purity replaces the common hierarchy between the Hebrew language, taken to be holy, and all other languages, and is probably connected to the high status of the vowels in Greek and Coptic literature.[48]

An example of a distinction that the Hekhalot literature makes between ordinary language and the language of purity occurs in the second part of the paragraph discussed above about the creation of the world from one letter of the ineffable name: "I call upon you once again in a name greater than all your names, [a name] that is nice and pleasant, in your master's name, since one letter is omitted (from) His name with which He created and founded everything and He sealed with it all his creations, and this is its interpretation: YWRN TWKPN WHDWRN AŠŠ MKṢTT MG MSṢYY MNYKYY PYPG HWGYY HSS PṢS YH SAMYNNSYH KTW HWHS and its interpretation in the language of purity, in *yod he*, how is it to be read? YHWH YW HWH HW YHWH YH HYH YHWH ḤY WHYY HYW HYH YH HHW YW ḤY HYH YH YHWH YWH."[49]

This source belongs to a treatise named *Sar ha-Panim* (The prince of presence) to which it is part of a series of adjurations. The source describes the importance of one of the names of God, a name also attributed to *Sar ha-Panim*. This name has two layers: the first and lower layer involves sequences of all the alphabetic letters where some kind of *nomina barbara* can be found. The higher layer, "the language of purity," contains sequences of letters of the ineffable name. The language of purity is, then, a translation of the ordinary alphabet into a higher one composed of only three letters—the letters of the ineffable name—and it is similar to the successions of vowels found in Greek and Coptic amulets as well as in sources from the Nag-Hammadi library.

Examining the notions of twenty-two names and twenty-two seals that were mentioned in the source from 3 Enoch from this perspective suggests that those seals refer to a succession of twenty-two letters of the ineffable name and not the twenty-two letters of the alphabet. An interesting example of a Hekhalot text discussing the notion of twenty-two letters at two levels—a lower one, comprising *nomina Barbara*, and higher one, comprising *he*, *yod*, and *waw*—is found in *Hekhalot Zutartei*: "These are the twenty-two letters that are twenty-two names from one letter of the Torah. TŠRK, ṢP'S, NMLKHY, ṪḤZ, WHDGBA, for with YA the Lord (כי ביה אדני) Lord YA (אדני יה), *WYHW YH WHY WHYW WHYH HYH YH*. H(oly) H(oly) H(oly)."[50]

The section begins with statements about the twenty-two letters, saying that they stem from a letter in Torah. After the enumeration of the twenty-two letters in reverse order, a phrase is cited connected with Isa. 26:4, a verse that refers in both the rabbinic literature and *Seder Rabbah de Bereishit* to the creation of the world from the letters of the ineffable name. Immediately following the three words כי ביה אדני, a mirror image of the last two ineffable names אדני יה appears, and subsequently a sequence of twenty-two letters of the ineffable name *yod*, *he*, and *waw*.[51] Interpolating this section according to my suggested interpretation results in the following:

> These are the twenty-two letters
> that are twenty-two names from one letter of the Torah.
> TŠRK, ṢP'S, NMLKHY, ṪḤZ, WHDGBA,
> for with YA the Lord (כי ביה אדני)
> Lord YA (אדני יה),
> WYHV YH WHY WHYW WHYH HYH YH.
> H(oly) H(oly) H(oly).[52]

According to this passage, there exists a mirror to the letters of the alphabet in a higher rank of letters: those of the ineffable name. This reading evokes parallels in the distinction between the twenty-two Hebrew letters and those of the ineffable name, as well as between the seventy languages and the language of purity. As we have seen, in the context of the Hekhalot literature, the twenty-two letters do not necessarily refer to the Hebrew alphabet but might refer to combinations of twenty-two letters composed of the letters *he*, *yod*, and *waw*.[53]

The interpretation presented above is reinforced by a reading of Gnostic sources such as *The Gospel of the Egyptians*, a treatise from the Nag-Hammadi library in which we find sequences of vowels. In this text, we find both a description of the ineffability of the name of "the aeon of the aeons" as well as successions of vowels, each one composed of twenty-two letters: "Domedon Doxomedon came forth, the aeon of aeons, . . . he [who came] forth from the silence, while he rests in the silence, he whose name [is] in an [invisible] symbol. [A] hidden, [invisible] mystery came forth iiiiiiiiiiiiiiiii[iii] ēēēēēēēēēēēēēēēēēēēē[ēē o]oooooooooooooooooo oo uu[uuu]uuuuuuuuu uuuuuuuu eeeeeeeeeeeeeeeeeeeeee aaaaaaa[aaaa]aaaaaaaaaaa ōōōō ōōōōō[ōō] ōōōōōōōōōōō."[54]

The fact that this text presents successions of precisely twenty-two letters cannot be considered coincidental, especially because such a succession is also found in the quotation from "The Discourse of the Eighth and the Ninth" quoted above. Why, then, would a text of Greek/Coptic origin specify a succession of exactly twenty-two vowels? We have before us testimony to a realm of engagement and mutual influence between Hebrew/Aramaic and Greek/Coptic notions. I suggest that, at first, the Greek/Coptic hierarchy between the vowels and the consonants influenced Hebrew or Aramaic sources, sources that symbolized the heavenly language by a succession of twenty-two *matres lectionis*. In other words, Greek/Coptic notions had an influence on how, in the Hebrew or Aramaic sources, the hierarchy of the letters was conceived: the ordinary language composed of twenty-two letters contrasted with a higher language composed of twenty-two *matres lectionis*, which are also the letters of the ineffable name. In a second stage, these sources from Nag-Hammadi readapted a Semitic combination of twenty-two vowels.

With all this in mind, let us return to the Hekhalot literature, specifically to the section from 3 Enoch. It is now clear, following the abovementioned review, that its main interest is in the letters of the ineffable name engraved on the throne that God gave to Metatron. The twenty-two seals are most likely made up of combinations of the engraved letters. In view of the above discussion concerning the hierarchy where the language of purity consists of twenty-two letters composed of vowels, or of the letters of the ineffable name, it is reasonable to assume that the twenty-two seals that this passage describes do not correspond to the whole alphabet but reproduce only the letters *he, yod*, and *waw*.

Memar Marqah

Samaritan texts, especially those found in the collection of Samaritan homilies *Memar Marqah* (תיבת מרקה), are an additional source, one that is culturally and geographically close to the Jewish world.[55] Here we find an abundance of different kinds of discussions about letters. *Memar Marqah* is a collection of homilies arranged in six books, of which the first five deal with Moses, beginning with the revelation of God in the burning bush and ending with the death of Moses after the journey through the desert; the sixth book, which is not part of this chronology, is called the "Homily of the Twenty-Two Letters." According to Samaritan tradition, this composition is attributed to the poet Marqah, who lived sometime between the second and fourth centuries CE.[56] Scholars are divided over the date of composition of the book, with suggestions ranging from the first to the ninth centuries.

On the basis of his comprehensive research into Samaritan Aramaic, Zeev Ben-Ḥayyim claims that the book is composed of different sections written beginning in the first centuries CE and continuing until the last centuries of the first millennium.[57] Ben-Ḥayyim notes that these kinds of traces point to large gaps in time, not only between the different sections but also within them.[58] Of greater relevance for our inquiry is his assumption that the dating of the contents of the book cannot be deduced from the dating of its actual writing,[59] since it is possible that material formulated in later Aramaic reflects ancient traditions of which no written evidence remains. Like the rabbinic literature, the Samaritan *Memar Marqah* contains a few midrashim about the creation of the world from the ineffable name or from one of its letters. Jarl Fossum, in *The Name of God and the Angel of the Lord*, has demonstrated that some of those beliefs are very early and can be traced to the first century CE. With regard to the creation of the world from the name of God, in the fourth book of *Memar Marqah*, Moses says to God: "O Thou who hast crowned me with Thy light and magnified me with wonders and honored me with Thy glory and hid me in Thy palm and brought me into the Sanctuary of the Unseen and vested me with Thy name, by which Thou didst create the world."[60]

In addition to this source describing the creation of the world from the name of God, there are depictions of the creation of the world solely from the letter *he* of the name—for example: "*Ascribe greatness to our God* (והבו גדל לאלהינו) (Deut. 32:3). The great prophet Moses made it the gateway to all praises. In it (והבו) is contained Genesis, as well as what is like it. *Waw* (ו) represents the six days and everything created in them. *He* (ה) is the name that all creatures arose. *Bet* (ב) is the two worlds, the first world and the second world. *Waw* (ו) is the end."[61]

The letters *waw* and *he* from the word והבו are each purported to be connected to the creation of the world. The numerical value of *waw* indicates the six days of creation; *he* indicates the name from which the world was created.

It seems that as in the rabbinic corpus, so in the Samaritan literature; in the first stage, the belief was that the world was created by the name of God; in the second stage, that belief was amalgamated with a new notion about the importance of the letters of the name of God. The fact that we can find these beliefs in both Jewish and Samaritan sources demonstrates that there is a context; we catch the reflection of an environment in which the name of God was identified as a succession of letters.

Sefer Yeṣirah and the Ineffable Name

As I have mentioned, *Sefer Yeṣirah* as a rule does not show any interest in the letters of the ineffable name, but there is one exception. In the first chapter of *Sefer Yeṣirah*, one finds an explicit narrative about the sealing (חתימה) of the six directions of the world with different combinations of the letters of the ineffable name *he*, *waw*, and *yod*. What the sealing referred to in this text is unclear; it does not state that it is the chaos that was sealed by the name of God, as in other myths referred to above, and this sealing certainly does not correspond to the creation of the world from letters. It nevertheless seems that this tradition, which has parallels in Jewish and Gnostic sources,[62] asserts that the name of God guarantees the existence of the three dimensions of space: "Five—he sealed above. He chose three simple letters and fixed them in his great name—YHW. And he sealed with them the six edges (of the universe), and turned upward and sealed it with YWH. Six—he sealed below. He turned downward and sealed it with YWH. Seven—he sealed the east. He turned in front and sealed it with HYW. Eight—he sealed the west. He turned behind and sealed it with HWY. Nine—he sealed the south. He turned to his right and sealed it with WYH. Ten—he sealed the north. He turned to his left and sealed it with WHY."[63]

The preface to this section about the sealing of the dimensions of the world with the ineffable name suggests that the ineffable name had a role of some sort in the creation in *Sefer Yeṣirah*. Nevertheless, a careful reading the last paragraph reveals that the creation of the world from the ineffable name has a problematic status in *Sefer Yeṣirah*. In this paragraph, which appears in all manuscripts of *Sefer Yeṣirah* known to me, the letters of the ineffable name have a low status in the hierarchy of the letters, which brings to mind the low rank of the vowels in the hierarchy of the letters as depicted by Marcus. According to the above paragraph from *Sefer Yeṣirah*, God took three letters of the twelve simple letters and only subsequently affixed them to his name and sealed the six half-dimensions of the world with them.

This tortuous formulation seemed to Peter Hayman to be a later addition and led him to claim that, in all likelihood, it did not feature in the early versions of the paragraph.[64] But it is impossible to confirm or refute Hayman's hypothesis, since we do not have in our possession any evidence of versions of *Sefer Yeṣirah* without this articulation. The very claim of *Sefer Yeṣirah* that the world was sealed with the letters of the ineffable name is problematic in this context, since *Sefer Yeṣirah* evidently does not assign high status to the letters of the ineffable name, making such a claim incongruous. This anomaly will not be solved by reconstructing a hypothetical fluent version of the text. It is, rather, a diligent reading of the words and examination of their meaning that finally establishes that what we have before us is a text contesting other approaches to the creation of the world from letters. It seems that alongside the presentation of its own approach to the creation of the world from the twenty-two letters of the alphabet, *Sefer Yeṣirah* refers to "the other approach," with which it does not identify, in an attempt to override it and make it accord with its own method. *Sefer Yeṣirah* adapts the inadmissible doctrine of the creation of the world from the letters of the ineffable name to its own approach, the creation of the world from the twenty two-letters, by stressing that the origin of the three letters *he*, *waw*, and *yod* is, in fact, the twelve simple letters. If we read the claim of *Sefer Yeṣirah* as it is, with no attempt at reconstructing an unknown editorial orientation, we discover a provocative contention that presents a hierarchy of letters: while *Sefer Yeṣirah* presents the well-known belief that the world was sealed with the letters of the name of God, it claims that these letters are but a segment of a larger whole. This claim is congruent with its general point of view about the ascendancy of the twenty-two letters.

For hundreds of years, in many contexts, the letters of the ineffable name were strictly written in Paleo-Hebrew script; they were employed as amulets, they were written on the miter of the high priest, and their utterance was prohibited.[65] Despite their potency, they are for *Sefer Yeṣirah* three letters from the largest and least defined group of letters, designated as the "simple" letters. Additional support for this claim derives from the fact that in the body of the book, in the third chapter, we find a different tradition from that of the first chapter, according to which the world was sealed by the letters *alef*, *mem*, and *shin*.[66] In addition, if Ithamar Gruenwald's thesis according to which *Sefer Yeṣirah*'s first chapter is an independent composition that was integrated into the book, is correct, it follows that the first composition, describing the sealing of the world with the ineffable name, was edited to make it conform to the contents of the entire book, which deals with the twenty-two letters.[67]

Summary

The creation of the world with the name of God, as described in the Apocrypha literature, is probably an outcome of the ontological qualities that the ineffable name of God absorbed from the biblical literature onward.[68] The belief that the world was created by this name is not surprising, in light of the following facts: in the late Second Temple period, the pronunciation of the tetragrammaton was considered to be secret;[69] it was written, because of its holiness, in Paleo-Hebraic characters, even in square Hebrew texts and in Greek texts;[70] and it was considered to have the highest magical qualities. In the second stage, as I have argued throughout this chapter, under the influence of Greek and Coptic perceptions of the importance of the vowels, the name of God was seen not only as a noun or written unit but as a sequence of Hebrew vowels (*matres lectionis*). That was probably the reason for the evolution of this myth of creation: from the view that the world was created from the name of God into a myth of the creation of the world from the letters of the name of God. In this respect, it is interesting to see that transfer of knowledge between Hebrew/Aramaic and Greek/Coptic contexts in this matter was rapid and transformative. Texts from the Nag-Hammadi library, in which there are successions of twenty-two vowels, make prompt mutual influence seem likely.

Another example of mutual influence can be found in *Pistis Sophia*, where combinations of the letters of one of the Greek forms of the ineffable name (ϊαω) are juxtaposed with a description of the sealing of the dimensions of the world by the ineffable name, in a similar manner to that of *Sefer Yeṣirah*: "Then Jesus stood with his *disciples* beside the water of the *ocean* and pronounced this prayer, saying: Hear me, my Father, thou father of all fatherhoods, thou *infinite* Light: αεηιουω. ϊαω. αωϊ. ωϊα. . . . And Jesus cried out as he turned to the four corners of the world with his *disciples* . . . and he said: ϊαω ϊαω ϊαω. This is its *interpretation*: iota, because the All came forth; alpha, because it will return again—omega, because the completion of all completions will happen."[71] In this text, written in Greek around the third century CE, the ineffable name of God is a sequence of different combinations of the Greek vowels that sealed the cosmos. This is a further case of Greek influence on Jewish perception, followed by a Jewish influence on Greek texts.

My main goal in this chapter was to demonstrate that the creation of the world from the letters of the ineffable name was the main tradition concerning the creation of the world from letters to be found in late antique rabbinic sources. This tradition has two derivations: first, the name of God has ontological qualities; and second is the priority of the Hebrew *matres lectionis* over the other letters. These two assumptions are absent from *Sefer Yeṣirah*: the name of God does not play a significant role in *Sefer Yeṣirah*;

Chapter 3

The Creation of the World from Twenty-Two Letters and the Syriac Context of *Sefer Yeṣirah*

The Creation of the World from Twenty-Two Letters

Sefer Yeṣirah is a composition written in a fluent Hebrew before the tenth century and therefore would seem to belong to the known Jewish literary corpus of late antiquity. Nevertheless, *Sefer Yeṣirah* differs from these sources in crucial respects: *Sefer Yeṣirah* uses a different terminology, it articulates its arguments in a totally different manner, and it does not refer to rabbinic figures. The differences between *Sefer Yeṣirah* and the other Jewish sources are reflected also in the core issue of the book: its discussions about the role of the twenty-two letters in the creation of the world. Unlike most of the Jewish literature in late antiquity, in which it is rare to find texts that explicitly refer to the creation of the world from all the twenty-two letters of the alphabet, most of *Sefer Yeṣirah* is dedicated to this matter, as in the following example: "Twenty-two letters: He carved them out, he hewed them, he weighed them and exchanged them, he combined them and formed with them the life of all creation and the life of all that would be formed."[1]

Whereas there are substantial differences between *Sefer Yeṣirah* and other Jewish sources about the specific letters that serve in the creation of the world in a few non-Jewish sources, in the Samaritan *Memar Marqah*—and, especially, in the sixth-century Christian composition *The Mysteries of the Greek Letters*—we find the same tradition as in *Sefer Yeṣirah*, the creation of the world from all twenty-two letters. To contextualize *Sefer Yeṣirah*, we will begin our discussion with *Memar Marqah*, which mentions this tradition only once, as part of a description of another, more dominant, tradition about the creation of the world from the ineffable name and its letters; then we will turn to *The Mysteries of the Greek Letters*, which discusses this tradition extensively and comprehensively.

Memar Marqah

Along with the discussions in *Memar Marqah* about the creation of the world from the name of God and its constituent letters, there is a midrash containing an account similar to those in *Sefer Yeṣirah*. At the beginning of the fourth book of *Memar Marqah*, in a discussion about the term "and spoke" (וידבר) [Deut. 31:1] and the role of number twenty-two in the creation:

> [T]wenty-two corresponding to twenty-two which Moses wrote on the stones which are at the beginning of this word *waw, yod, dalet, bet* (וידב), and *resh* (ר) in its end. It was the seal, for they were concealed until Moses the prophet came and God revealed them through him. Every commandment is reinforced by *wayedaber* (וידבר) and every blessing by *R* (ר) strengthened. If it had not been for Moses all this would not have been known and nothing would have been declared of what was sent down. The enumeration *W* (ו) represents the six days, which were a storehouse for all that was created. *Y*'s (י) value is revealed before you—no need to repeat it here. *D* (ד)—by it the heavens were perfected and by *B* (ב) every glorious thing was magnified in the world, both the opening and closing of it—of what had passed and of what was yet to come. In the beginning it closed and it opened. It closed what was passed and it opened what was yet to come.[2]

According to this midrash, the letters were concealed from the day of the world's creation and revealed only when Moses came down with the stone tablets on which they were engraved. The revelation of writing according to this midrash is not simply the discovery of a graphic means of phonetic representation—significant as that may be—but rather the revelation of the mystery of creation and the secret of the universe. All of creation is founded upon the twenty-two letters, and all that was done during the world creation by God was in the numerical value of the letters *WYDB* (וידב). Consequently, the midrash demonstrates how this numerical value, twenty-two, stands for the sum of foundational elements in the creation of the world: *waw*—the six days of creation; *yod*—as is evident from other places in *Memar Marqah*, the representative letter of the name of God in creation, or the ten foundations of the creation of the world; *dalet*—the fourth day, on which heaven and earth were completed; and *bet*—the first letter in the Torah, representing the separation between the primordial world (inquiry into which is prohibited) and the created world. The midrash refers to the familiar biblical narrative of creation and demonstrates how central parts of it are, in a veiled way, based on the number twenty-two. It is important to note that the twenty-two letters are not associated with the act of creation through the speech of God, but rather specifically with the numerical foundations whose sum is twenty-two. It appears that writing with its twenty-two signifiers constitutes evidence for the central status associated with the number twenty-two and not the other way around. In other words, the number twenty-two is at the root of creation, and writing, first expressed in the Ten Commandments, can be seen as harboring mysteries associated with this number.

This midrash from *Memar Marqah* about the alphabet and the number twenty-two as the secret number of the creation is indeed an important parallel to *Sefer Yeṣirah*, but its contribution to the contextualization of *Sefer Yeṣirah* is minimal. The midrash is the only example in *Memar Marqah* of the role of this number in creation, is not developed elsewhere, and has no parallel, as far as I know, in Samaritan literature. Moreover, *Memar Marqah* does not reveal the origins of the midrash, and the only thing that can be concluded from it is that the tradition about the role of the number twenty-two was known during the first millennium CE in different contexts, including a Samaritan one.

The Mysteries of the Greek Letters

The Mysteries of the Greek Letters, as noted, is probably the most detailed composition about the importance of the number twenty-two and the twenty-two letters in the creation of the world.[3] The book repeatedly emphasizes that the sources of its main insights about the letters are Semitic—Hebrew and (in most cases) Syriac, and hence only twenty-two letters are considered. For example, inspired by the Book of Jubilees,[4] *The Mysteries of the Greek Letters* claims that twenty-two letters point to the number twenty-two, which is the foundation of the creation of the world:

> There are twenty-two letters according to the number of the twenty-two works, which God created in the entire creation, which are the following: Concerning the twenty-two works, which God created:
>
> 1. The first and highest heaven
> 2. The earth beneath the abyss
> 3. The water above and below the firmament
> 4. Another earth that is dry
> 5. The spirit above the water
> 6. The darkness above the abyss
> 7. Light that is called fire
> 8. The firmament that is named heaven
> 9. Separation between the two waters
> 10. The revealing of the earth from the depth
> 11. The sprouting out of the plants
> 12. Fruit-bearing trees with seeds in them
> 13. Stars
> 14. Sun and moon

> 15. Their placement in the heaven
> 16. Fish
> 17. Birds
> 18. Sea monsters
> 19. Wild beasts
> 20. Reptiles
> 21. Cattle
> 22. Man
>
> Behold, twenty-two works of God. Because of that, the Jews enumerate twenty-two books of the Old [Testament].[5]

It seems that this paragraph construes creation similarly to *Sefer Yeṣirah*, insofar as the twenty-two letters allude to the twenty-two creations of God in making the world.

The Mysteries of the Greek Letters differs from *Memar Marqah* in three main criteria: first, it does not mention the letters of the ineffable name, and we have no indication that the authors of this treatise were aware of the existence of that tradition. Second, the importance of the letters and the numbers they symbolize are discussed throughout the book. Third, *The Mysteries of the Greek Letters* refers explicitly to its origins and is thus very helpful in the contextualization of *Sefer Yeṣirah.*

The similarities between *Sefer Yeṣirah* and *The Mysteries of the Greek Letters* pertain to the role of subgroups of letters as standing for numbers: the letters, in these cases, are important because of their numerical value. Like the division of the twenty-two letters in *Sefer Yeṣirah* into three, seven, and twelve, *The Mysteries of the Greek Letters,* following the Greek traditions, divides the letters according to a linguistic criterion, into the seven vowels and the fifteen consonants; and, in other cases, to fourteen, according to another criterion.[6] For example, in a discussion of the seven Greek vowels, the book asserts that these letters correspond to the seven creatures capable of making sounds: "There are only seven voiced letters [=vowels], since God created in the creation seven beings that have a voice."[7]

As to the fifteen consonants, the book argues that these letters lack the quality of articulation and correspond to the fifteen created things unable to make sound: "Fifteen are the voiceless letters [=consonants], since fifteen are the voiceless realities among the created things of the world."[8]

The importance of *The Mysteries of the Greek Letters* goes far beyond its points of similarity with *Sefer Yeṣirah* and the fact that they both transmit the tradition of creation from twenty-two letters. Its significance lies in its semi-reflective nature, so that, in some cases, this long and detailed treatise explicitly indicates its origins. These pointers enable us to locate the origins of the tradition that the world was created from twenty-two letters.

The Mysteries of the Greek Letters elevates the Greek letters. Nevertheless, as we have stated, its real concern is with the Hebrew and Aramaic languages, and it therefore supports the tradition that the world was created from twenty-two letters—according to their count in Hebrew and Syriac. In this text, we encounter words of praise and many mythical tales connected mainly to letters designated as "Syriac." In the course of a discussion about the shape of the letters, we read: "Not only by form, but also by their very names in the Syriac language, do these letters clearly reveal the mystery of Christ."[9]

More explicitly, the text describes a myth according to which the Syriac letters are divine. In its eclectic style, *The Mysteries of the Greek Letters* adopts a myth, whose roots are in the ancient Near East, regarding books that the ancients buried prior to the flood. These books, in which all human knowledge up to that date was stored, came to light after the flood.[10] This narrative is incorporated into the Greek tale about Cadmus, who introduced writing to the Greeks.[11] According to that tale, God wrote the Syriac letters on a stone tablet and buried it in the ground. Cadmus found the tablet inscribed with the letters, the root of all knowledge, and disseminated it in Palestine among the Phoenicians. "This Syriac language and its twenty-two letters existed among men until the building of the Tower of Babel and the division of languages. Later, the characters of the Hebrew letters were carved in accordance with the Syriac letters, not by a man or men but by the hand and finger of God, on a certain stone tablet, like the tablets of the Law. The Greeks accompanying Cadmus found this tablet after the flood. And then through this [tablet] the instruction of the letters became known as *Palaestina Prima* in Phoenicia."[12]

The commentary asserts the originality and primacy of the Syriac letters, an assertion that frequently arises in the author's contemplation of the names of the letters in the Syriac language.[13] In an attempt to clarify the reason for concentrating on the Greek alphabet, which is also the language of the book, the author of *The Mysteries of the Greek Letters* argues for a parallel between the Greek and the Syriac alphabets: "Listen attentively how the Greek pronounces fourteen of the names of the letters in accordance with the Syrians, softening only the rough breathing of their speech."[14]

These excerpts make clear that God spoke with the first man in Syriac and engraved the Syriac letters on the holy stone tablets with his own hands. This is indicative of the importance of these letters for this Greek treatise. Although it is also notable that *The Mysteries of the Greek Letters* presents certain traditions about the Hebrew letters, these traditions are treated as local and are succinctly stated, unlike those dealing with the Syriac letters; the Hebrew letters do not have mythic status.

The Mysteries of the Greek Letters is an eclectic book, and most of the traditions presented in it are gathered from outside sources rather than being original formulations of the author. On the subject of creation from letters, there is no doubt that the author accommodates a Semitic tradition, since he argues that the world was created from twenty-two letters and not from twenty-four. One can assume on the basis of this evidence that the book's assertion that the world was created from twenty-two letters is originally Syriac.

To stress the importance of the Syriac dialect, I want to shed light on another, earlier tradition than that mentioned by the Syriac church fathers, found in the writings of Eusebius of Caesarea (ca. 265–340), whose aim was to prove that the Greeks borrowed knowledge from other peoples and especially from the Hebrews:[15] "For by copying different sciences from different nations, they got geometry from the Egyptians, and astrology from the Chaldeans, and other things again from other countries; but nothing among any other nations like the benefit which some of them found from the Hebrews."[16]

In line with this approach, Eusebius demonstrates that the Greeks did not invent their alphabet, either, but borrowed its letters from other peoples, as two traditions testify. According to the first, which is well known, Cadmus, who was a Phoenician, brought the letters to the Greeks. The second and lesser-known tradition is that the Syrians endowed the world with the Greek letters. Eusebius tries to prove that "Phoenicians" and "Syrians" are designations for the Hebrews from whom the letters reached the Greeks: "First therefore he who introduced to the Greeks the common letters, even the very first elements of grammar, namely Cadmus, was a Phoenician by birth, from which circumstance some of the ancients have surnamed the alphabet Phoenician. But some say that the Syrians were the first who devised letters. Now these Syrians would be Hebrews who inhabited the neighboring country to Phoenicia, which was itself called Phoenicia in old times, but afterward Judaea, and in our time, Palestine."[17]

Eusebius's aim is clearly to prove that the Hebrews are the originators of any significant Greek knowledge. What is interesting for our purposes is that along with the well-known traditions concerning Cadmus and the Phoenicians, there were other traditions claiming a Syriac origin for the letters. It seems that as part of this general trend, Eusebius attributed the first tradition to the Hebrews when he argued that Phoenicia is no other than Palestine and that the Syrians are Jews.

Reading, hence, both Eusebius and *The Mysteries of the Greek Letters* demonstrates clearly that in late antiquity, there was a well-known narrative according to which the primal letters are Syriac. This narrative, which *The Mysteries of the Greek Letters* accepts and Eusebius rejects, is not surprising in light of the fact that, as Milka Rubin has demonstrated, the sole Christian milieu that held Aramaic to be holy, giving it preference over Hebrew, was that of the Syriac church fathers.[18] These facts can serve as good starting points for explaining, in terms of the history of ideas, how it could be that a Hebrew composition discussing the twenty-two letters of the alphabet was written under Christian-Syriac and not vice versa.

Parallels Between Syriac Texts and *Sefer Yeṣirah*

Although the available evidence is far from complete, there is good reason to suppose that Syrian traditions ascribed importance to the letters of the alphabet in a manner similar to *Sefer Yeṣirah*.[19] I would like to consider three sources that conjointly can help us outline a context that can be reasonably assumed to be the matrix for the evolution of a composition like *Sefer Yeṣirah*. I will first deal with a section from a hymn ascribed to Ephrem,[20] belonging to an anthology of hymns of birth whose similarity to *Sefer Yeṣirah* has been briefly noted by Elliot Wolfson[21] and Eliane Ketterer.[22] Then I will discuss the importance of a few lines from one of Narsai's *mêmrâ* that bear a great resemblance to *Sefer Yeṣirah* and that were discussed by Nicolas Séd.[23] Finally, I will consider in some detail an East Syriac source of the late sixth century that was recently discussed by Adam Becker.

The hymn ascribed to Ephrem (ca. 306–373) is important for our purposes since it provides a formidable parallel to *Sefer Yeṣirah*. The hymn showers words of praise on the letter *yod*, which begins the names of Jesus, John, and Joseph, as well as the letter *mem*, which is the first letter of the name of Maria as well as the term "Messiah." The hymn also praises the number ten, which is the numerical value of the letter *yod*, and the number six, both of which are described as perfect symbols. It relates that these two numbers designate Jesus and thus fulfill an important role in the world, indicating the hidden role of Jesus in the created world. The assertion about the role of ten and six is, in the hymn, based on two examples: the decimal counting system, limited in its digits but not in its capacity to count; and space, which is composed of six half-dimensions: up, down, north, south, east, and west, where each of these half-dimensions is infinite. "And as numbers/ have only ten degrees,/ creation has six sides,/ height depth and the four corners which are full of you."[24]

This paragraph has interesting parallels in *Sefer Yeṣirah*, and a comparison of the texts seems to indicate that *Sefer Yeṣirah* had a more refined version and would consequently seem to be based on a later source: "The ten *sefirot* are the basis and their measure is ten for they have no limit: dimension of beginning and dimension of end, dimension of good and dimension of evil, dimension of above and dimension of below, dimension of east and dimension of west, dimension of north and dimension of south. And a unique Lord, a trustworthy divine king, rules over them all from his holy abode forever and ever."[25]

Two main points of similarity between *Sefer Yeṣirah* and the Syriac hymn deserve notice. The first parallel concerns three central themes discussed in both: the importance of the number ten, the three dimensions with six extremities, and the status of the deity. The second correspondence is in the order of appearance of the themes in these sections, which is identical for both: beginning with the decimal counting system, continuing with the dimensions of space, and ending with the status of the deity. Hence we can say that this significant similarity goes beyond mere coincidence and testifies to a mutual influence or to the effect of a third source, whether textual or oral, on the two texts.[26] Moreover, it seems that the Syriac hymn has a less edited version than its counterpart in *Sefer Yeṣirah*, as the number of dimensions of space in the hymn is the original number six. In *Sefer Yeṣirah*, by contrast, two additional dimensions have been appended—the dimension of time (beginning and end) and the dimension of ethics (good and evil), which indicates a later development in which the number of dimensions of space (six) had been manipulated in order to accommodate the assertion regarding the crucial importance of the number ten in this part of *Sefer Yeṣirah*.

Another especially interesting Syriac text addressing the letters in the creation of the world was briefly discussed in the 1960s by Nicolas Séd. In an article about the Jewish origins of a *mêmrâ* (verse homily) about the creation by the fifth-century poet and theologian Narsai, who was head of the school of Edessa and later the founder of the famous school of Nisibis, Séd notes a parallel between a few lines in this *mêmrâ* and *Sefer Yeṣirah*. In the *mêmrâ* , Narsai describes the five letters of the first word in Genesis, "In the beginning" (ܒܪܫܝܬ) as stones that were hewed by an iron of spirit. Narsai says that a vast house was built upon those stones: "I saw the five letters that he set down at the beginning of the verse (Gen. 1:1). . . . / With the iron toll of the spirit he hewed the signs like stones/ And built upon them a house, vast from top to bottom."[27]

These lines of the *mêmrâ* contain two images similar to those in *Sefer Yeṣirah* that deserve special attention. First, we find the image of hewing stone from spirit in a famous description in *Sefer Yeṣirah* about creation ex nihilo: "He formed substance from chaos, and he made it with fire and it exists, and he *hewed out great columns from intangible air*."[28]

The second image with a parallel in *Sefer Yeṣirah* is of letters as stones used to build a house. In *Sefer Yeṣirah*, the image is of letters combined in different ways, just as stones are joined variously in order to build different houses: "How did he combine them?—two stones build two houses; three build six houses; four build twenty-four houses; five build 120 houses; six build 720 houses; seven build 5,040. From here on, go out and ponder what the mouth cannot speak and what the eye cannot see and what the ear cannot hear."[29]

An examination of the above paragraphs cited from Syriac sources and *Sefer Yeṣirah* does not lend itself to the conclusion that one influenced the other but rather that they outline a cultural context in which these images were known. *Sefer Yeṣirah* and these Syriac sources employed each for its unique purposes.

I would like to draw attention to a source discussed by Adam Becker in his book on the school of Nisibis.[30] According to Becker, the preoccupation with letters in this source is parallel to Jewish sources and especially to *Sefer Yeṣirah*. Two comments on Becker's assertion should be made before proceeding to the source itself. First, as we have seen in Chapter 1, the presumption that the world was created by alphabetic letters was, in late antiquity, no more prevalent in Jewish than in non-Jewish sources. Hence, coming upon a non-Jewish source from late antiquity or from the early Middle Ages addressing the letters need not necessarily lead to the assertion that this non-Jewish source had a Jewish influence. Second, while there is a strong and fascinating similarity between the sources—a similarity that we will further consider—the sources nevertheless frequently differ in their narratives as well as in their mythic and cosmogonic imagery. Like the former sources, the complex relations between these two sources apprise us of an extensive shared cultural context in which both were written.

"The Cause of the Foundation of the Schools" is a treatise written in the late sixth century, in the city of Nisibis, and is one of the most important documents that we have for understanding the world of Eastern Christianity in Syria of that period. This is a translation of the source under discussion:[31]

> In a similar manner, we have a practice, after we have a child read the simple letters and repeat them, we join them one to another and from them we put together names that he may read syllable by syllable and be trained. Thus also that eternal teacher did, after he had them repeat the alphabet, then he arranged it [the alphabet] with the great name of the construction of the firmament and he read it in front of them that they might understand that he is the creator of all of them, and as he orders them, they complete his will, and because they are quick-witted, they receive teaching quickly. In six days, he taught them a wholly accurate teaching; at one time in the gathering together of the waters and in the growth of the trees; at another in the coming into being of the creeping things; and then at another in the creation of the animals and in the division of the luminaries, with these then also in (the creation of) the birds of wing, until he made them comprehend the number ten; and he taught them again something else in the creation of the human being; and from then on he handed over to them the visible creation, that like letters they might write them in their continuous variations and read syllable by syllable with them the name of the creator and organizer of all. And he let them go and allowed them to be in this spacious house of the school, which is of the earth.[32]

There are many similarities between this source and *Sefer Yeṣirah* on a thematic level and in exact terminology. First, a term that is seemingly straightforward but is nevertheless of great significance: "simple letters" (ܐܬܘ̈ܬܐ ܦܫܝ̈ܛܬܐ). Nehemya Allony has remarked in "Zunz, Krauss, and Scholem Teach Their Theories of *Sefer Yeṣirah*" that a central problem in the determination of the time and context of *Sefer Yeṣirah* derives from the unique terms employed in the text, unknown to us from other sources of that period.[33] I would like to add that the flowing Hebrew of *Sefer Yeṣirah* can be deceptive. Describing letters lacking specific titles as "simple," though perhaps sounding reasonable to the reader who is proficient in modern Hebrew, is an unusual word choice in the context of the period of *Sefer Yeṣirah.* As Allony stresses, the expression "simple letters" is not to be found in Jewish sources prior to the tenth century. It is, then, remarkable to find just that expression in a Syriac source dating from the late sixth century discussing the role of the letters of the alphabet in the creation of the world.

Moreover, the source twice describes how the combination of one letter with another jointly creates the name of the God from which the world was created, a matter that, in this manner, is not to be found in Jewish texts besides *Sefer Yeṣirah.* It is precisely *Sefer Yeṣirah* that describes how all the letters combine into one name, in all likelihood the great name of God: "Twenty-two letters. . . . How did he weigh and exchange them? *Alef* with them all, and them all with *alef*; *bet* with them all, and them all with *bet*. . . . And they all rotate in turn. The result is that they go out by 221 gates. The result is that all creation all speech go out by one name."[34]

In "The Cause of the Foundation of the Schools," God is described as the one who combined all the letters and formed his name with them: "Thus also that eternal teacher did, after he had them repeat the alphabet, then he arranged [the alphabet] with the great name"; similarly, in *Sefer Yeṣirah*, the twenty-two letters and their combinations "go out by one name."

Another resemblance between the sources according to which the deity teaches ten things (ܡܢܝܢܐ ܕܥܣܪܐ) to the angels and we can thus see that the rare combination of twenty-two letters and the number ten appear in the same context, is in a source about the creation of the world from or by the letters together with this number.[35]

The last sources show interesting similarities of images, ideas, and notions to those that can be found in *Sefer Yeṣirah.* As for the contribution of these similarities to the contextualization of *Sefer Yeṣirah*, most of them—such as the notion of the creation of the world from twenty-two letters, the comparison between letters, stones, and houses, the depiction of the six half-dimensions, and precise notions like "simple letters"—are absent from the rabbinic sources and from the Hekhalot literature. Nevertheless, these similarities do not indicate any direct influence of one source on another but rather conjointly outline a context within which *Sefer Yeṣirah* could have crystallized.

Soft and Hard: The Double Letters in Their Context

In the sixth century or a little earlier, the famous Greek grammatical treatise by Dionysius Thrax, "Art of Grammar," was translated into Syriac.[36] It was probably due to this treatise and its discussions of the aspirated and unaspirated consonant that early Syriac scribe-scholars and grammarians defined *BGD KPT* as double letters.[37] Accordingly, Shlomo Pines, in his article about the similarity between the doctrine of the *sefirot* in *Sefer Yeṣirah* and the Pseudo-Clementine homilies, argued that the early version of *Sefer Yeṣirah* cannot be dated prior to this period: "[T]he earliest relevant Syriac treatises dealing with the grammatical phenomenon of double letters go back to the beginning of the sixth century. If that is the case, and if our supposition as to the connection between the Hebrew and the Syriac conception of the 'double letters' is accepted, the redaction of the *Sefer Yezira* must have been produced at that time or later."[38]

Although Pines designates the earliest possible period in which a grammatical rule showing the existence of double letters was known, the origin of the seven double letters mentioned in *Sefer Yeṣirah* remains open: Was this pericope authored by the composer of *Sefer Yeṣirah*, or is it a citation inspired by the cultural environment in which the book was composed? A clarification of a fact that has been long known in the *Sefer Yeṣirah* scholarship but has unfortunately remained in the margins of research can solve this problem. It seems that not only does *Sefer Yeṣirah* formulate a phonetic rule first formulated by the Syriac grammarians but that *Sefer Yeṣirah* employs grammatical terminology that is, in effect, Syriac. To demonstrate this last assertion, I will first cite *Sefer Yeṣirah* discussing the seven double letters: "Seven double letters: *bet*, *gimel*, *dalet*; *kaf*, *pe*, *resh*, *taw*. . . . [T]hey are pronounced with the tongue in two different positions, for they represent two categories of opposites: *bet/vet*, *gimel/ghimel*, *dalet/dhalet*, *kaf/khaf*, *pe/fe*, *resh/rhesh*, *taw/thaw*, corresponding to soft and hard (*rakh ve-qashe*), a paradigm of strong and weak. They are opposites. The opposite of life is death; the opposite of peace is evil; the opposite of wisdom is folly."[39]

The authors or editors of *Sefer Yeṣirah* characteristically use the doubling of the letters to point out paired opposites such as wisdom and folly or peace and evil, to demonstrate that the letters are the foundation of the created world and to prove the book's opening statement that God created the world from the thirty-two paths. The first example given of these opposites is soft and hard, or, in the words of *Sefer Yeṣirah*: *rakh* and *qashe* (רך וקשה). This wording or a proximate one appears in each version of *Sefer Yeṣirah* and may have decisive significance for the determination of the origin of the double letters. In Syriac literature, we encounter two signs that direct the pronunciation of the double letters *BGD KPT* toward either plosive or fricative, designated in Aramaic *rukkakha* (ܪܘܟܟܐ) for a soft enunciation and *qushshaya* (ܩܘܫܝܐ) for a hard one, and adapted to Hebrew, *rakh* and *qashe*.[40] While this last distinction concerning the origin of the words "soft" and "hard" has been mentioned in the *Sefer Yeṣirah* scholarship, it has remained marginal.

To the best of my knowledge, no scholar has formulated the simple significance of this fact: if *Sefer Yeṣirah* quotes a phonetic rule concerning the existence of a group of double letters first articulated in any Semitic language in Syriac literature, and in so doing uses the terminology of Syriac grammar, it follows that *Sefer Yeṣirah* belongs to that cultural context. Among dozens of papers dedicated to *Sefer Yeṣirah*, I have found only five researchers who mention the parallel between the Syriac *rukkakha* and *qushshaya* and *Sefer Yeṣirah*'s *rakh* and *qashe*, and even they avoid drawing any conclusion from it.[41]

The first to mention this parallel was Wilhelm Bacher, who wrote that the words "hard" and "soft" are close to Syriac terms coined in the late seventh century by Jacob of Edessa but that there is nothing pointing to a Syriac influence on *Sefer Yeṣirah*.[42] Bacher's view, from the end of the nineteenth century, calls for a few comments. First, it is not clear who first coined the terms *rukkakha* and *qushshaya*. Since we do not have enough information about Syriac grammar prior to the tenth century, it would be hard to determine where and when those terms were first used.[43] We can, however, say that while there is no evidence that Jacob of Edessa used those terms,[44] there are manuscripts that go back to the late sixth century that do distinguish between the two pronunciations of the letters *BGD KPT*.[45] The fact that *rukkakha* and *qushshaya* were widely employed only after the tenth century is of crucial importance: it means that the author or editor of *Sefer Yeṣirah* wrote the composition before this terminology was widespread and therefore had accurate and detailed knowledge of Syriac grammar very early on.

Shlomo Morag, responding to a paper on the subject of double letters by Yehuda Liebes, mentions the terms *rukkakha* and *qushshaya*: "What is the nature of the terms *rakh* and *qashe*, which the author of *Sefer Yeṣirah* uses regarding the geminated pronunciation of *BGD KPRT*? It is simple: in the Arabic terminology used to describe the Tiberius pronunciation, the term *qafif* (*qal*) designates the fricative pronunciation. . . . The opposite of *kal* is *kaved* or *qashe*; the opposite of *qashe* is *rakh* or *qal*. Thus the use of the Hebrew terms *rakh* and *qashe* developed in order to designate the pronunciations of the fricative and plosive with a *dagesh*. Compare further the terms *rukkakha* and *qushshaya*, employed in Syriac for the designation of these pronunciations."[46]

Morag is aware that in Jewish sources, we do not encounter such terms as *rakh* and *qashe* to designate the letters *BGD KPT*. To support his argument that the author of *Sefer Yeṣirah* knew the Jewish scribe-scholars in Babylon or Tiberius, he constructs an especially circuitous route for the evolution of the words *dagesh* and *rafi* rather than simply considering the possibility that the author of *Sefer Yeṣirah* translated the terms *rukkakha* and *qushshaya* directly from Aramaic to Hebrew. According to Morag, *Sefer Yeṣirah* adapted Arabic terms to Hebrew terms that are coincidentally identical to the Syriac. It is surprising that this fact did not lead Morag to the straightforward conclusion that *Sefer Yeṣirah* used Syriac terminology. There is no reason to take such a tortuous path when one can simply say that *Sefer Yeṣirah* was composed by Jews who lived in the same cultural context as that of the early Syriac scribe-scholars and therefore adapted their terminology.

In a book on astrology and other sciences practiced by Jews in late antiquity and the beginning of the Middle Ages, Meir Bar-Ilan dedicates a number of lengthy chapters to *Sefer Yeṣirah* and states in a footnote that we encounter the terms "hard" and "soft" in Syriac literature but that it is possible that the Syrians borrowed these terms from the Hebrew or that both languages obtained them from the Greek. The schematic division suggested by Bar-Ilan is possible in any investigation of directions of influence among sources.[47] However, it is highly unlikely that the author of *Sefer Yeṣirah* would translate the Greek terms of aspirated letters[48] and unaspirated letters[49] into the same words as the Syriac scribe-scholars with no variation. Although in Hebrew and in Arabic, proximate terms to designate two types of pronunciation did develop, none resembled *rakh* and *qashe*. Even less probable is the hypothesis that the Syriac scribe-scholars drew their knowledge about the double letters from Hebrew and employed terms for this purpose coined by hypothetical Hebrew grammarians.[50] We possess no knowledge of a Jewish preoccupation with grammatical themes or *massorah* before the Jewish scribe-scholars in Babylon and Tiberius.

It can be conclusively stated that no Hebrew source, aside from *Sefer Yeṣirah*, describes the hard and the soft letters with the terms *rakh* and *qashe*, although we have Syriac sources employing these terms.[51] An interesting example demonstrating the distinction—and, indeed, tension—between the regular Hebrew terms and the Syriac terms is to be found in MS. Parma 2784 (de Rossi 1390), a manuscript from 1286 (the earliest version of the short recension of *Sefer Yeṣirah*): "Seven double letters. . . . They are pronounced with the tongue in two different positions, for they represent two categories of opposites: *bet/vet*, *gimel/ghimel*, *dalet/dhalet*; *kaf/khaf*, *pe/fe*, *resh/rhesh*, *taw/thaw*, *dagesh* and *rafi*, *rakh* and *qashe*."[52]

The addition of the words *dagesh* and *rafi*, as the Tiberians were accustomed to designate the pronunciations, alongside the words *rakh* and *qashe*, leads to the conclusion that foreign terminology caught the attention of a copyist of *Sefer Yeṣirah*, who subsequently added the common Jewish terms *dagesh* and *rafi*.

The authors/editors of *Sefer Yeṣirah* are not aware of the Jewish terminology but are well aware of the Syriac one. *Sefer Yeṣirah*, with all its interest in phonetics and grammar, does not refer to medieval Hebrew grammatical issues, such as the Hebrew vocalization (*niqqud*).[53] These facts lead to the conclusion that the main structure of *Sefer Yeṣirah* was created after the evolution of the first stages of Syriac grammar and before the evolution of Hebrew grammatical terms, thus around the seventh century.

Sefer Yeṣirah's Context

The most interesting issue that ensues from the reading of the last three chapters, especially in consequence of the comparison conducted between *Sefer Yeṣirah* and Syriac literature, concerns the identity of the authors/redactors of the early version of *Sefer Yeṣirah*. Because the information in our possession is limited, it would be irresponsible to attempt to describe a detailed portrait on the basis of preliminary and discrete elements that we have succeeded in revealing. On the other hand, we cannot abstain from drawing conclusions and indicating directions that may advance scholarship on this subject and that might be confirmed or rejected in future scholarship.

From what is known, *Sefer Yeṣirah* is structured by a cosmogonic approach to the creation of the world from all twenty-two letters of the alphabet, an approach connected to Syriac Christianity, and the book contains many parallels to Syriac literature. The basic division of the letters in *Sefer Yeṣirah* according to *immot*, doubles, and simples, demonstrates that the authors/redactors of the book were exposed, at a very early stage in the development of Syrian grammar, to the definition of the letters *BGD KPT* as double letters and that they employ the exact Syrian terms for the double pronunciation of those letters: soft (*rakh*) and hard (*qashe*). The acquaintance of *Sefer Yeṣirah* with the ideas of the intellectual elite that generated Syrian grammar leads to the conclusion that *Sefer Yeṣirah* developed in its early stages in an area in which Greek texts were translated into Syriac and in which Syriac grammar was developed (north Mesopotamia): it might be in the West, in Edessa; or, as Shlomo Pines has argued, in the East, in Nisibis.[54] But it would be impossible to determine an exact location at this stage in the scholarship of *Sefer Yeṣirah* with our minimal knowledge about the Jews in that area.[55] I cannot determine with certainty that north Mesopotamia was the area in which the core of *Sefer Yeṣirah* was developed; yet it seems, from all that has been described until now, as the most tenable context.

If *Sefer Yeṣirah* was composed in north Mesopotamia, more light can be shed on its relation to rabbinic literature. *Sefer Yeṣirah* does not indicate a conversance with rabbinical literature. Even those scarce citations of rabbinic literature found in *Sefer Yeṣirah* could possibly be no more than later additions that were appended to the composition by subsequent Jewish readers who were more acquainted with rabbinic literature. *Sefer Yeṣirah* is not similar to rabbinic literature with regard to its style, makes no mention of rabbinical figures, differs completely in its method of presentation, and makes minimal use of biblical sources as prooftexts.

A comparative consideration of the tension between Hekhalot literature and rabbinic literature may emphasize this issue with regard to *Sefer Yeṣirah*. Some scholars have considered the Hekhalot literature as a product of an alternative milieu to that of the rabbinic circles.[56] Even if we were to accept this approach, the Hekhalot literature seems to be in internal opposition to rabbinic literature: the names of the heroes of the Hekhalot literature are those of the rabbinic sages, and many parallels, in terms of content and form, exist between the Hekhalot literature and rabbinic literature, which together outline the intellectual proximity between these two corpora despite clear differences between them.

In contrast to the Hekhalot literature, *Sefer Yeṣirah* does not seem to be a composition that rebels against rabbinic literature; rather, it appears to have scant acquaintance with it, if any.[57] *Sefer Yeṣirah* does not express attraction, acceptance, rejection, or opposition toward rabbinic literature, and as such, it is a non-rabbinic Jewish composition.[58] Concomitant with the above, from the reading of *Sefer Yeṣirah*, there is no indication that the alternative Jewish context of *Sefer Yeṣirah* reflects a revolt against the Jewish ritual, possesses antinomistic tendencies, or should be considered a Christian-Jewish text.[59] All we can say is that *Sefer Yeṣirah* was originated by Jews who wrote in a fluent Hebrew and who were distant from the Jewish communities of Palestine and Babylon in which rabbinic literature in all its branches—Talmudic literature, Hekhalot literature, midrash, Jewish-magical literature and *piyyut*—was generated.[60]

If the last conclusions are correct, *Sefer Yeṣirah* is evidence for non-rabbinic Jewish literature written or edited by Jews who left no additional historical or literary evidence and who lived in north Mesopotamia around the seventh century.

Summary

Investigating the possibility that *Sefer Yeṣirah* is mentioned in a *piyyut* by Elazar Birabi Qilir, Ezra Fleischer argues that *Sefer Yeṣirah* was, in all likelihood, composed slightly before the period of Saadya and that it makes no sense to date it any earlier: "The cosmogonic doctrine of the book conveys great regard for the letters of the alphabet, and in the history of the Jewish people there is no period when that regard is greater than that of R. Saadya. Dating this book to too early a date dislodges it from the cultural context of which it is probably an organic part. Although it is indeed possible that a truly great work could anticipate its time and be at a distance from it, it is rather difficult to assume this without concrete evidence."[61]

Fleisher's statement is based on two assumptions: first, discussion of the letters was popular only from the days of Saadya. Second, *Sefer Yeṣirah* was composed in a known Jewish context. In previous chapters, we saw that Fleischer's first assumption concerning the late period in which preoccupation with the letters flourished is incorrect; his second assumption implying that *Sefer Yeṣirah* evolved in known Jewish circles also should be rejected. No small number of researchers of *Sefer Yeṣirah* have assumed that the cultural context of this unique text should not be sought in known Jewish sources but rather in alternative cultural contexts.[62] We can now say that this alternative context is that of Syriac Christian letter discussions. In other words, it is possible to understand the singularity of *Sefer Yeṣirah* in two opposing ways: the first is to see it as a unique composition, evolved in a known Jewish environment, whose authors or editors succeeded in removing most of its identifying Jewish signs. The second possibility is to take it as a treatise that does not in any way attempt to conceal its cultural context but whose context became, with time, largely unknown to its readers and interpreters.

Since *Sefer Yeṣirah* employs many physiological, linguistic, astrological, cosmological, and other terms to articulate its various arguments, there is no evident reason to believe that there is in this text any attempt at concealment. It therefore seems more correct to endorse the possibility that the singularity of *Sefer Yeṣirah* in the eyes of its readers and interpreters emerged precisely because of its estrangement from the cultural context in which its essential foundations evolved. I conclude that the most likely provenance of *Sefer Yeṣirah* is Syriac Christianity in north Mesopotamia sometime around the seventh century.

Chapter 4

Sounds of Silence: *Sefer Yeṣirah* Before the Tenth Century

If the formation of *Sefer Yeṣirah* occurred around the seventh century, as we demonstrated in Chapter 3, approximately three hundred years passed before rabbinic luminaries would pen their commentaries on it, in the tenth century. It is difficult to outline the history of *Sefer Yeṣirah* during that long period in any detail: we cannot find any definite reference to *Sefer Yeṣirah* in Jewish or non-Jewish sources of that time. A further impediment, no less relevant to such a historical reconstruction, is the lack of Jewish manuscripts dating from the "silent era of Jewish manuscripts," between the second and eighth centuries. That deficiency can only confirm that the canonical Jewish texts written in that period that survived in later manuscripts, because of their status, did not quote or refer to *Sefer Yeṣirah*; the deficiency is not indicative of the status of *Sefer Yeṣirah* among the Jews of that period.

In this chapter, I will present an analysis of two unique textual exceptions that can shed light on how *Sefer Yeṣirah* was understood during its "dark period," before the tenth century. The first source is a short commentary inserted into some recensions of *Sefer Yeṣirah* before the tenth century. The second source is the well-known ninth-century epistle of Agobard of Lyon.

A Gloss Within *Sefer Yeṣirah*: The Section of the "Interpretation of the Holy Names"

The precise chronological sequence of the editing of *Sefer Yeṣirah* cannot be determined with the modest evidence available to us. Nevertheless, the very occurrence of such a process of editing is quite palpable: every reader can see that the book contains different layers and disparate wordings. I propose that this gap between the different layers of *Sefer Yeṣirah* and our inability to accurately outline how *Sefer Yeṣirah* was edited offers us an invaluable aperture. In the next few lines, I would like to examine a single paragraph belonging to a very late layer of *Sefer Yeṣirah*, which gives us an interesting overview of how *Sefer Yeṣirah* was read before the tenth century. The paragraph deals with the interpretation of a list of holy names, so we will call it the "interpretation of the holy names" section.

This section is uniquely different from other parts of *Sefer Yeṣirah* that also reflect rabbinic or Hekhalot material; it is different in wording, terminology, and the manner in which it was integrated into some of the recensions of *Sefer Yeṣirah*. This is perhaps why Yehudah ben Barzillai Barceloni (end of the eleventh–beginning of the twelfth centuries) designates it as a later segment of commentary inserted into *Sefer Yeṣirah*.[1] The section appears in some of the early recensions of *Sefer Yeṣirah*: in the tenth-century manuscript of *Sefer Yeṣirah* found in the Cairo Geniza[2] and in the tenth-century commentaries to *Sefer Yeṣirah* of Saadya[3] and Shabbetai Donnolo;[4] undoubtedly, the section existed in that early period. However, the paragraph is not found in the eleventh-century recension of *Sefer Yeṣirah* in Ms. Vatican 299, the second earliest manuscript of *Sefer Yeṣirah*. It seems, therefore, that this section was inserted only into some of *Sefer Yeṣirah*'s recensions before the tenth century.

Below is a translation of the version of the "interpretation of the holy names" section from the tenth-century manuscript from the Cairo Geniza, with corrections made in accordance with other manuscripts.[5]

> [These are the twenty-two letters] by which carved out [YH] WH [Ṣevaoth], God of Israel, the living God, El Shaday, high and lofty dwelling forever and holy is his name

[YH] two names
YH WH four names
Ṣevaoth—he is a sign in his host
God of Israel—he is a minister before God
Living God—Three have been called living, [living] God, running [living] water, tree of life
El Shaday—El–hard
Shaday—so far sufficient
High—for he dwells in the height of the universe, higher than the highest
And Lofty (and supports)—for he lifts and supports both above and below, for all (lift) are below and what they lift is above, but he is above and what he lifts is below, and he lifts and supports all his universe
Dwelling forever—for his kingdom is eternal and has no end
Holy his name—[for he is holy] and his servants are holy and every day they say to him, holy, holy, holy.[6]

Such lists of interpretations of holy names can be found in other Jewish sources from late antiquity and the early Middle Ages,[7] and the *Sefer Yeṣirah* "interpretation of holy names" section, partly based on Isa. 57:15, resembles them.

This section is important for two reasons: first, this is a list of ten holy names that do not appear in this order, other than in *Sefer Yeṣirah*. Second, the list of those names appears twice in *Sefer Yeṣirah*, at the very beginning of the book[8] and at the end, and was interpreted only in the latter case. It seems that the interpretation of the holy names in *Sefer Yeṣirah* was inserted at a later stage, after the list of holy names was already a part of *Sefer Yeṣirah*.

This section, which contains original interpretations unknown from other sources, is considered to be an integral part of *Sefer Yeṣirah*, in Saadya's commentary, written in the first third of the tenth century, as well as in the tenth-century manuscript of *Sefer Yeṣirah* from the Cairo Geniza. It constitutes important evidence about the intellectual world of some of *Sefer Yeṣirah*'s early readers.

Peter Hayman refers to this paragraph in his edition and interpretation of *Sefer Yeṣirah*, noting that it seems to consist of "traditional" midrashic perceptions, traces of which can be found in rabbinic literature.[9] The majority of themes mentioned in the "interpretation of the holy names" section refer to rabbinic literature; this is the case with the explanation of the name "Ṣevaoth—he is a sign in his host" (צבאות—אות בצבא(ות) שלו);[10] the comment "Shaday—so far sufficient" (שדי—עד כ[א]ן די);[11] the explanation of the three who have been called living: "[living] God, running water, and tree of life" (אלהים [חיים], מים חיים ועץ חיים);[12] the detailed argument about the name "Lofty" (supports): "for he lifts and supports both above and below, for all (lift) are below and what they lift is above, but he is above and what he lifts is below, and he lifts and supports all his universe" (שנושא וסובל מעלה ומטה שהכל נשואים למטה ומשואן למעלה והוא למעלה ונישא למטה ונושא וסובל את כל העולם כולו);[13] and also the argument that "God" (*el*, אל) is "hard" (קשה), indirectly based on the talmudic reading of the preposition *el* as an indicator for "hard" things.[14] Along with these midrashic sources, which reflect well-known rabbinic sources and are thus of minimal help in characterizing the spiritual world of the editor of the section, I want to point to two unique interpretations that can teach us more about the intellectual world and theoretical substratum that are their point of origin.

I will begin with a discussion of "God of Israel—he is a minister before God" (אלהי ישראל—שר בפני אל), and in Yehudah Barzillai's version: "a minister in the heavenly entourage" (שר בפמליא של מעלה). Reflecting on this interpretation, Barzillai saw it as a heresy deriving from a copyist's error. According to Barzillai, this interpretation seems to argue that there are "two powers in heaven": if the God of Israel is only a minister in the heavenly entourage and there is a higher God above him, it could lead the innocent reader to a binitarian approach, according to which there is a lesser God, the demiurge, that is, God of Israel, and a higher one—*the* God: "And that which is written—'God of Israel is a minister in his heavenly entourage'—is, according to our humble opinion, a grave mistake in the recension, and whoever wrote this way erred and misconstrued his recension so as to 'kill' whoever has no knowledge. Since one cannot describe our Creator, blessed be his Name, with the term 'minister,' since a minister is someone who has someone greater above him . . . . But why should this interpreter want to write it in this way? He should have written 'God of Israel is the God of his entourage.'"[15]

Barzillai, hence, seems to understand "God of Israel" as a heavenly minister belonging to an entourage to be referring to a pleromatic vision, according to which the God of Israel is a minister representing Israel and is subordinate, similar to ministers of other nations, to a higher heavenly being. I have no doubt that Barzillai's comment accurately conveys the way in which this paragraph was understood by many readers of *Sefer Yeṣirah*. Moreover, it seems that such an understanding of the original version led to the change from שר בפני אל to שר בפמליא של מעלה.

The formulation שר בפני אל need not be read in this alarming manner. As I have demonstrated in detail elsewhere,[16] the wording שר בפני אל initially referred to the well-known myth of Jacob's apotheosis. This myth, traces of which can be found in rabbinic literature, early *piyyut*, and Hekhalot literature,[17] certainly shows that the interpreter is drawn to one of the boldest mythical sources in rabbinic literature, in which Jacob has undergone an apotheosis. For instance, in b. Megilah, we find a midrash on the biblical description of Jacob building the altar on his return to Shechem from Laban's home, after his struggle with the angel and the meeting with Esau: *And he erected there an altar, and [he] called it [him] El, the God of Israel.*[18] To the question that emerges from this verse concerning the grounds for Jacob naming the altar "El, the God of Israel," the midrash replies that it is not Jacob who is the subject of this verse but rather God calling Jacob "El": "R. Aḥa said in the name of R. Eliezer: Whence do we know that the Holy one, blessed be He, calls Jacob 'god'? As it is written 'He called him El, the God of Israel.'"[19]

In this midrash from b. Megilah, as well as in other sources of late antiquity, Israel, Jacob, is apotheosized and considered to be a mediator between the people of Israel and God. Interestingly, in the "interpretation of the holy names" in *Sefer Yeṣirah*, this radical myth is articulated unequivocally, where the depiction of the God of Israel as no more than a prince before the highest God rests on the acquaintance with the designation of Jacob as God of Israel.

An additional intimation of the editor's spiritual world can be found in another reading from the "interpretation of the holy names" section—dealing with the number of letters in the ineffable name: "[YH] two names YHWH four names." Converting "letters" into "names," especially when dealing with the ineffable name, while not common in rabbinic literature, has been shown by Karl Grözinger to exist in Hekhalot literature. According to Grözinger,[20] letters and names became synonymous as a consequence of the use of long sequences of letters for holy names. Indeed, a close equivalent of the matter at hand can be found in one of the later compositions of Hekhalot literature—*Seder Rabbah de-Bereishit*, where a rabbinic midrash about the creation of the world from the letters *yod* and *he* is presented in wording and terminology similar to those of the "interpretation of holy names" section, reading as follows:[21] "'In the beginning [בראשית, *bereishit*], when God created' (Gen. 1:1). Do not read 'in the beginning [*bereishit*]' but rather 'created six [ברא-שית, bara-shit].' And thus you find 'In the beginning' six letters from which heavens and earth were created. As it says: '*for with YH YHWH created the worlds*' [Isa. 26:4], YH two YHWH four therefore—six. Therefore you have learned that by these six names the Holy one, blessed be He, created the heavens and the earth."[22]

In the preceding paragraphs, we have shown that the manner of interpretation of two names in the "interpretation of the holy names" section indicates something of the spiritual world of the early readers of *Sefer Yeṣirah*. The interpretation of the name "God of Israel" reveals a connection to the myth of Jacob's apotheosis, and the interpretation of the ineffable name reveals the use of terminology known from Hekhalot literature. This layer presents, therefore, a minute but significant trace of a spiritual world in which midrash, myth, and mysticism were inseparable.

To highlight the "interpretation of the holy names" section in the history of the reception of *Sefer Yeṣirah*, I will refer to a short text that shows that the substance of this section also found expression in channels external to *Sefer Yeṣirah*. As with other commentaries quoted in the writings of *Ḥasidei Ashkenaz* and circles close to them, there are probably traditions of interpreting *Sefer Yeṣirah* not in our possession.[23] I will refer to a short but important paragraph from a commentary to *Sefer Yeṣirah* written by Elhanan ben Yaqar of London (first half of the thirteenth century), in which he interprets a list of holy names at the beginning of *Sefer Yeṣirah* similar to the list under discussion. His account states that these letters refer to the theophonic names of the angels and not to God Himself. This prompts one to assume that this was an attempt to moderate the interpretation of "God of Israel," about which, as we have mentioned above, Barzillai was also troubled. We quote from Elhanan ben Yaqar:

> Ṣevaoth—He is a sign in His host, YHWH is engraved on the crown, in accordance with: "Holiness to YHWH" [Exod. 39:30].
>
> God of Israel—its interpretation: the ministers on high are named "El" like Michael, Gabriel, and the other holy [angels] who serve [God].
>
> El—its interpretation: strong.
>
> Šaday—[He who] brings everything into being and is omnipotent.
>
> High and lofty—it is an epithet of the bearer who, being above, bears the one under [him], unlike the [usual] way of the bearers who are under and their burden above.
>
> Dwelling forever and holy—its interpretation: He dwells in Eternity.[24]

Examination of *Sefer Yeṣirah* manuscripts confirms that the "interpretation of holy names" section, once inserted into *Sefer Yeṣirah*, preserved its wording, form, and content over the centuries and that differences between the quotations about the interpretation of names in the various versions of *Sefer Yeṣirah* are minor. It is therefore of utmost importance to note the deviation in this excerpt's citation of the holy names interpretation, suggesting that Elhanan ben Yaqar was in possession of a different version of the interpretation. One possibility is that after the section interpreting *Sefer Yeṣirah* had been mistakenly inserted into the body of *Sefer Yeṣirah*, it continued to evolve separately and independently of *Sefer Yeṣirah*, with alterations being made over the next three hundred years. Consequently, in the thirteenth century, Elhanan ben Yaqar probably had a different version of this interpretation and not the one that had been inserted into *Sefer Yeṣirah*. In other words, the interpretation of *Sefer Yeṣirah*, a section of which had found its way into *Sefer Yeṣirah* itself, was probably known between the tenth and thirteenth centuries as an independent source of interpretation and was available to Elhanan ben Yaqar, who integrated it into his commentary. Its fate was similar to other *Sefer Yeṣirah* commentaries in the possession of *Ḥasidei Ashkenaz* and their close circles, and did not survive independently.

The Epistle of Agobard of Lyon

Another useful source in showing how *Sefer Yeṣirah* was understood in the Jewish world before the tenth century is Agobard of Lyon's famous epistle, a letter about the Jews and their beliefs, which has been discussed by numerous scholars of Judaism in the last 150 years.[25] The invaluable significance of this text for an understanding of the evolution of mythical and mystical knowledge in the Jewish world from the Islamic East to the communities based in Western Christendom at the turn of the first millennium can hardly be overestimated. In the following paragraphs, I would like to refer to one matter in Agobard's epistle: the description of the Jews' relation to alphabetic letters:

> They also say that their deity is corporeal and is distinguished by his limbs and his corporeal features and that, like us, he hears with one body part, sees with another, and speaks or does whatever else he does with yet another; and thus the human body was fashioned in the image of God, except that he has inflexible, rigid fingers, inasmuch as he does no work with his hands. He sits like some terrestrial king on a throne borne by four beasts, and he is housed in some sort of great palace. He even thinks many vain and pointless thoughts, which, because they all come to naught,

> turn into demons. As we have said, they relate countless abominations concerning their god, such that they worship an image which they have fashioned and erected for themselves in the folly of their hearts, not the true, completely unalterable God, of whom they are totally ignorant.
>
> They believe that the letters of their alphabet exist eternally and that before the beginning of the world they received different tasks, over which they were supposed to preside in this world. The law of Moses was written many eons before the world came into being. They further maintain that there are many terrestrial worlds, many hells, and many heavens. They assert that one of these, which they call "racha," that is, the firmament, supports God's mill, in which manna is ground for food for the angels. They call another one "araboth," in which they contend that the Lord resides, and, according to them, this is what is written in the Psalm, "lift up a song to him who rides upon the *araboth*" (Ps. 68:5). God therefore has seven trumpets, one of which measures a thousand cubits.[26]

Agobard attributes beliefs to the Jews, some of which can be traced back to rabbinic sources as well as to the Hekhalot; others are unknown to us from earlier Jewish sources. Among these beliefs are that the alphabetical letters had a crucial role in the creation of the world and in the created world. He gives three criteria explaining the role that alphabetical letters have for the Jews:

> a. The letters have existed eternally (*litteras quoque alfabeti . . . existere sempiternas*).
>
> b. The letters were allotted tasks before the world was created (*ante mundi principium impetrasse diversa ministeria*).
>
> c. The tasks allotted to the letters before the world was created are to be administered by them in the created world (*quibus eas oporteat in seculo presidere*).

Agobard's claims regarding Jewish perceptions of the importance of the alphabet prior to and after the creation of world, as well as their coronation as head of creation, can contribute to our understanding of *Sefer Yeṣirah*'s reception history. As we noted in Chapter 2, Jewish literature of late antiquity and the early Middle Ages identifies the letters by which the world was created as those of the ineffable name. There is no known Jewish cosmogonic source prior to the ninth century that explicitly makes a claim concerning the alphabet and includes all three criteria defined by Agobard. All other Jewish sources known to us from late antiquity, such as rabbinic literature, *piyyutim*, Hekhalot literature, or *Letters of Rabbi Akiva* (Version A and Version B), do not conform to this description.[27] In *Sefer Yeṣirah*, on the other hand, one does find a clear-cut and elaborate description of God having thirty-two *netivoth* prior to the world's creation, consisting of ten *sefirot* and the twenty-two letters. From the second chapter onward, *Sefer Yeṣirah* depicts the central role of the twenty-two letters in the creation of the world and in setting it in order, as well as their coronation as head of the created world. Repetitive wording points out the three *immot* letters, the seven "doubles" and the twelve "simples." For example, *Sefer Yeṣirah* discusses the role of the letter *bet*: "He made *bet* rule, and bound to it a crown, and combined one with another, and formed with it Saturn in the universe, the Sabbath in the year, and the mouth in mankind."[28]

Although this ninth-century French bishop's short description of the letters of the alphabet does not directly quote *Sefer Yeṣirah*, only one Hebrew source known to us written before the tenth century contains a mythical scenario like Agobard's, and this source is *Sefer Yeṣirah*. So even if Agobard or his Jewish informants on these matters in ninth-century Lyon did not quote directly from *Sefer Yeṣirah*, they were well acquainted with its main mythical and cosmogonic traditions. Two points: first, in the ninth century, the ideas of *Sefer Yeṣirah* were known in the Jewish world and even in Europe; second, the depiction of the cosmogony of *Sefer Yeṣirah*, that is, the role of the letters of the alphabet in the creation of the world and in the created world, is in Agobard's epistle interwoven with issues that can be traced back to Hekhalot literature, *Shiur Koma*, the rabbinic *ma'aseh bereishit* and *ma'aseh merkavah*, and *Letters of Rabbi Akiva* version A, and with others not known from early Jewish sources but that nevertheless have clear mythical meaning, such as the descriptions of God's rigid fingers and his evil thoughts.[29] Although *Sefer Yeṣirah* does not show any affinity with early Jewish mystical and mythical lore, the context in which its main ideas were understood in the ninth century, approximately two hundred years after its crystallization, seems to be that of early Jewish mystical and mythical beliefs. We therefore conclude that in the ninth century, at the latest, approximately a hundred years before it was interpreted as a scientific treatise by its tenth-century Jewish commentators, *Sefer Yeṣirah* was considered part of the corpus of Jewish mystical and mythical traditions.

Summary: *Sefer Yeṣirah* Before the Tenth Century and the Hekhalot Material

In his article about *Sefer Yeṣirah* and the Hekhalot literature, Peter Hayman demonstrates that the two came from different milieus and that there is no justification for considering *Sefer Yeṣirah* as related to that textual corpus. He further asserts that Hekhalot material that can be found in *Sefer Yeṣirah* should be regarded as a later layer in the history of the evolution of this treatise. Our arguments seem to lead to the same conclusions but from a different angle. As we have seen, although it is difficult to outline the precise history of *Sefer Yeṣirah* in the Jewish world between the seventh and tenth centuries, some traces of it can be found, traces that attest to the fact that *Sefer Yeṣirah* was known in the Jewish world before the tenth century. The short interpretation of holy names inserted into the body of *Sefer Yeṣirah*, as well as the testimony of Agobard from Lyon, reveals that *Sefer Yeṣirah* was understood by its very early Jewish readers as part of Jewish mystical lore from late antiquity. Although *Sefer Yeṣirah* was not edited in a known Jewish milieu, it was accepted before the tenth century by Jews who seem to have understood it to contain mystical and mythical material. This conclusion also supports Haggai Ben-Shammai's assumption that Saadya's commentary to *Sefer Yeṣirah* was apologetic in nature and probably written in view of, and perhaps even as a reaction to, other *Sefer Yeṣirah* commentaries that were concerned with myth, mysticism, and magic: "It may be said that Saadya's goal in writing his Commentary on *Sefer Yeṣirah* was to detach the work from mythical, mystical, or magical elements which had possibly been attached to it by earlier commentators."[30]

Chapter 5

Reevaluating the Scientific Phase of *Sefer Yeṣirah*

Although the first commentaries on *Sefer Yeṣirah* were not homogeneous, they shared a perspective in seeing *Sefer Yeṣirah* as a sort of scientific-philosophical treatise and therefore differed essentially from the mythical, mystical, and magical commentaries on *Sefer Yeṣirah* written from the second half of the twelfth century onward by *Ḥasidei Ashkenaz* and the kabbalists. This departure has led scholars such as Joseph Dan to call the period between the tenth and twelfth centuries the "scientific phase" of *Sefer Yeṣirah*.[1]

In Chapter 4, I stated that before the tenth century, *Sefer Yeṣirah* was understood, at least by some of its readers, as part of Jewish mystical lore from late antiquity. My main goal in this chapter is to demonstrate that the well-known commentaries on *Sefer Yeṣirah* written between the tenth and twelfth centuries by prominent rabbinic figures such as Saadya Gaon, Dunash Ibn Tamim, Shabbetai Donnolo, Yehudah Barzillai, and Judah Halevi do not fully reflect the history of its reception. An overview of the history of the reception of *Sefer Yeṣirah* shows that, as with its early readers before the tenth century, and as with readers after the twelfth century, *Sefer Yeṣirah* was also understood by many of its readers between the tenth and twelfth centuries as a mythical, mystical, and magical book. Related to this is another important issue in *Sefer Yeṣirah*'s history of acceptance, which can be formulated as a question: Why did these leading rabbinical figures dedicate such long and detailed commentaries to *Sefer Yeṣirah*, a treatise that was supposedly unknown and anonymous? Throughout this chapter, I will demonstrate that a main motivation for writing those commentaries was to diminish the canonical status of *Sefer Yeṣirah*, which was considered by many, in all probability, to have a significance comparable only with that of the Torah. For some, it might even have been considered to be part of the Torah, which is probably the reason that it was attributed to Abraham the patriarch. As we will see, a narrative exists, according to which God created the world while contemplating *Sefer Yeṣirah*, which is said to have been an integral part of the Torah at that time. My argument will be that the early commentators of *Sefer Yeṣirah* did not simply interpret this treatise and that the scientific-philosophic commentaries to *Sefer Yeṣirah* that those rabbis wrote were, in effect, an attempt to supervise its content by changing the way in which it was understood by readers less bound by rabbinic norms.

Several important studies dedicated to various subjects in the history of *Sefer Yeṣirah* during those three centuries have appeared in the last twenty-five years, each of which has demonstrated that *Sefer Yeṣirah* was read through mystical, mythical, and magical lenses. Although none of these studies purports to give an extensive and detailed picture of the reception of *Sefer Yeṣirah*, pooling the research findings provides a more panoramic perspective on the acceptance of *Sefer Yeṣirah* prior to the late twelfth century. Here is a brief chronology of the advance in the research of the last quarter-century toward such a perspective.

In an article published in 1987, Yehuda Liebes argued that in the first half of the eleventh century, Rabbi Solomon Ibn Gabirol refers to *Sefer Yeṣirah* in liturgical poems in a way that reflects a kabbalistic approach.[2] In 1992, Elliot Wolfson argued that Shabbetai Donnolo's commentary on *Sefer Yeṣirah* gives a theosophical reading of the term *sefirot* in *Sefer Yeṣirah* similar to the kabbalistic use of the term.[3] In 1993, Klaus Herrmann published a segment of *Sefer Yeṣirah* commentary, preserved in the Cairo Geniza, written between the end of the tenth and the beginning of the eleventh centuries, in the spirit of the Hekhalot literature.[4] In 2000, Daniel Abrams noted that the commentary that Herrmann indicated was probably in the possession of the mystical circle close to those of *Ḥasidei Ashkenaz* and named "Unique Cherub

Circle" and that there is evidence for this in the *Beraita de Yosef ben Uziel* and in one of the commentaries on *Sefer Yeṣirah* by Rabbi Elhanan ben Yaqar of London.[5] Abrams's comment led Herrmann to return to the Geniza commentary segment in an article published in 2005, in which he concludes that because it was written no later than the end of the tenth century or the beginning of the eleventh, one can infer that—parallel to the so-called scientific phase of *Sefer Yeṣirah*—another more mystical interpretation was also in play, of which only fragments survived. That this interpretation was known between the eleventh and thirteenth centuries can be ascertained by its use in the writings of R. Elazar of Worms and in those of the "Unique Cherub Circle."[6]

The purpose of this chapter is to expand our understanding of the convoluted history of the reception of *Sefer Yeṣirah* between the tenth and twelfth centuries. To this end, we will investigate a midrashic tale about *Sefer Yeṣirah* that seems to be an introduction to the book and appears in one of its earliest manuscripts, the eleventh-century Vatican Ms. 299/4. I will then examine how R. Shlomo Yitzhaki (Rashi), in the eleventh century, deals with *Sefer Yeṣirah*, and then will discuss its concluding phrasing, which also appears in the Vatican manuscript of *Sefer Yeṣirah*.

The Early Manuscripts of *Sefer Yeṣirah* and Ms. Vatican 299

Although *Sefer Yeṣirah* was first cited in Jewish sources only from the tenth century, we have quite a few early and complete manuscripts of it, even by comparison with other Jewish compositions of late antiquity and the early Middle Ages that are cited in sources before the tenth century. The earliest manuscript of *Sefer Yeṣirah* was found in the Cairo Geniza and was published in its entirety by Nehemya Allony.[7] This version is the most similar to Saadya's commentary, containing three parts written as a vertical scroll. Apart from the paragraph discussed in the previous chapter, this manuscript does not reveal much about how it was read, since the manuscript contains no additional commentary, notes, or any other markings that might guide its interpretation. Ms. Vatican 299, written in Italy, is the second of the dated texts of *Sefer Yeṣirah*. This manuscript has been dated to the tenth century by scholars such as Ithamar Gruenwald and Peter Hayman.[8] With the publication of a comprehensive catalog of Jewish manuscripts from the Vatican library, Benjamin Richler, Malachi beit-Arié, and Nurit Pasternak have reevaluated its dating and determined it as belonging to the second half of the eleventh century.[9] The question of the dating of the manuscript is evidently highly relevant for the present study; nevertheless, both the earlier and the later date are sufficient support for the contention that mystical interpretations of *Sefer Yeṣirah* developed before the twelfth century.

The paramount importance allotted to Ms. Vatican 299 in our discussion derives from the fact that this version of *Sefer Yeṣirah* has a lengthy midrashic introduction dealing with Ben Sira and his connection to *Sefer Yeṣirah*, as well as a concluding phrase in a contemplative idiom. These additions make it possible to infer how *Sefer Yeṣirah* was read and understood at that stage. The significance of these interpretive sources will be clarified in due course; it is worth noting at this point that in a number of early manuscripts of *Sefer Yeṣirah*—those written before the fourteenth century—we see both the introductory and concluding additions of Ms. Vatican 299, and it therefore seems that many scribes viewed them as integral to *Sefer Yeṣirah*.[10]

The Midrash on *Sefer Yeṣirah* and Ben Sira

We open the discussion on Ms. Vat. 299 with a close reading of the midrash on *Sefer Yeṣirah* and Ben Sira. This midrash, in medieval phrasing, glorifies Ben Sira for having discovered forgotten chapters, books, and orders (*sedarim*). In this long and complex midrash, there is a description of God creating the world with the help of *Sefer Yeṣirah* and instructions about the correct way to learn *Sefer Yeṣirah*'s secrets, as well as an account of the achievements of the sages who learned *Sefer Yeṣirah* in *ḥavruta* (joint study)[11] for three years, studies that included the creation of an artificial man. The significance of this source for our study warrants the presentation of a complete translation for the reader's reference. I offer my translation of the whole midrash, which I have divided into two parts:[12]

Part 1

These are the five books and five chapters and five orders that Ben Sira revealed to Uziel his son and Yosef his grandson: *Sefer Yeṣirah*, *Sefer Tag[im]*, *Sefer Dikdukim*, *Sefer Pesikta Batrey Apey Miškan*, *Sefer Zerubavel*. Five chapters: *Perek R. Shimon Bar Yoḥay*, *Perek Avot de-Rabbi Natan*, *Perek Otiot de-Rabbi Akiva*, *Perek Ma'asse Miškan*, *Perek Dereḵ Ereṣ*. Five orders: *Seder Olam*, *Seder Tekufut*, *Seder Shaot*, *Seder Eibur*, *Seder Halakhot*. And when he had revealed all the secrets, all the heavenly entourage shook, and the Holy Spirit went forth and said: "Who revealed my mysteries to mankind?" Ben 'A.Ṣ.Š.T stood up and said: "I, Buzi ben Buzi." The Holy One, blessed be he, said to him: "That is enough for you!" At once Yosef sat down and wrote from 'A.Ṣ.Š.T those fifteen things, he wrote five books with a stylus; *Sefer Yeṣirah* with which the Holy One, blessed be he, created his world.

Part 2

"Who can utter the mighty doings of the Lord, or declare all his praise" (Ps. 106:2), and from here you learn that no one can utter his mighty acts and shew forth all his praise. Even the ministering angels cannot recount a fraction of his mighty acts or interpret what he contemplated and created and did. Since in the beginning when the Holy One, blessed be he, created the world, he was alone and a thought arose in him to create the world, and so he was engraving the foundations in the land but they did not last, until he created in the Torah—*Sefer Yeṣirah*, which he contemplated and understood with his wisdom, and thus he created the world. And his eyes were contemplating *Sefer Yeṣirah*, and his hands were wandering and building in the world. Although distinctly different, it is like a man who builds a building and he has a book [of instructions] and he reads it, so did the Holy One, blessed be he. And after he created his world and completed it, he left it [*Sefer Yeṣirah*] in the Torah, which was concealed from

the beginning, 974 generations before the creation of the world. When our Father Abraham was born, the ministering angels said before God, blessed be he: "Lord of the world, you have a friend in the world, you mean to keep something hidden from him?" The Holy One, blessed be he, replied forthwith: "Am I indeed hiding something from Abraham?" and he took counsel with the Torah and said: "Come, we shall wed you to my friend Abraham." And [the Torah] said before him: "No, until a humble man [i.e., Moses] will come and will marry[13] the humble one [=Torah]."[14] Thereupon the Holy One, blessed be he, took counsel with *Sefer Yeṣirah*, who said: "Yes," and he gave her to Abraham. And [Abraham] sat alone and studied *Sefer Yeṣirah* but could not understand a thing, until a heavenly voice went forth and said to him: "Are you trying to set yourself up as my equal? I am one, and I have created *Sefer Yeṣirah*, and it was read to me, and I did all that was written in it, but you by yourself cannot understand it. Take a companion and meditate on it, both of you, and you will understand it." Thereupon, Abraham went to Shem, his rabbi, and he sat with him three years, and they contemplated it and they knew how to create the world. And to this day, there is no one who can understand it alone, but only two sages. And even they will not understand it in less than three years. And when they understand it, they will be able to make everything their heart desires. And when Abraham understood it, he added wisdom upon wisdom and learned all the Torah. And Rava, too, wished to understand it alone. Rabbi Zera said: "But it is written: 'A sword [is] upon the liars,[15] and they shall dote.'[16] A sword upon 'Israel's enemies' who sit singly, each by himself, and concern themselves with the Torah.[17] If so, let us go and busy ourselves with *Sefer Yeṣirah*." And so they sat together, and contemplated it for three years and understood it, and one calf was created to them. And they slaughtered it and used it [for a feast] for the completion of the treatise. And when they slaughtered it, they forgot it [i.e., their understanding of the *Sefer*

> *Yeṣirah*]. They sat another three years and produced it again. And Ben Sira, too, wished to understand it alone; a heavenly voice went forth and said: "Two are better." He went to Jeremiah, and they studied it for three years and understood it, and a man was created before them, and on his forehead was written "But the Lord God is Truth [אמת, *emet*]" and in his hand was a knife and he erased the letter *alef* from *emet* [מת, dead]. Jeremiah said: "Why are you doing that? Can the Truth not be?" He said to them: "I will tell you a parable. What does this resemble? [It resembles] a man who was a builder and was wise. When the people saw him, they made him their king. A few days later, other people came and learned that craft, and [the people] abandoned the first one and followed the others. Likewise, the Holy One, blessed be he, may his name be exulted, contemplated *Sefer Yeṣirah* and created the world, and they made him king over his created beings. Yet now that you have come and have done the same thing, what would be the outcome? Everyone would leave him and would follow you. What would become of him who created you?" They said to him: "In that case, what should we do?" He answered: "Turn him [i.e., me] back." And that man became dust and ashes.

Dating the Midrash

This midrash has been discussed by leading scholars such as Gershom Scholem, Moshe Idel, Joseph Dan, and Yehuda Liebes.[18] Certain factors, however, have prevented scholars from comprehending the full significance of the midrash for the history of *Sefer Yeṣirah* before the twelfth century: errors in dating the midrash and the tendency to focus on its relation to the evolution of the legend of the Golem in the period before the writings of *Ḥasidei Ashkenaz*,[19] while giving insufficient attention to other themes in the midrash.

Most scholars who have discussed this midrash have based their dating of it on Yehudah Barzillai's interpretation of *Sefer Yeṣirah*, which quoted only the second half of the midrash.[20] However, as Joseph Dan has recently pointed out, we have at hand only one manuscript of Barzillai's commentary to *Sefer Yeṣirah*, and this midrash, which is quoted after the commentary, was probably not originally part of the commentary and was inserted as an appendix into the manuscript by a later editor.[21] Although Dan does not mention all the reasons for his assertion, we are led to the conclusion that this midrash is a later insertion, based both on the fact that the wording in this section of the manuscript is different from the rest of the commentary; and that neither the name of Ben Sira or the tale about him was mentioned in the body of Barzillai's commentary, although it could support some of its main ideas.[22] I part company, however, over Dan's misguided conclusion that the midrash's terminus *ad quem* should be the fourteenth century, the period of Ms. Padua,[23] the only manuscript of Barzillai's commentary to *Sefer Yeṣirah*. According to Ms. Vat. 299, the midrash's *terminus ad quem* is the late eleventh century, and, as we will demonstrate, the *terminus a quo* of the main part of the midrash could possibly be as early as the ninth century.

The Two Parts of the Midrash

A close reading of this version of the midrash, as well as of some later versions, reveals that it is composed of two separate midrashim dealing with *Sefer Yeṣirah*, unrelated in narrative, style, and terminology. In the first and shortest part of the midrash, *Sefer Yeṣirah* does not have an important role. One finds first a list of books, chapters, and *sedarim* of post-talmudic Jewish treatises, including *Sefer Yeṣirah*—all of which were revealed by Ben Sira and transmitted to his son Uziel and grandson Yosef. Then comes a description of God's wrath following the discovery of the books; and then an account of Ben Sira's grandson Yosef's transcription of these books from his grandfather's oral transmission.

The second part of the midrash, by contrast, deals solely with *Sefer Yeṣirah*. It consists of a detailed description of God using *Sefer Yeṣirah* to create the world, discusses the relation between *Sefer Yeṣirah* and the Torah, and recounts the prime role of Abraham, and not Ben Sira, as the first person to have been engaged with the book and to have understood its wisdom, together with his companion in study. The lack of continuity in the fabric of the two parts of the midrash is immediately obvious and is a clear indication of editing: the seam where the two midrashim are amalgamated is prominently located after the account of Ben Sira's grandson transcribing the books. What ensues is a text in which only *Sefer Yeṣirah* is discussed.

Although the two midrashim coalesce in a literary structure beginning and ending with Ben Sira, two distinct figures of Ben Sira, originating in two different traditions, can be distinguished. Ben Sira in the concluding part of the midrash is depicted as a contemporary of Jeremiah, just as he was portrayed in the *Tales of Ben Sira*. By contrast, Ben Sira of the first part is not related to Jeremiah and has the unknown nicknames Ben 'A.Ṣ.Š.T and Buzi ben Buzi, and, as in *The Alphabet of Ben Sira*, his offspring are named Uziel and Yosef.[24] The assumption that two different traditions concerning Ben Sira and *Sefer Yeṣirah* were amalgamated is further supported by the fact that in Ms. Vat. 299, immediately following the text in question, the same scribe copied an additional narrative about Ben Sira, unrelated to *Sefer Yeṣirah*: the first part of the *Tales of Ben Sira*.[25] It seems, therefore, that Ms. Vat. 299 contains a collection of traditions about Ben Sira, two of which were merged into one section serving as an introduction to *Sefer Yeṣirah*.

The First Midrash

As we have noted, the first of the two midrashim joined in Ms. Vat. 299 does not attach much significance to *Sefer Yeṣirah*: it is mentioned there as one treatise in a long list of treatises, and the only description that relates to *Sefer Yeṣirah* is a short sentence that tells how God created the world. To shed light on this midrash, I will refer to an article in which Israel Weinstock argues that it alludes to abu-Aharon[26] and that it describes how abu-Aharon brought the treatises in the above-mentioned list from the East to Europe.[27] Although we cannot make a direct connection between abu-Aharon and this midrash, it still seems likely that this part of the midrash is an etiological legend about the way in which some rabbinic as well as post-talmudic compositions arrived in Europe sometime in the early Middle Ages.

The Second Midrash

In contrast to the first midrash, *Sefer Yeṣirah* is central to the second, while the figure of Ben Sira is less important and, as will be demonstrated, his name was probably inserted only at a later stage. According to the midrash, it was Abraham who revealed *Sefer Yeṣirah* and who, together with his rabbi, Shem (the patriarch Shem, son of Noah), understood it to its core. This midrashic narrative is not surprising in light of the well-known tradition that *Sefer Yeṣirah* was written by Abraham, as well as the fact that he is the only biblical or postbiblical figure to be mentioned in *Sefer Yeṣirah*. The second half of this midrash depicts later rabbinic figures who utilized *Sefer Yeṣirah* for magical and mystical purposes, a theme that the author of the midrash obviously took from tractate Sanhedrin, in which we read about the sages creating a calf and an artificial human: "Rava created a man, and sent him to R. Zera. R. Zera spoke to him, but received no answer. Thereupon he said unto him: 'Thou art a creature of the magicians. Return to thy dust.' R. Ḥanina and R. Hoshaiah spent every Sabbath eve in studying *Sefer Yeṣirah* by means of which they created a third-grown calf and ate it."[28]

Tractate Sanhedrin says that R. Ḥanina and R. Hoshaiah created a calf and that Rava created an artificial human and sent him to R. Zera. In our midrash, though, the names of the rabbis were transposed, and instead of R. Ḥanina and R. Hoshaiah, it is Rava and Rabbi Zera who are depicted as having created a calf, while Ben Sira and Jeremiah are, in turn, said to have created a human, rather than Rava. The changed attributions in the second part of the midrash, including the highly significant role given to Ben Sira, probably serve the synthetic intent of harmonizing different traditions about Ben Sira. It seems that our midrash adheres to a clear chronological narrative, beginning with the creation of the world, proceeding to a tale about Abraham, and ending with one about talmudic sages. That the names of the prophet Jeremiah and Ben Sira appear after the talmudic sages seems to be, from a literary point of view, a late change made in the midrashic story. Scribal errors found in Ms. Vat. 299 indicate that our midrash was copied from an earlier manuscript.[29] Collating this evidence, then, leads to the conclusion that our midrash had an earlier version in which the name of Ben Sira was not mentioned.

Although the precise dating of the early version of this midrashic tale is an impossible undertaking, it can be safely assumed that since our midrash starts with a *ptiḥta* based on Pirkei de Rabbi Eliezer,[30] which was edited around the mid-eighth century,[31] the midrash was probably written between the ninth century and the time that this part of Ms. Vat. 299 was copied in the mid-eleventh century.

In the second midrash, one can find much evidence relating to the reception of *Sefer Yeṣirah*, by at least some of its readers, up to the late twelfth century. This midrash depicts the mystical and contemplative way of studying *Sefer Yeṣirah* in *ḥavruta* and extensively elaborates the story from Sanhedrin about the creation of a calf and an artificial man. To better comprehend the interpretive trends reflected in this midrash, I will focus on an issue that can be deduced from the midrash, a surprising one: the complicated relation of *Sefer Yeṣirah* with the primordial Torah. As some scholars have noted, *Sefer Yeṣirah* is exceptional in ignoring the biblical description of creation.[32] Although it refers to biblical verses, *Sefer Yeṣirah*, unlike other postbiblical Jewish sources, does not consider the Bible to be *the* canonical book. It seems, therefore, that the tension produced by the alternative to the biblical narrative presented by *Sefer Yeṣirah* is resolved in the midrash with the unification of the two books: the Torah and *Sefer Yeṣirah* belong together. According to this interpretation, the world was created by God after contemplating the Torah—*Sefer Yeṣirah*. The midrash based its tradition of the creation of the world by or from *Sefer Yeṣirah* on the well-known midrashic account according to which "The Holy One, blessed be He, was observing the Torah and creating the world."[33] Our midrash joined *Sefer Yeṣirah* to the Bible and says that God created the world by contemplating and learning *Sefer Yeṣirah*: "He created in the Torah—*Sefer Yeṣirah*, which he contemplated and understood with his wisdom, and thus he created the world. And his eyes were contemplating *Sefer Yeṣirah*, and his hands were wandering and building in the world. Although distinctly different, it is like a man who builds a building and has a book [of instructions] and reads it, so did the Holy One, blessed be he."

According to the midrash, immediately after the creation process, *Sefer Yeṣirah* was appended to the Torah, which existed from time immemorial. It necessarily follows that *Sefer Yeṣirah* does not refer to the biblical narrative, since it is itself a biblical composition: "And after he created his world and completed it, he left [*Sefer Yeṣirah*] in the Torah, which was concealed from the beginning, 974 generations before the creation of the world." This union did not last long, and a new division took place between the two, when the Torah refused to be given to Abraham, and *Sefer Yeṣirah* was given to him instead. According to the midrash, it is because of this refusal that *Sefer Yeṣirah* was not included in the Torah.

These last statements regarding the elevated status of *Sefer Yeṣirah*, ranking close or even equal to the Torah are in all probability early, and we can find them already in Shabbetai Donnolo's tenth-century commentary to *Sefer Yeṣirah*.[34] They may shed light on the claim made by Saadya[35] and, following him, also by Barzillai, that *Sefer Yeṣirah* in its previous format was not composed by Abraham and does not constitute a part of the Torah. Barzillai's arguments are more detailed, and he explicitly rejects the designation of *Sefer Yeṣirah* as part of the Torah:[36] "As for us, in our modest opinion, we were much amazed by this since if this book was already made in this form from the days of Abraham our father, and yet all the prophets who came after him did not mention this book and did not refer to it, neither by his name nor by theirs, as we find in Proverbs where it is written: 'These are other proverbs of Solomon that the officials of King Hezekiah of Judah copied' (Prov. 25:1). And this would not be possible. Moreover, what is the category of this book? If it were part of the Bible [it is not possible to consider it as part of the Bible], since it is not considered one of the Holy Books!"[37]

Barzillai goes on to make a connection between Abraham's knowledge of *Sefer Yeṣirah* and his knowledge of rabbinic law in general. Basing his conclusion on rabbinic sources, according to which Abraham knew the Oral Law, Barzillai asserts that Abraham knew *Sefer Yeṣirah* just as well as the talmudic tractate Avodah Zarah:[38] "And he learned many of the *halakhot* of *Yeṣirah* until he could write and compose from them many lengthy treatises. Nevertheless, he was not permitted to write it down by prophecy because it was part of the Oral Law. Just as he was studying at that time the tractate Avodah Zarah, until, at that time, this tractate contained six hundred chapters, and since it was part of the Oral Law he was not permitted to write [it down] but only to study it."[39]

This last argument is most interesting, for while Barzillai does not disassociate Abraham from *Sefer Yeṣirah*, a connection stated in *Sefer Yeṣirah*, he does demote *Sefer Yeṣirah*, ranking it together with other rabbinic sources. Barzillai not only reduces *Sefer Yeṣirah* to being part of the Oral Law but further diminishes its status in another section of his commentary, where he writes that wherever a dispute arises between rabbinic traditions and *Sefer Yeṣirah*, we should rule according to rabbinic traditions, since these traditions were more reliably transmitted: "If we see in [*Sefer Yeṣirah*] a saying that explicitly contradicts a saying that appears in the Talmud as *halakha*, we should not consider this [contradiction] as an uncertain case of which we do not know the solution. Since it is clear that it contradicts [the Talmud], it is certain and obvious that we rely on the Talmud and that we disregard the sayings of this book, and we reject the matter that disputes the sayings of the Talmud."[40]

Barzillai and the midrash entertain opposing narratives about the relation between *Sefer Yeṣirah* and the written Torah: The "midrash of *Sefer Yeṣirah* and Ben Sira" tries to join the two and maintain that *Sefer Yeṣirah* was part of the written Torah from the outset, while Barzillai claims that the version of *Sefer Yeṣirah* available to us today is late and fragmentary. It seems that Barzillai and the midrash are responding to existing opinion, which accords first-rank canonical status to *Sefer Yeṣirah*, comparable with the Torah. However, they take opposite stances with regard to this opinion, each according to his predilection.

That *Sefer Yeṣirah* was considered by many to be as important as the Bible may explain why prominent rabbinical figures wrote such long commentaries to this short, enigmatic composition, which was, until then, unheard of in Jewish literature. The purpose of some of the early commentaries on *Sefer Yeṣirah* was not solely to explain it but also to control and supervise its many versions, together with all the cosmogonic, theological, mystical, magical, and mythical meanings already associated with it in those Jewish circles where it was viewed as a canonical source of equal authority to the Torah.[41]

Rashi, *Sefer Yeṣirah*, and the Midrash About Ben Sira

We find another important piece of evidence for how *Sefer Yeṣirah* was understood by its early readers in the writings of one of the most important medieval Jewish commentators, R. Shlomo Yitzhaki (Rashi, 1040–1105). As is well known, Rashi made several references to *Sefer Yeṣirah*.[42] It seems from these references that Rashi saw *Sefer Yeṣirah* as part of the set of books belonging to *Sitrê Torah* (secrets of the Bible)[43] and as an authoritative source for interpreting discussions of the letters in rabbinic sources, whether these discussions were hermeneutic, mystical, or magical. As opposed to other early commentators on *Sefer Yeṣirah*, Rashi finds neither scientific nor grammatical and linguistic meaning in *Sefer Yeṣirah*, and he does not adopt an apologetic tone. A thorough examination of Rashi's approach to *Sefer Yeṣirah* shows that he was probably using an earlier version of the second part of the midrash about *Sefer Yeṣirah* and Ben Sira, which does not refer to the figure of Ben Sira. For example, in his famous interpretation of the creation of the artificial man by Rava in b. Sanhedrin (65b), Rashi wrote that Rava created a man: "By means of *Sefer Yeṣirah*, which taught him the letter combination of [the] name." Gershom Scholem and Moshe Idel see this quotation as proof of Rashi's view of *Sefer Yeṣirah* as a magical text and a guide to creating an artificial human,[44] a view that Idel thinks may be true to the original meaning of *Sefer Yeṣirah*.[45] The claim that a narrative of the creation of an artificial human can be found in *Sefer Yeṣirah* should be considered with caution, since it is not apparent in the book and is, at most, only a possibility. Another source by Rashi supporting the assumption that he was acquainted with an early version of our midrash is his interpretation of the verse in Job: "*God understands the way to it, and he knows its place*" (Job 28:23). In his interpretation of Job 28:12, Rashi identifies wisdom with the Torah; and in reading verse 23, he understands the ambiguous "God understood the way to it" (אלהים הבין דרכה) to mean not that God understood the way of the Torah but that God observed the Torah: "He looked in it and created the world with its letters; with their order and their balance, he created all creatures, as it is written in the secret of *Sefer Yeṣirah*."[46]

Rashi's interpretation raises three interesting questions. First, since Rashi regards the phrase "understands the way" to mean that God created the world by observing the Torah, how is it that he does not refer to the famous midrash that opens Genesis Rabbah ("The Holy One, blessed be he, was looking at the Torah and creating the world")?[47] Second, why did Rashi associate looking at the Torah while creating the world with *Sefer Yeṣirah*? And third, although Rashi refers several times to *Sefer Yeṣirah* in his interpretations of Talmud and Bible, this is the only occasion on which he uses the phrase "the secret of *Sefer Yeṣirah*," and thus it seems that "the secret of *Sefer Yeṣirah*" and *Sefer Yeṣirah* are not synonymous. The solution to these questions seems to be that Rashi knew the midrash in which God is described as having contemplated *Sefer Yeṣirah*, considered as part of the written Torah, and it is this midrash that he calls "the secret of *Sefer Yeṣirah*."[48]

A *piyyut* written by one of Rashi's disciples[49] says: "The learned persons who know to combine [the letters of] your ineffability"[50] (חכמי צירוף עילומך), and the interpretation is as follows: "The learned persons who know to combine [the letters of] your ineffability: The learned persons who know how to combine an exalted name . . . like people who are knowledgeable in *Sefer Yeṣirah*[51] and know how to combine the name and to create a world upon incantation."[52]

This quotation is interesting for two reasons: first, the link between *Sefer Yeṣirah* and magic seems obvious; second, the fact that *Sefer Yeṣirah* can stand for those who combine the letters of the ineffable name demonstrates how popular the use of *Sefer Yeṣirah* as a magical guide was. In other words, it seems that everyone knew that *Sefer Yeṣirah* was a book used by magicians, and the way in which the book was learned was a good illustration of the magicians' practice of combining the letters of the ineffable name.

Contemplating *Sefer Yeṣirah*

As a last example of how *Sefer Yeṣirah* was understood between the tenth and the twelfth centuries, I would like to discuss a mystical and contemplative way of learning *Sefer Yeṣirah*, which had certain magical implications and which was, as far as we know, popular at the same time as the scientific interpretation of *Sefer Yeṣirah*. The midrash on *Sefer Yeṣirah* and Ben Sira makes repeated use of the unique word צפיה to describe a praxis of learning *Sefer Yeṣirah*. This word, although popular in modern Hebrew, previously appeared solely in forthrightly mystical Jewish sources from late antiquity and the early Middle Ages, where it has the meaning of a mystical vision.[53] Hence, the use of this word in *Sefer Yeṣirah* leads us to examine a well-known paragraph that was added to most copies of *Sefer Yeṣirah* and thus became part of the book in a very early period. The paragraph appears in Ms. Vat. 299: "This is the book of the letters of Abraham our father, which is called 'The Laws of Creation.' There is no limit to the wisdom of everyone who will contemplate [דיצפי] it."[54]

Because this paragraph is common in *Sefer Yeṣirah* manuscripts, Ithamar Gruenwald, Peter Hayman, and, recently, Klaus Herrmann decided to treat it in their editions as an integral part of *Sefer Yeṣirah*, seeing it as the last paragraph of the treatise.[55] We find early twelfth-century evidence that this was the version of many manuscripts of *Sefer Yeṣirah* in Barzillai's commentary to *Sefer Yeṣirah*, which reads: "And we have found in many versions of 'The *Halakhot* of *Yeṣirah*' that we still have in our hands that it is written at the beginning of the book or at its end: 'This is the book of the letters of Abraham our father, which is called "Book of *Yeṣirah*."' There is no limit to the wisdom of whoever contemplates it" (כל דיצפי ביה).[56]

The verb *tsfah* (צפה)[57] in this context refers mainly to the wording of *Sefer Yeṣirah*, preserved in its short recension, as part of the description of Abraham. The verb *tsfah* appears in a similar context in a description of the magical and mystical abilities of Abraham, who had learned the wisdom of *Sefer Yeṣirah* and had thereby become equal to God.[58] It is further stated that Abraham had succeeded in using this wisdom (ועלתה בידו), which brought him into an incomparable mystical proximity to God, manifested by God seating him on his lap and calling him his son.[59] In the words of the short version of *Sefer Yeṣirah*: "When Abraham our father contemplated [צפה], and observed, and saw, and investigated, and understood, and carved, and hewed, and combined, and formed, and succeeded, the Lord of all was revealed to him. And He made him sit in his lap, and kissed him upon his head. He called him his friend and named him his son."[60]

It seems that in the eleventh century, at the latest, as manifested in the second midrash, as well as in the concluding paragraph of *Sefer Yeṣirah*, it was clear to some of *Sefer Yeṣirah*'s readers that this treatise had mystical and magical qualities that could be implemented using contemplative means. The concluding paragraph describes in a straightforward manner that it is not only Abraham who succeeded in the magical act by contemplating *Sefer Yeṣirah* but that whoever contemplates the book will attain immeasurable wisdom.[61]

Summary

My main goal in Chapters 4 and 5 has been to demonstrate that the attempt to historically reconstruct the manner in which a highly influential treatise such as *Sefer Yeṣirah* was understood, by focusing on the uncritical reading of a limited section of the rabbinical elite, while giving no consideration to the way *Sefer Yeṣirah* was understood in other social layers in the Jewish world, is methodologically problematic. Even a short passage in a midrash with mythical and magical meanings can be more significant in understanding the reception of *Sefer Yeṣirah* than a long and detailed commentary by one of the early scientific-philosophical readers of *Sefer Yeṣirah*: Saadya, Dunash Ibn Tamim, Shabbetai Donnolo, Yehudah Barzillai, and Judah Halevi. Such is the case with: "This is the book of the letters of Abraham our father, which is called 'The Laws of Creation.' There is no limit to the wisdom of everyone who will contemplate it," which entered very early on into most recensions of *Sefer Yeṣirah* and became part of the book.[62] Research should lend a critical ear to quiet voices and testimonies, records of which were lost over the years and which have left behind only traces and echoes. The important studies written by Yehuda Liebes, Haggai Ben-Shammai, Elliot Wolfson, Klaus Herrmann, and Daniel Abrams[63] over the last thirty years, as well as the insights presented in these two chapters, show that it would be far from true to say that at the end of the twelfth century, a change took place in how *Sefer Yeṣirah* was understood—from its reception as a scientific treatise to a treatise that was read in mystical terms. The appearance of the mystical commentaries to *Sefer Yeṣirah* from the end of the twelfth century should not be understood as a fundamental change in the way *Sefer Yeṣirah* was read in the Jewish world, a new stage in its interpretation. As is frequently the case in the scholarship on Jewish mysticism, researchers are deceived by the textual inventory, since the early mystical references to *Sefer Yeṣirah* survived to only a limited extent and were eclipsed by the big scientific commentaries. Unfortunately, the lack of extensive textual evidence about the mystical ways *Sefer Yeṣirah* was read before the twelfth century is part of a wider phenomenon: the paucity of textual evidence concerning the mystical world of the Jews from the geonic period to the end of the twelfth century.[64]

Epilogue

Throughout this book, I have sought to chart the developmental path of *Sefer Yeṣirah*, one of the most influential compositions in the history of Jewish thought, on the basis of a critical examination of its sources, context, and reception.

I examined the sources of *Sefer Yeṣirah* through the lens of the preoccupation with alphabetic letters in Jewish and non-Jewish texts of late antiquity. Contrary to the accepted scholarly assumption that *Sefer Yeṣirah* developed from—or, at the very least, drew on—the same roots as the account of the creation of the world from letters in rabbinic tradition, I contend that on this essential issue, *Sefer Yeṣirah* is different from that tradition. In contrast to the rabbis' belief that the world was created from the letters of the ineffable name, *Sefer Yeṣirah* stresses that the world was molded from all twenty-two letters of the alphabet. In *Sefer Yeṣirah*, the letters of the ineffable name are designated as no more than "three simple letters."

My claim is that the cultural sources of *Sefer Yeṣirah* are not rabbinic; I maintain that the sources of *Sefer Yeṣirah* can be located in the world of Syriac Christianity around the seventh century. I support my claim based on a careful examination of three critical factors: first, we have sound evidence to the effect that accounts of the creation of the world from the twenty-two letters were developed in Syriac sources. Second, quite a few concrete parallels exist between *Sefer Yeṣirah* and Syriac sources. Third, the group of double letters BGD KPRT, one of three secondary groups defined by *Sefer Yeṣirah*, is formed on the basis of a rule determined by Syriac grammarians and scribal scholars, and there is no indication that this group of letters had been defined grammatically prior to the sixth century. Furthermore, *Sefer Yeṣirah* not only makes use of a set of letters first defined by Syriac grammarians but also employs the exact linguistic terms they coined to distinguish between soft and hard enunciation: *rakh* and *qashe*—a Hebrew adaptation of the Syriac terms *rukkakha* and *qushshaya*.

A few scholars have argued in recent years that the problem of contextualizing *Sefer Yeṣirah* will not be solved by finding concrete parallels between *Sefer Yeṣirah* and other sources but only by locating *Sefer Yeṣirah* in its most probable cultural environment: the ninth-century Arabic renaissance.[1] A thoughtful reading of their studies has left me unconvinced, for two reasons: first, the dubious rationale for preferring the assumption of the Arabic writings of the Abbasid context rather than an earlier or even contemporary Syriac Christian one.[2] Second, an Arabic-Islamic context: the Islamic science of letters was prevalent only from the late ninth to the beginning of the tenth centuries. This is quite a late period in the history of *Sefer Yeṣirah*. By that period, *Sefer Yeṣirah* was already interpreted, had had many recensions, and had received canonical status.[3]

It is difficult to determine who the people who wrote or edited *Sefer Yeṣirah* were, and caution is called for in trying to assign them to any definitive circle. All we can assert is that *Sefer Yeṣirah* and the rabbinic literature, as it is known to us today, do not exhibit any great affiliation. Although there is no indication that *Sefer Yeṣirah* attempts to conceal its context, nothing in it bespeaks any great awareness of the rabbinic world. *Sefer Yeṣirah* is a kind of relic suggesting the existence of another Jewish context, one we could glean almost nothing of from reading the composition. It is an intimation that arouses our curiosity and can certainly spark our imagination; yet we should be careful in turning such a germinal trace into a detailed profile that might only be imaginary.

What can we say about the authors/editors of *Sefer Yeṣirah*? We can determine that they were Jews, as they had a good mastery of the Hebrew language and did not refer to any kind of Christian dogma.[4] We can also say that they were clearly part of the intellectual renaissance in the world of Syriac Christianity in north Mesopotamia. I find it hard to accept the assumption that the authors/editors of *Sefer Yeṣirah* concealed their context. As philologists, we need at least a minimal confidence in our tools and should be confident that any attempt by the authors or editors of any text to conceal their real cultural context would be to no avail. Terminology, notions, paradigms, and beliefs will find their way into any text, even one that was written by a wary writer. Sensitivity to the manner in which certain concepts are employed, together with discrimination of the linguistic register used, should suffice to uncover what has been obscured.

Therefore, as I noted in the conclusion of Chapter 3, our main difficulty in apprehending the context in which *Sefer Yeṣirah* crystallized comes from the fact that this world is foreign to us, and not from the intrinsic nature of the composition. Another fact that is rarely taken into account in discussions of Jewish thought in late antiquity and the early Middle Ages is that there are very few, and only short, fragments of Hebrew manuscripts from the long period known as "the silent era," spanning approximately six hundred years, between the second and eighth centuries. Although this paucity of Hebrew manuscripts is unfortunate and hampers scholarship in presenting a broad view of the world of Jewish thought in this period, it should enlighten us about the material that has endured. Naturally, the Jewish writings known to us today are those that were in some way canonized and that engaged Jews for hundreds of years. In this respect, *Sefer Yeṣirah* is an exceptionally interesting composition; despite the fact that it was not written in rabbinical circles, it was canonized in the tenth century and thus survived.

To probe the ensuing stages in the reception of *Sefer Yeṣirah*, a critical examination of the parallel development of Jewish thought is necessary. In the first stage of its reception, from the tenth century, there were four or five commentaries dedicated to *Sefer Yeṣirah* that can roughly, even if not rigorously, be defined as philosophical-scientific in nature. In the second stage, from the end of the twelfth century, tens of commentaries were written; in this case, we can say that they generally deal with mystical subjects. This shift actually took place in the crystallization of the Jewish canon but does not reflect how *Sefer Yeṣirah* was understood by other readers. From the ninth century, mainly as a consequence of encounters with the Muslim world, a certain kind of writing evolved among Jews employed by the rabbinic and intellectual elite, who generally wrote in a Jewish-Arabic dialect. In the late twelfth century, though, in western Europe, different genres of writing evolved; mystical and mythical in nature, they were mostly written in Hebrew. The commentaries written from within both these trends reflect changes that were occurring in the Jewish canon, but they do not reflect the way that *Sefer Yeṣirah* was understood by readers beyond these specialist circles. It is important to keep in mind that the canon of Jewish thought, like every canon, exerts a kind of violence and imposes a certain paralysis in defending its frame. Beyond the strong and clear voices, the softer tones become inaudible; the force of the canon can erase whatever does not belong to it.

The goal of this book was to extricate *Sefer Yeṣirah* from the shackles of the Jewish canon—both the rabbinic canon of late antiquity and the medieval canon of Jewish thought. On the basis of philological research, supported by an exacting investigation of texts, I aspired to demonstrate that *Sefer Yeṣirah*, in its early stages of crystallization, did not belong to the rabbinic world and that its history cannot be understood by referring to the great changes that took place in the world of Jewish thought in the Middle Ages. I hope that in so doing, I have not only contributed to an understanding of *Sefer Yeṣirah* but also to strengthening the proposition that in late antiquity and in the Middle Ages, there existed other arenas of Jewish thought that flourished in the hidden valleys between and beyond the high mountains of the canon.

Appendix 1

Sefer Yeṣirah and the Early Islamic Science of Letters

Excellent scholars such as Steven Wasserstrom and Zvi Langermann have put forward an important methodological argument about the contextualization of *Sefer Yeṣirah*.[1] The claim, which I agree with, is that any examination of the context of *Sefer Yeṣirah* cannot rely solely on textual parallels; substantial attention needs also to be given to the wider cultural context in which such a treatise could have been written. Throughout this book, I have demonstrated why the Christian-Syriac atmosphere of around the seventh century is the most probable context for *Sefer Yeṣirah*'s creation. As I state in the epilogue, I do not see any reason to prefer the Arabic context of the Abbasid period to an earlier Syriac Christian one.[2]

Many suggestions have been made throughout the years for contextualizing *Sefer Yeṣirah*, and the Islamic option is only one of them.[3] In recent years, this option has become the most prevalent, especially because of the impact of Wasserstrom's and Langermann's remarks on methodology. Therefore, I want to offer some clarifications about it, in the hope of contributing to future *Sefer Yeṣirah* scholarship.

The matter that has attracted the most scholarly attention with regard to the Islamic context of *Sefer Yeṣirah* is the origin of the triad of letters A-M-Š, which are called *ammot*, *immot*, or *ummot*. *Sefer Yeṣirah* claims that this triad is an acronym of three of the four elements: "Three *immot* letters:

alef, mem, shin . . . He made *alef* rule over air [*ruaḥ*]. . . . He made *mem* rule over water [*mayim*]. . . . He made *shin* rule over fire [*esh*]."[4]

The *alef* stands for air (*awir/ruaḥ*).[5] The *mem* stands for water (*mayim*), and the *shin* is the second letter in fire (*esh*), since *alef* was already used for air. *Sefer Yeṣirah*'s own explanation of the triad seems insufficient to a number of researchers whose domain of expertise concerns the relationships and connections between the medieval Muslim and Jewish worlds. Louis Massignon was the first to propose an alternative, connecting this triad of letters in *Sefer Yeṣirah* and the three Arabic letters *ʿayn*, *mīm*, and *sīn*.[6] These Arabic letters refer, according to Massignon, to three heretic Shiite groups named after three central figures in Muslim tradition: *ʿayn* stands for ʿAlī, the fourth caliph, whom Shiites considered to be Muhammad's heir. *Mīm* stands for Muhammad. And *sīn* stands for Salmān the Persian, one of the prophet Muhammad's friends and a central and elevated figure among the Shiʿa. So for Massignon, these letters represent three ancient heretical Shi'a groups: the group giving the most importance to Muhammad was called *Mīmiyya*, those elevating ʿAlī above the others were called *ʿAyniyya*, and the group devoted to Salmān the Persian was called *Sīniyya*. Following Massignon, other important researchers, such as Paul Kraus,[7] Henry Corbin,[8] Nehemya Allony,[9] and Steven Wasserstrom,[10] have supported this explanation and added that among the Shiʿa, the relation between ʿAlī and Muhammad is thought to be parallel to the relation between Aharon and Moses.[11] They therefore contend that the Jewish A-M-Š, where the letters *alef* and *mem* correspond to Aharon and Moses, can be seen as a transformation of the Shiite tradition of the letters ʿ-M-S.

This explanation is interesting but problematic. An examination of this thesis in a perspective broader than the alleged connection between A-M-Š and ʿ-M-S shows how convoluted and far-fetched a comprehensive comparison between *Sefer Yeṣirah* and Muslim sources addressing the science of letters, in fact, is.

I will begin my discussion of the Islamic influence on *Sefer Yeṣirah* with the letters ʿ-M-S and proceed to a general overview of the subject.

Examining the asserted link A-M-Š/ʿ-M-S from the perspective of *Sefer Yeṣirah* shows, as Yehuda Liebes has argued, that this explanation is not probable: *Sefer Yeṣirah*, at least until its final sections, shows no interest in biblical or later figures.[12] The assumption that the letters ʿ-M-S were replaced by A-M-Š to represent names of biblical figures such as Aharon and Moses is distant from the general attitude of the book. We might add that an exchange of letters seems even less probable than an exchange of names: although the exchange of a *shin* with a *sīn* is frequent, the exchange between *ʿayn* and *alef* is rare. It therefore seems that the hypothesis of the transformation of ʿ-M-S and -M-Š is unconvincing from a philological as well as a literary perspective.

Nevertheless, the crux of the problem with this explanation does not have to do with *Sefer Yeṣirah*. It has, rather, to do with intra-Islamic considerations that make it difficult to assume that *Sefer Yeṣirah* was composed in an Islamic context, in which the letters ʿ-M-S left their mark.

As indicated above, Massignon claims that the triad A-M-Š in *Sefer Yeṣirah* is parallel to the triad ʿ-M-S, representing, in his view, the initials of the names of three heretical groups in Shiʿa Islam: *Mīmiyya*, *ʿAyniyya*, and *Sīniyya*. Massignon bases his argument on an Arabic composition named *Kitāb al-Mājid* (The book of the glorious one). The book is included in the alchemical corpus attributed to Jābir Ibn Ḥayyān (the alleged disciple of the sixth Shiite *imām*, Jaʿfar al-Ṣādiq, d. 765), which was composed between the mid-ninth and the mid-tenth century.[13] In *Kitāb al-Mājid*, there is a discussion in which the letters *ʿayn*, *mīm*, and *sīn* are mentioned, along with two corresponding groups of devotees: "those who adhere to the *ʿayn*" (*aṣḥāb al-ʿayn*) and "those who adhere to the *sīn*" (*aṣḥāb al-sīn*).[14] Massignon argues that the letters and groups mentioned in *Kitāb al-Mājid* reflect the names of the three Shii heretical groups mentioned above, and therefore assumes that these groups, with their corresponding letters, were known at a relatively early stage and could have influenced the triad A-M-Š in *Sefer Yeṣirah*. However, as some scholars have noted, Massignon's conclusions are exaggerated.[15] These scholars have demonstrated that the earliest mention of relevant heretical Shii groups is in the writings of the Persian historian Muhammad al-Shahrastanī (1086–1153), of the first half of the twelfth century. It is notable that al-Shahrastanī mentions only two groups: the *Mīmiyya* and *ʿAyniyya*, and he does not refer to the *Sīniyya*.

Approximately twenty-five years ago, in his first paper on *Sefer Yeṣirah* and early Islam, Steven Wasserstrom went back to Massignon's argument and tried to correct it. He claimed that the letters *mīm*, *ʿayn*, and *sīn* in *Kitāb al-Mājid* do not refer to Shi'a heretical groups, which were referred to as such only from the twelfth century onward, but only to the names of ʿAlī, Muhammad, and Salmān the Persian.[16] But a reading of *Kitāb al-Mājid* shows that the interpretation offered by Wasserstrom should at least be reexamined for two reasons: first, in *Kitāb al-Mājid* the letters *ʿayn*, *mīm*, and *sīn* do not appear as a sequence of three letters in the order ʿ-M-S. Second, the context of the discussion in *Kitāb al-Mājid* seems to be alchemical, and it is difficult to see how this context relates to the figures of Muhammad, ʿAlī, and Salmān or theological theories concerning them. Although this issue demands further research, it is clear that the connection made by Massignon is historically anachronistic. As a rule, the triad ʿ-M-S, as an encoding with theological significance in this same order of letters, *ʿayn*, *mīm*, and *sīn*, comes much later. It is a *Nuṣayrī* (*ʿAlawī*) triad whose purpose is to indicate the precedence of ʿAlī over Muhammad and Salmān in *Nuṣayrī* theology.[17]

I turn from this discussion of the well-known scholarly argument concerning the particular comparison between ʿ-M-S and A-M-Š to take a broader view of the suggestion that the composition of *Sefer Yeṣirah* was influenced by Islam. The Islamic preoccupation with the science of letters seems to have begun in the eighth century, influenced by Jewish, Syriac, and Greek traditions. It was nevertheless only from the mid- to late ninth century onward that this preoccupation took hold in Shiʿa and Sunni mysticism, when one can find detailed discussions in writing about the letters.[18]

Saadya finished writing his commentary on *Sefer Yeṣirah* in 931 and was apparently not the book's first commentator. From a textual perspective, at the beginning of the tenth century, *Sefer Yeṣirah* was already a mature text, as indicated by its various versions, abundant in commentaries that percolated the text via glosses. It already had high canonic status: many important Jewish writers, such as Isaac Israeli and his disciple Dunash Ibn Tamim, Saadya, and Shabbetai Donnolo, dedicated lengthy commentaries to *Sefer Yeṣirah*, which demonstrates the centrality that *Sefer Yeṣirah* had acquired in this period. Each of these authors was situated geographically in a different continent and had use of a different recension of *Sefer Yeṣirah*.

As we have seen, the different recensions of *Sefer Yeṣirah* used by the last three commentators are not different with regard to the exchange of letters or omissions, or minor additions, but rather embody a completely different editorial structure and are substantially different volumes, such that one version is twice the length of another. The variations in the recensions of *Sefer Yeṣirah* were already a central issue in the early stages of its interpretation, to the extent that Saadya wrote that one of his goals in writing about *Sefer Yeṣirah* was to establish a definite version of the book. Many leading scholars of *Sefer Yeṣirah*, such as Ithamar Grunewald, Peter Hayman, and Steven Wasserstrom, have assumed, as I have argued in my conclusion, that *Sefer Yeṣirah* was not composed in the circles of rabbinic learning.[19]

In addition to the entire complex textual evolution that I have described, *Sefer Yeṣirah* went through a transformation of context from a nonrabbinic to a rabbinic milieu. If we examine the relevant time span, we will see that in order to connect *Sefer Yeṣirah* and the Islamic science of letters, we would have to lay them together in a procrustean bed that stretches their limbs and distorts their form until they can no longer be recognized. Had *Sefer Yeṣirah* been edited in the late ninth or early tenth centuries, the days of Saadya, one could have seen it as related to the increasing preoccupation with the science of letters in Islam at that time; but at that time, it was already considered to be a canonic book.

From all the above, I see no philological or historical reason to justify what seems to be an artificial advance of a Muslim context in order to delay *ad absurdum* the date of *Sefer Yeṣirah*.

Appendix 2

Sefer Yeṣirah's Long Version, According to Ms. Vatican 299/4, 66a–71b, with the English Translations of Peter A. Hayman

1. Yah, the Lord of hosts, the God of Israel, the Living God, God Almighty, *high and exalted, dwelling for ever, and holy is his name* (Isa. 57:15), carved out thirty-two wondrous paths of wisdom. He created his universe with three groups of letters (*separim*): with *seper* and *seper* and *seper.*

1. שלשים ושנים נתיבות פלאות חכמה חקק יה י״י צבאות אל[ה]י ישר[אל] א[לה]ים חיים אל שדי רם ונישא שוכן עד וקדוש שמו ברא את עולמו בשלשה ספרים בספר וספר וספר.

2. The ten *sefirot* are the basis and the twenty-two letters are the foundation.

2. עשר ספירות בלימה ועשרים ושתים אותיות יסוד.

3. The ten *sefirot* are the basis—the number of the ten fingers, five opposite five, and the covenant of unity is exactly in the middle by the word of the tongue and mouth and the circumcision of the flesh.

3. עשר ספירות בלימה מספר עשר אצבעות חמש כנגד חמש וברית ייחוד מכוונת באמצע במילת לשון ופה ובמילת המעיר.

4. The ten *sefirot* are the basis—ten and not nine, ten and not eleven. Understand with wisdom, and be wise with understanding. Test them and investigate them. Know and ponder and form (a mental image). Get the thing clearly worked out and restore the Creator to his place. And their measure is ten for they have no limit.

4. עשר ספירות בלימה עשר ולא תשע עשר ולא אחת עשרה הבין בחכמה וחכום בבינה בחון בהם וחקור בהן דע וחשוב וצור והעמד דבר על בוריו והשב יוצר על מכונו ומידתן עשר שאין להן סוף.

5. The ten *sefirot* are the basis: restrain your heart from thinking; restrain your mouth from speaking. And if your heart races return to the place where you started, and remember that thus it is written: *And the living creatures ran to and fro* (Ezek. 1:14). And concerning this matter a covenant was made.	5. עשר ספירות בלימה בלום ליבך מלהרהר בלום פיך מלדבר ואם רץ ליבך שוב למקום שיצאתה ממנו וזכור שכך נא[מר] והחיות רצוא ושוב ועל דבר זה נכרת ברית
6. And their measure is ten for they have no limit. Their end is fixed in their beginning, and their beginning in their end, as the flame is bound to the burning coal. Know and ponder, and form (a mental image) that the Lord is unique and the Creator one, and he has none second to him; and before one, what can you count?	6. ומידתן עשר שאין להן סוף נעוץ סופן בתחילתן ותחילתן בסופן כשלהבת קשורה בגחלת דע וחשוב וצור שאדון יחיד והיוצר אחד ואין לו שיני ולפני אחד מה אתה סופר.
7. The ten *sefirot* are the basis and their measure is ten for they have no limit: dimension of beginning and dimension of end, dimension of good and dimension of evil, dimension of above and dimension of below, dimension of east and dimension of west, dimension of north and dimension of south. And the unique Lord, a trustworthy divine king, rules over them all from his holy abode for ever and ever.	7. עשר ספירות בלימה ומידתן עשר שאין להן סוף עומק ראשית ועומק אחרית עומק טוב ועומק רע עומק רום ועומק תחת עומק מזרח ועומק מערב עומק צפון ועומק דרום ואדון יחיד אל מלך נאמן מושל בכולן ממעון קדשו ועד עדי עד.
8. The *ten sefirot* are the basis. Their appearance is like the sight of lightning, and their end?—they have no limit. His word is in them *as though running* (Ezek. 1:14), and they pursue his command like the storm wind, and before his throne they bow down.	8. עשר ספירות בלימה צפייתן כמראה הבזק ותכליתן אין בהן קץ דברו בהן כרצוא ולמאמרו כסופה ירדופו ולפני כסאו הן משתחוים.
9. The ten *sefirot* are the basis and the twenty-two letters are the foundation: three mothers, seven double (letters), and twelve simple (letters). And the Spirit is one of them.	9. עשר ספירות בלימה ועשרים ושתים אותיות יסוד שלש אימות ושבע כפולות ושתים עשרה פשוטות ורוח אחת מהן.

10. The ten *sefirot* are the basis: one—the Spirit of the Living God. *His throne is established from of old* (Ps. 93:2). Twice blessed is the name of the Life of the Worlds. Voice, and air (*ruah*) and speech—this is the Holy Spirit (*ruah*).

10. עשר ספירות בלימה אחת רוח א[לה]ים חיים נכון כסאו מאז [fol. 66b] ברוך ומבורך שמו שלחי העולמים לעולם ועד קול ורוח ודיבור זו היא רוח הקודש.

11. The ten *sefirot* are the basis: one—the Spirit of the Living God; two—air from the Holy Spirit; three—water from air; four—fire from water; and above and below, east and west, north and south.

11. עשר ספירות בלימה אחת רוח א[לה]ים חיים שתים רוח מרוח הקודש שלוש <מים> מרוח ארבע אש <מ>מים ורום ותחת ומזרח ומערב וצפון ודרום.

12. Two—air from Spirit: he carved and hewed in it the four winds of heaven—east and west, north and south. And the air is in each one of them.

12. שתים רוח מרוח חקק וחצב בה ארבע רוחות השמים מזרח ומערב צפון ודרום ורוח בכל אחת מהן.

13. Three—water from air: he carved and hewed in it *tohu* and *bohu*, mud and mire. He made them like a sort of garden-bed. He erected them like a sort of wall, and he wove them like a sort of ceiling. And he poured out snow over them and it became dust, for it is said: *For to the snow he says, "Become earth"* (Job 37:6). *Tohu* is a green line which surrounds the world. *Bohu* is the slimy stones sunk in the abyss between which the water comes out (*b. Ḥag.* 12a, *y. Ḥag* 77c).

13. שלוש מים מרוח חקק וחצב בה תוהו ובהו רפש וטיט עשאן כמין ערוגה הציבן כמין חומה וסיככן כמין מעזיבה ויצק שלג עליהן ונעשה עפר שנ[אמר] כי לשלג יאמר הוי ארץ תוהו זה קו ירוק שמקיף את העו[לם] בוהו אילו אבנים מפולמות המשוקעות בתהום ומביניהן המים יוצאין.

14. Four—fire from water: he carved them and hewed in it the throne of glory, and the *Ofanim* and the *Serafim*, and the holy living creatures, and the ministering angels. And from the three of them he founded his abode, as it is said: *he makes his angels winds, his servants a flaming fire* (Ps. 104:4).

14. ארבע אש ממים חקק וחצב בה כסא כבוד ואופנים ושרפים וחיות הקודש ומלאכי השרת ומשלשתן ייסד מעונו עושה מלאכיו רוחות משרתיו אש לוהט.

15. Five—he sealed above. He chose three simple letters and fixed them in his great name—YHW. And he sealed with them the six edges (of the universe), and turned upwards and sealed it with YHW. Six—he sealed below. He turned downwards and sealed it with YWH. Seven—he sealed the east. He turned in front and sealed it with HYW. Eight—he sealed the west. He turned behind and sealed it with HWY. Nine—he sealed the south. He turned to his right and sealed it with WYH. Ten—he sealed the north. He turned to his left and sealed it with WHY.

15. חמש חתם רום בירר שלוש פשוטות וקבען בשמו הגדול יוד הי ויו וחתם בהן שש קצוות ופנה למעלה וחיתמו ביהו. שש חתם תחת ניפנה למטה וחיתמו ביוה. שבע חתם מזרח ניפנה לפניו וחיתמו בהיו .שמינית חתם מערב ניפנה לאחריו וחיתמו בהוי. תשיעית חתם דרום ניפנה לימינו וחיתמו בויה. עשר חתם צפון נפנה לשמאלו וחיתמו בוהי.

16. These ten *sefirot* are the basis: one—the Spirit of the Living God; two—air from the Spirit; three—water from air; four—fire from water; and the height above and below, east and west, north and south.

16. אילו עשר ספירות בלימה אחת רוח א[לה]ים חיים. שתים רוח מרוח. שלוש מים מרוח. ארבע אש ממים ורום מעלה ותחת מזרח ומערב צפון ודרום. חסלת.

17. The twenty-two letters are the foundation: three primary letters, seven double (letters), and twelve simple (letters). They are carved out by the voice, hewn out in the air, fixed in the mouth in five positions: Alef, Ḥet; He, Ayin; Bet, Waw, Mem, Pe; Gimel, Yod, Kaph, Qof; Dalet, Tet, Lamed, Nun, Taw; Zayin, Samek, Sade, Resh, Shin. They are bound to the tip of the tongue as the flame to the burning coal. Alef, He, Ḥet, Ayin are pronounced at the back of the tongue and in the throat. Bet, Waw, Mem, Pe are pronounced between the teeth and by the tip of the tongue. Gimel, Yod, Kaph, Qof are cut off a third of the way up the tongue. Dalet, Tet, Lamed, Nun, Taw are pronounced by the tip of the tongue with the voice. Zayin, Samek Sade, Resh, Shin (are pronounced) between the teeth with the tongue relaxed.

17. עשרים ושתים אותיות יסוד שלוש אימות ושבע כפולות ושתים עשרה פשוטות חקוקות בקול חצובות ברוח קבועות בפה בחמשה מקומות. אח הע בומף גיכק דטלנת זסצרש קשורות בראש הלשון כשלהבת בגחלת אה חע משתמשות בסוף הלשון ובבית הבליעה בומף [fol. 67a] משתמשות בין שפתים ובראש הלשון. גיכק על שליש הלשון נכרתות. דטלנת בראש הלשון משתמשות עם הקול. זסצרש בין שיניים ובלשון ישן.

18. The twenty-two letters are the foundation. They are fixed on a wheel with two hundred and twenty-one gates. The wheel rotates backwards and forwards. And this is the sign of the matter: if for good, above pleasure, and if for evil, below pain.

18. עשרים ושתים אותיות יסוד קבועות בגלגל במאתים ועשרים ואחד שערים חוזר הגלגל פנים ואחור וזה סימן לדבר אם לטובה למעלה מנגע ואם לרעה למטה מנגע <נ"ל מענג>.

19. Twenty-two letters: he carved them out, he hewed them, he weighed them and exchanged them, he combined them and formed with them the life of all creation and the life of all that would be formed. How did he weigh and exchange them?—Alef with them all, and them all with Alef; Bet with them all, and them all with Bet; Gimel with them all, and them all with Gimel. And they all rotate in turn. The result is that they go out by two hundred and twenty-one gates. The result is that all creation and all speech go out by one name.

19. עשרים ושתים אותיות חקקן חצבן שקלן והמירן וצרפן וצר בהן נפש כל היצור ונפש כל העתיד לצור כאיצד שקלן והמירן אלף עם כולן וכולן עם אלף בית עם כולן וכולן עם בית גימל עם כולן וכולן עם גימל וכולן חוזרות חלילה נמצאו יוצאות במאתים ועשרים ואחד שערים נמצא כל היצור וכל הדיבור יוצא בשם אחד.

20. He formed substance from chaos, and he made it with fire and it exists, and he hewed out great columns from intangible air. This is the sign:

20. יצר מתוהו ממש ועשאו באש וישנו וחצב עמודים גדולים מאויר שאינו נתפש זה סימן.

21. אל בת גש דר הק וץ זף חע טס ין כם אב גת דש הר וק זץ חף טע ים כן לס אג דת הש ור זק חץ טף יע כם לן בם אד בג הת וש זר חק טץ יף כע לס מן אה בד ות זש חר טק יץ כף לע מס גן או בה גד זת חש טר יק כץ לף מע נס אז בו גה חת טש יר כק לץ מף נע דס אח בז גו דה טת יש כר לק מץ נף סע אט בח גז דו ית כש לר מק נץ סף הע אי בט גה דז הו כת לש מר נק סץ עף אך בי גט דח הן לת מש נר סק עץ וף אל בך גי דט הח וז מת נש סר עק פץ אם בל גך די הט וח נת סש ער פק זץ אן בם גל דך הי וט זח סת עש פר צק אס בן גם דל הך וי זט עת פש צר חק אע בס גן דם הל וך זי חט פת צש קר אף בע גס דן הם ול זך חי צת קש טר אץ בף גע דס הן ום זל חך טי קת רש אק בץ גף דע הם ון זם חל טך רת יש אר בק גץ דף הע וס זן חם טל יך שת. [fol. 67b] אש בר גק דץ הף וע זס חן טם יל כת את בש גר דק הץ וף זע חס טן ים כל.

22. He looks and exchanges; he makes all creation and all speech one name. And a sign for the matter: twenty-two objects in one category (or body).

22. צופה ומימיר עושה את כל היצור ואת כל דיבור שם אחד וסימן לדבר עשרים ושתים חפצים בגוף אחד. חסלת.

23. Three primary letters: Alef, Mem, Shin. Their basis is the scale of acquittal and the scale of guilt, and the language of law holds the balance between them.

23. שלוש אימות אמש יסודן כף זכות וכף חובה ולשון חק מכריע בינתיים.

24. Three primary letters: Alef, Mem, Shin—a great secret, hidden and ineffable, and sealed with six seals. And from it goes out fire, water and air, and it is wrapped up in male and female. Know and ponder and form (a mental image) that fire evaporates water.

24. שלוש אימות אמש סוד גדול מכוסה ומופלא וחתום בשש טבעות וממנו יוצאין אש מים ורוח ומחותל בזכר ונקבה דע וחשב וצור שהאש נושא מים.

25. Three primary letters: Alef, Mem, Shin. The offspring of heaven is fire; the offspring of air is the Spirit; the offspring of earth is water; fire above, water below, and air is the balancing item.

25. שלוש אימות אמש תולדות השמים אש תולדות אויר רוח תולדות ארץ מים אש למעלה מים למטה ורוח חק מכריע בינתיים.

26. Three primary letters: Alef, Mem, Shin. Mem lifts up, Shin hisses, Alef is the balancing item.

26. שלוש אימות אמש מם רוממת, שין שורקת, אלף חק מכריע בינתיים.

27. Three primary letters: Alef, Mem, Shin. And from them were born three fathers from whom everything was created.

27. שלוש אימות אמש ומהן נולדו שלושה אבות שמהם נבראו הכל.

28. Three primary letters—Alef, Mem, Shin—in the universe: air, and water and fire. Heaven was created first from fire, and earth was created from water, and air was created from the Spirit, holding the balance between them.

28. שלוש אימות אמש בעולם רוח ומים ואש שמים נבראו תחילה מאש, וארץ נבראת ממים, ואויר נברא מרוח מכריע בינתיים.

29. Three primary letters—Alef, Mem, Shin—in the year: fire, water and air. Heat was created from fire, cold was created from water, humidity is the air holding the balance between them.

29. שלוש אימות אמש בשנה אש מים ורוח חום נברא מאש, קור נברא ממים, רוויה רוח מכריע בינתיים.

---

30. Three primary letters—Alef, Mem, Shin—in mankind. The head was created from fire, the belly from water, and the chest is the air holding the balance between them.

30. שלוש אימות אמש בנפש ראש נברא מאש, ובטן ממים, וגיויה רוח מכריע בינתיים.

---

31. Three primary letters: Alef, Mem, Shin. He carved them, hewed them, combined them and sealed with them the three primary letters in the universe, and the three primary letters in the year, and the three primary letters in mankind, male and female.

31. שלוש אימות אמש חקקן חצבן צרפן וחתם בהן שלוש אימות בעולם ושלוש אימות בשנה ושלוש אימות בנפש זכר ונקבה.

---

32. He made Alef rule over air (*ruah*), and bound to it a crown, and combined them with each other, and formed with them air (*awir*) in the universe, and humidity in the year, and the chest in mankind, male and female—male with Alef, Mem, Shin, and female with Alef, Shin, Mem.

32. המליך את אלף ברוח וקשר לו כתר וצרפן זה בזה וצר בהן אויר בעולם ורווייה בשנה וגיויה בנפש זכר ונקבה זכר באמש ונקבה באשם.

---

33. He made Mem rule over water, and bound to it a crown, and combined them with each other, and formed with it earth in the universe, cold in the year, and the belly in mankind, male and female.

33. המליך את מם במים וקשר לו כתר וצרפן זה בזה וצר בו ארץ בעו[לם] וקור בשנה ובטן בנפש [fol. 68a] זכר ונקבה.

---

34. He made Shin rule over fire, and bound to it a crown, and combined them with each other, and formed with it heaven in the universe, heat in the year, and the head in mankind, male and female.

34. המליך את שין באש וקשר לו כתר וצרפן זה עם זה וצר בו שמים בעולם וחום בשנה וראש בנפש זכר ונקבה.

35. How did he combine them?—AMŠ, AŠM, MAŠ, MŠA, ŠMA, ŠAM—heaven/fire, air/spirit, earth/water. Man's head is fire, his belly water, his heart spirit (or air).

35. כאיזה צד צרפן אמש אשם מאש משא שמא שאם שמים אש אויר רוח ארץ מים ראשו שלאדם אש בטנו מים לבו רוח.

36. Three primary letters: Alef, Mem, Shin. There was formed with Alef: spirit, air, humidity, the chest, law, and the tongue (or language). There was formed with Mem: earth, cold, the belly, and the scale of acquittal. There was formed with Shin: heaven, heat, the head, and the scale of guilt. This is Alef, Mem, Shin. The end.

36. שלוש אימות אמש נוצר עם אלף רוח אויר רוויה וגיויה וחוק ולשון. נוצר עם מם ארץ קור ובטן וכף זכות. נוצר עם שין שמים וחום וראש וכף חובה זה אמש. חסלת.

37. Seven double letters: Bet, Gimel, Dalet; Kaph, Pe, Resh, Taw. Their basis is life and peace, wisdom, wealth, prosperity, beauty and mastery. They are pronounced with the tongue in two different positions, for they represent two categories of opposites: Bet/Vet, Gimel/Ghimel, Dalet/Dhalet, Kaph/Khaph, Pe/Fe, Resh/Rhesh, Taw/Thaw, corresponding to soft and hard, a paradigm of strong and weak. They are opposites. The opposite of life is death; the opposite of peace is evil; the opposite of wisdom is folly; the opposite of wealth is poverty; the opposite of prosperity is desolation; the opposite of beauty is ugliness; and the opposite of mastery is slavery.

37. שבע כפולות בגד כפרת יסודן חיים ושלום וחכמה ועושר זרע וחן וממשלה ומתנהגות בשתי לשונות שהם כפולות שלתמורות בית בית גימל גימל דל דל כף כף פה פה ריש ריש תיו תיו כנגד רך וקשה תבנית גיבור כנגד חלש. והן תמורות: תמורת חיים מוות, תמורת שלום < נ"ל מלחמה> רע, תמורת חכמה איולת, תמורת עושר עוני, תמורת זרע שממה, תמורת חן כיעור, תמורת ממשלה עבדות.

38. Seven double letters: Bet, Gimel, Dalet; Kaph, Pe, Resh, Taw. Seven and not six, seven and not eight—six directions corresponding to the six sides (of a cube), and the Holy Temple set in the middle. *Blessed be the glory of the Lord from his place* (Ezek. 3:12). He is the place of his world, but his world is not his place. And he supports them all.

38. שבע כפולות בגד כפרת שבע ולא שש שבע ולא שמונה מכוון שש צלעות לששה סדרים והיכל קדוש מוכן באמצע ברוך כבוד י'י ממקומו הוא מקומו של עולמו, ואין עולמו מקומו והוא נושא את כולן.

39. Seven double letters: Bet, Gimel, Dalet; Kaph, Pe, Resh, Taw. He carved and hewed them, he combined them, weighed them and exchanged them, and he formed with them the planets in the universe, the days in the year, and the apertures in mankind, by sevens.

39. שבע כפולות בגד כפרת חקקן וחצבן צרפן שקלן והמירן וצר בהן כוכבים בעו[לם] וימים בשנה ושערים בנפש שבעה שבעה.

40. How did he combine them?—two stones build two houses; three build six houses; four build twenty-four houses; five build one hundred and twenty houses; six build seven hundred and twenty houses; seven build five thousand and forty houses. From here on go out and ponder what the mouth cannot speak, and what the eye cannot see, and what the ear cannot hear.

40. כאיזה צד צרפן שתי אבנים בונות שני בתים שלוש בונות ששה בתים, ארבע בונות עשרים וארבע בתים, חמש בונות מאה ועשרים בתים שש בונות שבע מאות ועשרים בתים, שבע בונות חמשת אלפים וארבעים בתים. מיכאן ואילך צא וחשוב מה שאין [68b] הפה יכולה לדבר ומה שאין העין יכולה לראות ומה שאין האוזן יכולה לשמוע.

41. He made Bet rule, and bound to it a crown, and combined one with another, and formed with it Saturn in the universe, the sabbath in the year, and the mouth in mankind. He made Gimel rule, and bound to it a crown, and combined one with another, and formed with it Jupiter in the universe, the first day of the week in the year, and the right eye in mankind. He made Dalet rule, and bound to it a crown, and combined with another, and formed with it Mars in the universe, the second day of the week in the year, and the left eye in mankind. He made Kaf rule, and bound to it a crown, and combined one with another, and formed with it the Sun in the universe, the third day of the week in the year, and the right nostril in mankind. He made Pe rule, and bound to it a crown, and combined one with another, and formed with it Venus in the universe, the fourth day of the week in the year, and the left nostril in mankind. He made Resh rule, and bound to it a crown, and combined one with another, and formed with it Mercury in the universe, the fifth day of the week in the year, and the right ear in mankind. He made Taw rule, and bound to it a crown, and combined one with another, and formed with it the Moon in the universe, the sixth day of the week in the year, and the left ear in mankind.

41. המליך את בית וקשר לו כתר וצרפן זה עם זה וצר בו שבתי בעו[לם] ושבת בשנה ופה בנפש. המליך את גימל וקשר לו כתר וצרפן זה עם זה וצר בו צדק בעו[לם] ואחד בשבת בשנה ועין ימין בנפש. המליך את דל וקשר לו כתר וצרפן זה עם זה וצר בו מאדים בעולם ושיני בשבת בשנה ועין שמאול בנפש. המליך את כף וקשר לו כתר וצרפן זה עם זה וצר בו חמה בעו[לם] ושלישי בשבת בשנה ואף ימין בנפש. המליך את פה וקשר לו כתר וצרפן זה עם זה וצר בו נוגה בעו[לם] ורביעי בשבת בשנה ואף שמאול בנפש. המליך את ריש וקשר לו כתר וצרפן זה עם זה וצר בו כוכב חמה בעו[לם] וחמישי בשבת בשנה ואוזן ימין בנפש. המליך את תיו וקשר לו כתר וצרפן זה עם זה וצר בו לבנה בעו[לם] וששי בשבת בשנה ואוזן שמאל בנפש.

42. And with them were carved out seven firmaments, seven earths, seven hours and seven days. Therefore he loved the seventh above everything under heaven.

42. ובהן נחקקו שבעה רקיעים ושבע ארצות ושבע שעות ושבעה ימים לפיכך חיבב שביעי לכל חפץ תחת השמים.

43. These are the seven planets in the universe: Sun, Venus, Mercury, Moon, Saturn, Jupiter, Mars. And the seven days: the seven days of creation. And the seven apertures in mankind: two eyes, two ears, two nostrils, and the mouth. And the seven firmaments: Wilon, Raqia, Shehaqim, Zebul, Ma'on, Makon, Arabot. And the seven earths: 'adama, 'arqa, tebel, neshiyya, siyya, heled, 'eretz. He split up the witnesses and made each one stand by itself—the universe by itself, the year by itself, mankind by itself.

43. ואילו הן שבעה כוכבים בעו[לם]: חמה, נוגה, כוכב חמה, לבנה, שבתי, צדק, מאדים. ושבעה ימים שבעת ימי בראשית, ושבעה שערים בנפש שתי עינים ושתי אזנים ושתי נחיריים ופה. ושבעה רקיעים: וילון, רקיע, שחקים, זבול, מעון, מכון, ערבות. ושבע ארצות: אדמה ארקא, תבל, נשייה, צייה, חלד, ארץ. חיצה את העדים והעמידן אחה אחד לבדו, עולם לבדו, שנה לבדה, נפש לבדה.

44. Seven double letters: Bet, Gimel, Dalet; Kaf, Pe, Resh, Taw. There was formed with Bet: Saturn, the sabbath, the mouth, life and death. There was formed with Gimel: Jupiter, the first day of the week, the right eye, peace and evil. There was formed with Dalet: Mars, the second day of the week, the left eye, wisdom and folly. There was formed with Kaf: the Sun, the third day of the week, the right nostril, wealth and poverty. There was formed with Pe: Venus, the fourth day of the week, the left nostril, prosperity and desolation. There was formed with Resh: Mercury, the fifth day of the week, the right ear, beauty and ugliness. There was formed with Taw: the Moon, the preparation of the sabbath, the left ear, mastery and slavery. This is Bet, Gimel, Dalet; Kaf, Pe, Resh, Taw.

44. שבע כפולות בגד כפרת נוצר עם בית שבתי שבת ופה וחיים ומוות. נוצר עם גימל צדק ואחד בשבת [69a] ועין ימין ושלום ורע. נוצר עם דל מאדים ושיני בשבת ועין שמאל וחכמה ואיולת. נוצר עם כף חמה ושלישי בשבת ואף ימין ועושר ועוני. נוצר עם פה נוגה ורביעי בשבת ואף שמאל וזרע ושממה. נוצר עם ריש כוכב חמה וחמישי בשבת ואוזן ימין וחן וכיאור. נוצר עם תיו לבנה וערב שבת ואוזן שמאל וממשלה ועבדות זה בגד כפרת.

45. Twelve simple letters: He, Waw, Zayin, Ḥet, Tet, Yod, Lamed, Nun, Samek, Ayin, Sade, Qof. Their basis is sight, hearing, smelling, time, eating, sexual intercourse, action, walking, anger, laughter, thought and sleep.

45. שתים עשרה פשוטות הוזחטילןסעצק יסודן ראייה שמיעה הריחה ושהות ולעיטה ותשמיש מעשה והילוך רוגז ושחוק הירהור ושינה.

46. Twelve simple letters: He, Waw, Zayin, Ḥet, Tet, Yod, Lamed, Nun, Samek, Ayin, Sade, Qof. Twelve and not eleven.

46. שתים עשרה פשוטות הוזחטילןסעצק שתים עשרה ולא אחת עשרה.

---

47. Twelve diagonal lines, radiating out to the six faces (of a cube), separating in each direction:—the south-eastern line, the upper eastern line, the lower eastern line, the lower northern line, the north-western line, the upper northern line, the lower western line, the upper western line, the upper western line, the lower western line, the lower southern line, the upper southern line. And they expand continually for ever and ever and *they are the arms of the universe* (cf. Deut. 33:27).

47. שנים עשר גבולי אכלוסין מופצלין לששה סדרים מופסקין בין רוח לרוח גבול מזרחית דרומית גבול מזרחית רומית גבול מזרחית תחתית גבול צפונית תחתית גבול ~~צפונית~~ צפונית מערבית גבול צפונית רומית גבול מערבית תחתית גבול מערבית רומית גבול מערבית רומית גבול מערבית תחתית גבול דרומית תחתית גבול דרומית רומית ומרחיבין והולכין עד עדי עד והן הן זרועות עולם.

---

48. Twelve simple letters: He, Waw, Zayin, Ḥet, Tet, Yod, Lamed, Nun, Samek, Ayin, Sade, Qof. He carved them, he combined them, he hewed them, he weighed them and exchanged them, and formed with them the constellations, the months, and the principal (bodily) organs: two exultant ones, two babbling ones, two deliberating ones and two rejoicing ones. They are the internal organs and the two hands and feet. He made them a sort of lawsuit, he arranged them in battle array, *one opposite the other* (Qoh. 7:14). Three—each one stands by itself; seven—three are at loggerheads with three, and one is the law which holds the balance between them. Twelve stand in battle array: three are hostile but three love; three give life but three kill. And the divine, trustworthy king rules over them all—one on top of three, and three on top of seven, and seven on top of twelve. And they all adhere to each other. And the sign for the matter is: twenty-two objects in one body.

48. שתים עשרה פשוטות הוזחטילןסעצק חקקן צרפן חצבן שקלן והמירן וצר בהן מזלות וחדשים ומנהיגין שני עליזים ושני לועזים ושני נועצים ושני עליצים והן קורקבנין ושתי ידים ושתי רגלים [fol. 69b] עשאן כמן מריבה ערכן כמן מלחמה זה לעומת זה. שלשה אחד אחד לבדו עומד שבעה שלשה חלוקין על שלשה ואחד חוק מכריע בנתיים שנים עשר עומדין במלחמה שלשה אויבים ושלשה אוהבים שלשה מחיים ושלשה ממיתים ואל מלך נאמן מושל בכולן אחד על גבי שלשה ושלשה על גבי שבעה ושבעה על גבי שנים עשר וכולן אדוקין זה בזה וסימן לדבר עשרים ושנים חפצים בגוף אחד.

49. Twelve simple letters: He, Waw, Zayin, Ḥet, Tet, Yod, Lamed, Nun, Samek, Ayin, Sade, Qof. He carved them and hewed them out, he combined them, weighed them and exchanged them, and formed with them the twelve constellations in the universe, the twelve months in the year, and the twelve principal organs in mankind. These are the twelve constellations in the universe: Aries, Taurus, Gemini, Cancer, Leo, Virgo, Libra, Scorpio, Sagittarius, Capricorn, Aquarius, Pisces. And the twelve months are: Nisan, lyar, Sivan, Tammuz, Av, Elul, Tishri, Marheshvan, Kislev, Tevet, Shevat, Adar. These are the twelve principal organs in mankind: two hands, two feet, two kidneys, the liver, the gall, the spleen, the gullet, the intestines and the stomach.

49. שתים עשרה פשוטות הוזחטילןסעצק חקקן וחצבן צרפן שקלן והמירן וצר בהן שנים עשר מזלות בעולם ושנים עשר חדשים בשנה ושנים עשר מנהיגים בנפש. ואילו הן שנים עשר מזלות טלה, שור, תאומים, סרטן, אריה, בתולה, מאזנים, עקרב, קשת, גדי, דלי, דגים. ושנים עשר חדשים ניסן, אייר, סיון, תמוז, אב, אלול, תשרי, מרחשוון, כסליו, טבת, שבת, אדר. אילו הן שנים עשר מנהיגין בנפש: שתי ידים, שתי רגלים, שתי כליות, כבד, ומרה טחול, המסס, קרקבן, וקיבה.

52. He made He rule, and bound to it a crown, and combined one with another, and formed with it Aries in the universe, Nisan in the year, and the liver in mankind. He made Waw rule, and bound to it a crown, and combined one with another, and formed with it Taurus in the universe, Iyyar in the year, and the gall in mankind. He made Zayin rule, and bound to it a crown, and combined one with another, and formed with it Gemini in the universe, Sivan in the year, and the spleen in mankind. He made Ḥet rule, and bound to it a crown, and combined one with another, and formed with it Cancer in the universe, Tammuz in the year, and the gullet in mankind. He made Tet rule, and bound to it a crown, and combined one with another, and formed with it Leo in the universe, Av in the year, and the right kidney. He made Yod rule, and bound to it a crown, and combined one with another, and formed with it Virgo in the universe, Elul in the year, and the left kidney in mankind. He made Lamed rule, and bound to it a crown, and combined one with another, and formed with it Libra in the universe, Tishri in the year, and the intestines in mankind. He made Nun rule, and bound to it a crown, and combined one with another, and formed with it Scorpio in the universe, Marheshvan in the year, and the stomach in mankind. He made Samek rule, and bound to it a crown, and combined one with another, and formed with it Sagittarius in the universe, Kislev in the year, and the right hand in mankind. He made Ayin rule, and bound to it a crown, and combined one with another, and formed with it Capricorn in the universe, Tevet in the year, and the left hand in mankind. He made Sade rule, and bound to it a crown, and combined one with another, and formed with it Aquarius in the universe, Shevat in the year, and the right foot in mankind. He made Qof rule, and bound to it a crown, and combined one with another, and formed with it Pisces in the universe, Adar in the year, and the left foot in mankind.

52. המליך הי וקשר לו כתר וצרפן זה עם זה וצר בו טלה בעולם וניסן בשנה וכבד בנפש. המליך את ויו וקשר לו כתר וצרפן זה עם זה וצר בו שור בעו[לם] ואייר בשנה ומרה בנפש. המליך את זיין וקשר לו כתר וצרפן זה עם זה וצר בו תאומים בעו[לם] וסיון בשנה וטחול בנפש. המליך את חית וקשר לו כתר <וצרפן זה בזה> וצר בו סרטן בעו[לם] ותמוז בשנה [fol. 70a] והמסס בנפש. המליך את טית וקשר לו כתר וצרפן זה בזה וצר בו אריה בעולם ואב בשנה וכוליה של ימין. המליך את יוד וקשר לו כתר וצרפן זה עם זה וצר בו בתולה בעו[לם] ואלול בשנה וכוליה שלשמאל בנפש. המליך את למד וקשר לו כתר וצרפן זה עם זה וצר בו מאזנים בעולם ותשרי בשנה וקרקבן בנפש. המליך את נון וקשר לו כתר וצרפן זה עם זה וצר בו עקרב בעו[לם] ומרחשוון בשנה וקיבה בנפש. המליך את סמך וקשר לו כתר וצרפן זה עם זה וצר בו קשת בעו[לם] וכסליו בשנה ויד ימין בנפש. המליך את עין וקשר לו כתר וצרפן זה בזה וצר בו גדי בעו[לם] וטבת בשנה ויד שמאל בנפש. המליך את צדי וקשר לו כתר וצרפן זה בזה וצר בו דלי בעו[לם] ושבט בשנה ורגל ימין בנפש. המליך את קוף וקשר לו כתר וצרפן זה בזה וצר בו דגים בעו[לם] ואדר בשנה ורגל שמאול בנפש.

54. Twelve simple letters: He, Waw, Zayin, Ḥet, Tet, Yod, Lamed, Nun, Samek, Ayin, Sade, Qof. There was formed with He: Aries, Nisan, the liver, sight and blindness. There was formed with Waw: Taurus, Iyyar, the gall, hearing and deafness. There was formed with Zayin: Gemini, Sivan, the spleen, smelling and anosmia (?). There was formed with Ḥet: Cancer, Tammuz and the gullet. There was formed with Tet: Leo, Av, the right kidney, eating and hunger. There was formed with Yod: Virgo, Elul, the left kidney, action and paralysis. There was formed with Lamed: Libra, Tishri, the intestines, sexual intercourse and impotence. There was formed with Nun: Scorpio, Marheshvan, the stomach, walking and lameness. There was formed with Samek: Sagittarius, Kislev, the right hand, anger and equanimity. There was formed with Ayin: Capricorn, Tevet, the left hand, laughter and sadness. There was formed with Sade: Aquarius, Shevat, the right leg, thought and thoughtlessness. There was formed with Qof: Pisces, Adar, the left leg, sitting and insomnia (?).

54. שתים עשרה פשוטות הוזחטילנסעצק. נוצר עם הי טלה ניסן וכבד וראייה וסמיות. נוצר עם ויו שור אייר ומרה ושמיעה וחרשות. נוצר עם זיין תאומים סיון וטחול וריחה וסרחות. נוצר עם חית סרטן תמוז והמסס. נוצר עם טית אריה אב וכוליה של ימין לעיטה ורעבתנות. נוצר עם יוד בתולה אלול וכוליה של שמאל ומעשה וגידמות. נוצר עם למד מאזנים תשרי וקרקבן תשמיש וסריות. נוצר עם נון עקרב מרחשוון וקיבה והילוך וחיגרות. נוצר עם סמך קשת וכסליו יד ימין ורוגז וניטול כבד. [fol. 70b] נוצר עם עין גדי טבת ויד שמאל ושחוק וניטול טחול. נוצר עם צדי דלי שבט רגל ימין והירהור וניטול הלב. נוצר עם קוף דגים אדר ורגל שמאל וישיבה ומעות.

55. This is He, Waw, Zayin, Ḥet, Tet, Yod, Lamed, Nun, Samek, Ayin, Sade, Qof. And they all adhere to the Hook, the Celestial Sphere, and the heart.

55. זה הוזחטילנסעצק וכולן אדוקין בתלי וגלגל ולב.

56. By them Yah Weh, the God of Israel, the Living God, Almighty, *high and lofty, dwelling for ever, and holy is his name* (Isa. 57:15) carved out (the universe). Two names 'Yah-Weh'; four names: 'hosts'—it is a sign in his host. 'God of Israel'—he is a prince before God; 'Living God'—Three are called living: the Living God, running water, the tree of life. 'God Almighty'—a strong God who has sufficient so far: 'high'—for he dwells in the height of the universe, higher than the highest; and 'lofty'—for he lifts and supports both above and below, for all who lift are below and what they lift is above, but he is above and what he lifts is below, and he lifts and supports all his universe; 'dwelling for ever'—for his kingdom is eternal and has no end; 'holy his name' and his servants are holy, and every day they say to him, *holy, holy, holy* (Isa. 6:3).[1]

56. שבהן חקק יה וה אלהי ישראל אלהים חיים אל שדי רם ונישא שוכן עד וקדוש שמו שני שמות יה וה ארבעה שמות צבאות אות בצבאות שלו אלהי ישראל שר בפני אל אלהים חיים שלשה נקראו חיים אלהים מים חיים עץ חיים אל שדי אל קשה שדי עד כן די רם שהוא יושב ברומו שלעולם ורם על הרמים ונישא וסובל שנושא וסובל מעלה ומטה שהכל נשואים למטה ומשואן למעלה והוא למעלה ונישא למטה ונושא וסובל את כל העולם כלו שוכן עד: שמלכותו עדי עד ואן לה הפסק. קדוש שמו ומשרתיו קדושים ולו אומרים בכל יום קדוש קדוש קדוש.

57. Twelve below and seven above on top of them, and three on top of seven. And from the three of them he founded his abode. And they all depend on one—a sign for the One who has none second to him, a King unique in his universe, for he is one and his name one.

57. שנים עשר למטה ושבעה למעלה על גביהן ושלשה על גבי שבעה ומשלשתן ייסד מעונו וכולן תלויין באחד סימן לאחד ואין לו שני מלך יחיד בעולמו שהוא אחד ושמו אחד.

58. Three fathers and their offspring, and seven dominant ones and their hosts, and the twelve diagonal lines. And a proof for the matter—trustworthy witnesses: the universe, the year and mankind. The universe—its counting is by ten; the year—its counting is by ten; mankind—its counting is by ten. And there are twenty-two objects in each one. In the universe there are three: fire, air and water; and seven planets and twelve constellations. In the year there are three: cold, heat and the temperate state, the seven days of creation, and the twelve months. In mankind there are three: the head, the belly and the chest; and the seven exits, and the twelve principal organs.

58. שלשה אבות ותולדותיהן ושבעה כבשים וצבאותיהן ושנים עשר גבולי אכלוסין וראיה לדבר עדים נאמנים עולם שנה ונפש עולם ספירתו בעשרה שנה ספירתה בעשרה נפש ספירתה בעשרה ועשרים ושנים חפצים יש בכל אחד. בעולם שלשה אש רוח ומים ושבעה כוכבים ושנים עשר מזלות. בשנה שלשה קור וחום ורוויה שבעת ימי בראשית ושנים עשר חדשים בנפש שלשה ראש ובטן וגיויה שבעה שערים ושנים עשר מנהיגין.

59. There is a law of ten, three, seven and twelve. They are present in the Hook, the Celestial Sphere, and the heart. The Hook in the universe is like a king on his throne; the Celestial Sphere in the year is like a king in a province; the heart in mankind is like a king at war.

59. חק עשרה שלשה ושבעה ושנים עשר פקודין בתלי וגלגל ולב. תלי בעולם כמלך על כסאו, גלגל בשנה כמלך במדינה, לב בנפש כמלך במלחמה.

60. The sum of the matter: in some cases these are combined with those, and those with these; these are opposites of those, and those of these; these correspond to those, and those to these; and if these do not exist, neither do those. *So God has created every object, one opposite the other* (cf. Qoh. 7:14): good opposite evil—evil from evil and good from good. Good brings evil to light and evil brings good to light. Good is stored up for the good.

60. כללו של דבר מקצת אילו נצטרפין עם אילו ואילו עם אילו. אילו תמורות אילו. ואילו תמורות אילו. אילו כנגד אילו, ואילו כנגד אילו. ואם אין אילו אין אילו. גם כל חפץ זה לעומת זה ברא א[לה]ים טוב לעומת רע רע מרע וטוב מטוב טוב מבחין את רע ורע מבחין את טוב טובה גנוזה לטובים.

61. When Abraham our father came, and looked, and saw, and investigated, and understood, and carved, and combined, and hewed, and pondered, and succeeded, the Lord of all was revealed to him. And he made him sit in his lap, and kissed him upon his head. He called him his friend and named him his son, and made a covenant with him and his seed for ever. *And he trusted in the Lord, and he accounted it to him for righteousness* (Gen. 15:6). And he invoked upon him the glory of the Lord, as it is written: *Before I formed you in the womb, I knew you, etc.* (Jer. 1:5). He made with him a covenant between the ten toes of his feet—it is circumcision. He made with him a covenant between the ten fingers of his hands—it is language. He bound twenty-two letters into his language, and the Holy One revealed to him the secret. He drew them out into water, he burned them into fire, he shook them into the air, he branded them into the seven, he led them into the twelve constellations.

61. וכיון שבא אברהם אבינו והיביט וראה וחקר והבין וחקק וצרף וחצב וחשב ועלתה בידו [fol. 71a] נגלה עליו אדון הכל והושיבו בחיקו ונשקו על ראשו קראו אוהבו ושמו בנו וכרת לו ברית ולזרעו לעולם והאמין בי״י ויחשבה לו צדקה וקרא עליו כבוד י״י דכת[יב] בטרם אצרך בבטן ידעתיך וגו' וכרת לו ברית בתוך עשר אצבעות רגליו והוא בשר מילה כרת לו ברית בתוך עשר אצבעות ידיו והוא לשון קשר עשרים ושתים אותיות בלשונו והק[ב״ה] גילה לו סוד משכן כמים דלקן כאש ריעשן כרוח ביערן כשבעה ניהגם בשנים עשר מזלות.

62. Air, temperate state and chest; earth, cold and the belly; heaven, heat and the head. This is Alef, Mem, Shin. Saturn, sabbath and the mouth; Jupiter, the first day of the week and the right eye; Mars, the second day of the week and the left eye; the Sun, the third day of the week and the right nostril; Venus, the fourth day of the week and the left nostril; Mercury, the fifth day of the week and the right ear; the Moon, the sixth day of the week and the left ear. This is Bet, Gimel, Dalet; Kaf, Pe, Resh, Taw. Aries, Nisan, the liver; Taurus, Iyyar, the gall; Gemini, Sivan, the spleen; Cancer, Tammuz, the gullet; Leo, Av, the right kidney; Virgo, Elul, the left kidney; Libra, Tishri, the intestines; Scorpio, Marheshvan, the stomach; Sagittarius, Kislev, the right hand; Capricorn, Tevet, the left hand; Aquarius, Shevat, the right foot; Pisces, Adar, the left foot. This is He, Waw, Zayin, Ḥet, Tet, Yod, Lamed, Nun, Samek, Ayin, Sade, Qof.

62. אויר רוויה וגיויה, ארץ קור ובטן, שמים חום וראש זה אמש. שבתי שבת ופה, צדק אחד בשבת ועין ימין, מאדים שיני בשבת ועין שמאל, חמה שלישי בשבת ואף ימין, נוגה רביעי בשבת ואף שמאל, כוכב חמה חמישי בשבת ואוזן ימין, לבנה שישי בשבת ואוזן שמאל. זה בגד כפרת. טלה ניסן כבד, שור אייר מרה, תאומים סיון טחול, סרטן תמוז המסס, אריה אב כוליה ימנית, בתולה אלול כוליה שמאלית, מאזנים תשרי קרקבן, עקרב מרחשוון קיבה, קשת כסליו יד ימין, גדי טבט יד שמאל, דלי שבת רגל ימין, דגים אדר רגל שמאל. זה הוזחטילןסעצק.

63. Three are hostile. These are they: the tongue, the liver and the gall. Three love: the eyes, the ears and the heart. Three give life: the two nostrils and the liver of the left side. Three kill: the two lower orifices and the mouth. There are three which are in man's control: the hands, the feet, and the mouth. There are three which are not in man's control: his eyes, his ears and his nostrils. Three things are heard by the ear and they are evil: cursing, blasphemy and an evil report. Three good things are heard by the ear: blessing, praise and a good report. There are three evil sights: an adulterous leer, an evil eye and a deceptive look. There are three good sights: modesty, a good eye, and a trustworthy look. Three things are bad for the tongue: He who speaks evil in the presence of his fellow, he who slanders, and he who speaks one thing with the mouth but another with the heart. Three things are good for the tongue: silence, reticence, and speaking the truth.

63. שלשה אויבים אילו הן לשון וכבד ומרה. שלשה אוהבים עינים ואזנים ולב. שלשה מחיים שני חוטמין וכבד של שמאל. שלשה ממיתים שני נקבים התחתונים והפה. שלשה שהן ברשותו ידים ורגלים והפה. שלשה שאין ברשותו עיניו ואוזניו וחוטמיו. שלשה שמיעות לאוזן והן רעות קללה וגידוף ושמועה רעה. שלשה שמיעות לאוזן טובות ברכה וקילוס ושמועה טובה. שלשה ראיות רעות עין נאפה ועין רעה ועין מגנבת. שלשה ראייות טובות בושה ועין טובה ועין נאמנת. שלשה ללשון רעות הדובר בפני ריעו רע והמלשין והמדבר אחד בפה ואחד בלב [fol. 71b]. שלוש ללשון טובות שתיקה ושמירת לשון ומדבר אמת.

Appendix 3

The Midrash About *Sefer Yeṣirah* and Ben Sira, According to Ms. Vatican 299/4, 65a–66a

(65a) אילו הן חמשה ספרים וחמשה פרקים וחמשה סדרים שגילה בן סירא לעוזיאל בנו וליוסף נכדו: ספר יצירה, וספר תגי'[ין], וספר דיקדוקין, וספר פסיקתא בתרי אפי משכן, ספר זרובבל. חמשה פרקים: פרק ר' שמעון בן יוחי, פרק אבות דר' נתן, פרק אותיות דר' עקיבה, פרק מעשה משכן, פרק דרך ארץ. חמשה סדרים: סדר עולם, סדר תקופות, סדר שעות, סדר עיבור, סדר הלכות. ומשגילה כל הרזים האילו רעשו כל צבא מרום, ויצאה רוח הקודש ואמרה: מי הוא שגילה סתריי לבני אדם? עמד בן עצש"ט[1] ואמ'[ר]: אני בוזי בן בוזי. אמ'[ר] לן הקב"ה: דייך מיד ישב יוסף וכתב מפי עצש"ט הללו חמשה עשר דברים, וכתבן בחרט חמשה ספרים ספר יצירה שיצר בו הקב"ה את עולמו. מי ימלל גבורות י"י וישמיע כל תהילתו[2]. מיכאן שאין לך שיכול לממל כל גבורותיו ולהשמיע (65b) כל תהילתו. ואפילו מלאכי השרת אינן יכולין לספר מקצת גבורות לדרוש שצפה וברא ועשה; שבתחילה כשברא את העו'[לם] היה הק[ב"ה] יחיד ועלה במחשבתו לברא העו'[לם] והיה מחרט יסודותיו בארץ ולא היה מתקיים, עד שברא בתורה ספר יצירה דצפה בו והבין בחכמתו ובכך יצר את העו'[לם], והיו עיניו צופות בספר יצירה וידיו משוטטות ובונות בעו'[לם]. להבדיל כאדם שבונה בינין ויש לו ספר ומסתכל בו, כן עשה הק[ב"ה]. וכיון שיצר את עולמו וסיימו היניחו (היניחו) בתורה שהיא גנוזה מראש קדם תשע מאות ושבעים וארבעה דורות לבריאת העולם. משנולד אברהם אבינו אמרו מלאכי' השרת לפני הק[ב"ה]: רבו'[נן] של עו'[לם] אהוב אחד יש לך בעו'[לם] ותכסה ממנו כלום? מיד אמר הק[ב"ה]: המכסה אני מאברהם[3]? ונמלך בתו'[רה] ואמ'[ר]: בואי ונשיאך לאברהם אהובי. אמרה לפניו (לפני): לאו עד שיבוא עניו וישא ענווה מיד נמלך הק[ב"ה] בספר יצירה ואמרה: הן, ומסרה לאברהם. והיה יושב יחיד ומעיין בספר יצירה

ולא היה יכול להבין בו כלום, עד שיצתה בת קול ואמ'[ר] לו: כלום אתה מבקש להשוות עצמך אלי? אני אחד ובראתי ספר יצירה והקרוני בו ועישיתי כל מה שכתוב בו, ואתה לא תוכל להבין יחיד קרב לעצמך חבר ותביטו בו שניכם ותבינו בו. מיד הלך אברהם לשם רבו וישב עמו שלוש שנים והביטיהו וידעו לצור את העולם. ועד עכשיו אין לך אדם שיבין בו יחיד אלא שני חכמים. ולא יבינוהו עד שלוש שנים. וכשיבינוהו יוכלו עשות כל מה שבליבם חפץ. וכשהבין בו אברהם הוסיף חכמה יתירה ולמד על התורה כולה ואף רבא רצה להבין בו יחיד. אמ'[ר] לו ר' זירא: והכת'[ב] חרב על[4] הבדים ונואלו[5], חרב על שנאיהם של ישר'[אל] שיושבין בד בבד ועוסקין בתורה[6]. אם כן נבוא ונעסוק בספר יצירה [וישבו[7]] שניהם. וצפו בו שלוש שנים והבינוהו ונברא להם עגל אחד. ושחטוהו ועשו בו סילק מסכתא. כששחטוהו נשתכח מהם. ישבו שלוש שנים (ישבו שלוש שנים) אחרות והחזירוהו. ואף בן סירא רצה להבין בו יחדי יצאתה בת קול ואמרה לו טובים (הם) השנים[8] הלך אצל ירמיהו ועסקו בו שלוש שנים והבינוהו ונברא א? אדם אחד לפניהם, וכתוב במצחו ויי' אלהים אמת[9]. ובידו סכין והיה מוחק א' שבאמת. אמ'[ר] ירמיהו למה אתה עושה כן: וכי ולא יכול להיות אמת? אמ'[ר] להם: אמשול לכם משל למה דומה לאדם שהוא בנאי וחכם ושרואין אותו בני אדם המליכוהו עליהם. לימים באו אחרים ולמדו את האומנות והניחו את הראשון וחזרו לאחרים גבי הקב"ה יתרומם שמו צפה בספר יצירה וצר את העולם והמליכוהו על ביריותיו וכשבאתם ועשיתם כמותו מה יהיה באחרית הדבר? ויניחהו ויחזרו לכם מי שיצר אתכם מה תהא עליו? אמרו לו: אם כן מה נעשה? אמ'[ר] להם: החזרוהו למפרע ונעשה אותו אדם עפר ואפר[10]. (66a) ויניחהו ויחזרו לכם מי שיצר אתכם מה תהא עליו אמרו לו אם כן מה נעשה אמ' להם החזרוהו למפרע ונעשה אותו אדם עפר ואפר.

Notes

INTRODUCTION

1. See, e.g., Yehuda Liebes, *Ars Poetica in "Sefer Yeṣirah"* (Jerusalem: Schocken, 2000), 229–242 [Hebrew].

2. See, e.g., Gershom Scholem, *Major Trends in Jewish Mysticism*, 3rd rev. ed. (New York: Schocken, 1995), 75; Joseph Dan, *History of Jewish Mysticism and Esotericism* (Jerusalem: Zalman Shazar Center for Jewish History, 2009), 2:573–574 [Hebrew]; Abraham Epstein, *Of the Jewish Antiquities: Studies and Monographs*, edited by Abraham M. Haberman (Jerusalem: Mosad Harav Kook, 1957), 183ff. [Hebrew].

3. See, e.g., Leo Baeck, "Zum *Sepher Jezira*," in *Aus drei Jahrtausende: Wissenschaftliche Untersuchungen und Abhandlungen zur Geschichte des jüdischen Glaubens*, 382–397 (Berlin: Schocken, 1938).

4. Meir Bar-Ilan, *Astrology and Other Sciences Among the Jews of Israel in the Roman-Hellenistic and Byzantine Periods* (Jerusalem: Mosad Bialik, 2010), 213–225 [Hebrew].

5. See, e.g., Shlomo Pines, "Points of Similarity Between the Exposition of the Doctrine of the *Sefirot* in the *Sefer Yezira* and a Text of the Pseudo-Clementine Homilies," *Proceedings of the Israel Academy of Science and Humanities* 7, no. 3 (1989): 63–142.

6. For a survey of nineteenth- and twentieth-century approaches to *Sefer Yeṣirah*'s time and context, see Nehemya Allony, "Zunz, Krauss, and Scholem Teach Their Theories of *Sefer Yeṣirah*," *Sinai* 74 (1974): 42–66 [Hebrew]. See also Y. Tzvi Langermann, "On the Beginning of Hebrew Scientific Literature and on Studying History Through *Maqbilot*," *Aleph* 2 (2002): 169–176; Steven M. Wasserstrom, "*Sefer Yesira* and Early Islam: A Reappraisal," *Journal of Jewish Thought and Philosophy* 3 (1993): 1–30; idem, "Further Thoughts on the Origins of *Sefer Yeṣirah*," *Aleph* 2 (2002): 201–221; Klaus Herrmann, *Sefer Jeẓira: Buch der Schöpfung* (Frankfurt: Verlag der Weltreligionen, 2008), 184–204.

7. Joseph Dan, "Three Phases of the History of the *Sefer Yezira*," *Frankfurter Judaistische Beiträge* 21 (1994): 7–29.

8. On the early commentaries on *Sefer Yeṣirah*, see, e.g., Joseph Dan, *Jewish Mysticism: Studies in Jewish Mysticism in Late Antiquity*, vol. 1 (Northvale, N.J.: Jason Aronson, 1998); Raphael Jospe, "Early Philosophical Commentaries on the *Sefer Yezirah*: Some Comments," *Revue des Études Juives* 149 (1990): 369–415; Haggai Ben-Shammai, "Saadya's Goal in His Commentary on *Sefer Yezira*," in *A Straight Pass: Studies in Medieval Philosophy and Culture: Essays in Honor of Arthur Hyman*, edited by Ruth Link-Salinger (Washington, D.C.: Catholic University of America Press, 1988), 1–9; Elliot R. Wolfson, "The Theosophy of Shabbetai Donnolo, with Special Emphasis on the Doctrine of *Sefirot* in His *SY Ḥakhmoni*," *Jewish History* 6 (1992): 281–316; Peter A. Hayman, ed., *Sefer Yesira: Edition, Translation and Text-Critical Commentary* (Tübingen: Mohr Siebeck, 2004), 25–32; Tzahi Weiss, "The Reception of *Sefer Yeṣirah* and Jewish Mysticism in the Early Middle Ages," *Jewish Quarterly Review* 103, no. 1 (2013): 26–46.

9. This remoteness of rabbinic Judaism contrasts with the Hekhalot literature, which, even if, as has been argued, it was not created by the sages, was written in relation or reaction to the rabbinic world, referring to the sages by name. For a survey of scholarly treatments of the Hekhalot literature, see Chap. 2, nn. 37–38.

10. On this matter, see Wasserstrom, "*Sefer Yesira* and Early Islam"; Ithamar Gruenwald, "Some Critical Notes on the First Part of *Sefer Yezira*," *Revue des Études Juives* 82 (1973): 477; *Sefer Yeṣirah*, 34; Bar-Ilan, *Astrology and Other Sciences*, 217.

11. Pines, "Points of Similarity."

12. Guy G. Stroumsa, "A Zoroastrian Origin to the *Sefirot*?," *Irano-Judaica* 3 (1994): 19; and cf., most recently, idem, "The Mystery of the Greek Letters: A Byzantine Kabbalah?," *Historia Religionum* 6 (2014): 35–44.

13. Ben-Shammai, "Saadya's Goal."

14. Klaus Herrmann, "Feuer aus Wasser zum Fortleben eines unbekannten *Sefer Yesira*-Kommentars in der Hekhalot-Literatur," *Frankfurter Judaistische Beiträge* 20 (1993): 43–95; idem, "An Unknown Commentary on the "Book of Creation" (*Sefer Yeṣirah*) from the Cairo Genizah and Its Re-Creation Among the *Ḥaside Ashkenaz*," in *Creation and Re-Creation in Jewish Thought*, edited by Rachel Elior and Peter Schäfer (Tübingen: Mohr Siebeck, 2005), 102–113.

15. Hayman, ed., *Sefer Yeṣira*, §§ 1–5, Ms. Vatican 299. All the quotations from *Sefer Yeṣirah* are according to Hayman's translation, with occasional corrections. For a recent English introduction to *Sefer Yeṣirah* content and history of acceptance, see Marla Segol, *Word and Image in Medieval Kabbalah: The Text, Commentaries and Diagrams of Sefer Yetsirah* (New York: Palgrave Macmillan, 2012), 21–37.

16. *Belimah*, employed here, is a rare Hebrew word appearing only once in the Bible (Job 26:7), where its meaning is also unclear. Hayman decided to translate it as "basis,"

claiming that *belimah* and *yesod* mean approximately the same (*Sefer Yeṣirah*, 66). For other interpretations of the word as "without anything" (בלי-מה) or restriction (as בלם, restrict, which appears in §5 or in modern Hebrew, בלימה, restriction), see Hayman's discussion (ibid.). Cf. Liebes, *Ars Poetica*, 55.

17. Liebes, *Ars Poetica*, 15.

18. On the number thirty-two, see Nicolas Séd, "Le Memar Samaritain, le *Sefer Yesira* et les 32 Sentiers de la Sagesse," *Revue de l'Histoire des Religions* 170 (1966): 159–184.

19. Liebes, *Ars Poetica*, 53–62.

20. *Sefer Yeṣirah*, §7, Ms. Vatican 299.

21. *Sefer Yeṣirah*, §17; 23; 37; 45, according to Ms. Vat. 299.

22. In the last foundation, the *shin* represents fire and not *alef*, since the *alef* was already occupy by the first foundations: air.

23. Shlomo Morag, "The Seven Double Letters BGD KFRT," *Proceedings of Israeli Society for Biblical Research* 8 (1960): 207–242 [Hebrew]; idem, "On the Seven Double Letters BGD KPRT and the Names Sarah-Sarai, Avram-Avraham," *Tarbiz* 63 (1994): 135–142 [Hebrew]; Geoffrey Khan, "The Pronunciation of *Reš* in the Tiberian Tradition of Biblical Hebrew," *Hebrew Union College Annual* 66 (1995): 67–80; Yehuda Liebes, "The Seven Double Letters *BGD KFRT*: On the Double *RESH* and the Background of *Sefer Yeṣirah*," *Tarbiz* 61 (1992): 237–247 [Hebrew]; Liebes, "Response to Shlomo Morag's Arguments," *Tarbiz* 63 (1994): 143–144 [Hebrew].

24. Dan, *Jewish Mysticism and Esotericism*, 2:623.

25. *Sefer Yeṣirah*, §§23–36.

26. Dan, *Jewish Mysticism and Esotericism*, 2:623.

27. Hayman translated: נפש כל העתיד לצור in the passive voice (maybe as לְצוּר), "the life of all that would be formed." But a better conjecture might be to translate it as active (לְצוֹר): "the life of all that will form."

28. *Sefer Yeṣirah*, §19, according to Ms. Vat. 299, with a few corrections of mine.

29. The letters.

30. Letters.

31. *Sefer Yeṣirah*, §40, according to Ms. Vat. 299.

32. Ibid., §§39–41.

33. Ibid., §32, with a few changes .

34. Ibid., §61. On this paragraph and its meanings, see Ronit Meroz, "Interreligious Polemic, Messianism, and Revelation in the Short Recension of *Sefer Yeṣirah*," *Da'at* 81–82 (2016): 1–37 [Hebrew].

35. Gershom Scholem, *On the Kabbalah and Its Symbolism*, translated by Ralph Manheim (New York: Schocken, 1965), 169–170.

36. Moshe Idel, *Golem: Jewish Magical and Mystical Traditions on the Artificial Anthropoid* (Albany, N.Y.: SUNY, 1990), 14–15.

37. See n. 46 below.

38. The relations and possible influences of Syriac Christianity on the rabbinic world have been discussed in a number of important works over the years. The matter is still under debate. See, e.g., Isaiah Gafni, "Nestorian Literature as a Source for the History of the Babylonian Yeshivot," *Tarbiz* 51 (1982): 567–576 [Hebrew]; Daniel Boyarin, *Socrates and the Fat Rabbis* (Chicago: University of Chicago Press, 2009), 138–141; Adam H. Becker, "The Comparative Study of 'Scholasticism' in Late Antique Mesopotamia: Rabbis and East Syrians," *AJS Review* 34 (2010): 91–113; Moulie Vidas, "Greek Wisdom in Babylonia," in *Envisioning Judaism: Studies in Honor of Peter Schäfer on the Occasion of His Seventieth Birthday*, edited by Ra'anan S. Boustan et al. (Mohr Siebeck: Tübingen, 2013): 287–305; Michal Bar-Asher Siegal, *Early Christian Monastic Literature and the Babylonian Talmud* (New York: Cambridge University Press, 2013); Yakir Paz and Tzahi Weiss, "From Encoding to Decoding: The AṬBḤ of R. Ḥiyya in Light of a Syriac, Greek and Coptic Cipher," *Journal of Near Eastern Studies* 74 (2015): 45–65.

39. See Chap. 5, pp. 89–90.

40. Joseph Kafiḥ, ed. and trans., *The Commentary of Saadya Gaon on* Sefer Yeṣirah (Jerusalem: Ha-Va'ad Le-Hotsaat Sifre Rasag, 1972), 34.

41. Israel Weinstock, "A Clarification of the Version of *Sefer Yeṣirah*," in *Temirin* vol. 1, edited by Weinstock (Jerusalem: Mosad Harav Kook, 1972), 11–13: Hayman, ed., *Sefer Yeṣirah*, 1–2.

42. On the possibility of there being more recensions, see Y. Tzvi Langermann, "A New Redaction of *Sefer Yeṣirah*?," *Kabbalah* 2 (1997): 49–63.

43. Daniel Abrams, *Kabbalistic Manuscripts and Textual Theory* (Jerusalem: Cherub Press, 2010), 447–454.

44. On this, see Chap. 4.

45. Gruenwald, "A Preliminary Critical Edition of *Sefer Yeṣirah*," 133.

46. Gruenwald, "Some Critical Notes," 479. On this distinction, see also Scholem, *Kabbalah and Its Symbolism*, 168–169; idem, *The Origins of the Kabbalah and the Book Bahir: Lectures of Gershom Scholem*, edited by Rivka Schatz (Jerusalem: Academon, 1962), 33 [Hebrew].

47. Ronit Meroz, "Between *Sefer Yezirah* and Wisdom Literature: Three Binitarian Approaches in *Sefer Yezirah*," *Journal for the Study of Religions and Ideologies* 18 (2007): 101–142.

48. Ibid., 130.

49. Cf. Hayman, ed., *Sefer Yeṣirah*, 6–7.

50. I do not agree with all Hayman's decisions regarding the content of this earliest version, but I think that he is right in his general attitude. See Hayman, ed., *Sefer Yesira*, 6–8. Cf. idem, "The Original Text of *Sefer Yeṣirah* or the 'Earliest Recoverable Text,'" in *Reflection and Refraction: Studies in Biblical Historiography in Honour of A. Graeme Auld*, edited by Robert Rezetko et al. (Leiden: Brill 2007), 175–186.

CHAPTER 1

1. For a survey of those claims, see Tzahi Weiss, *Letters by Which Heaven and Earth Were Created: The Origins and the Meanings of the Perceptions of Alphabetic Letters as Independent Units in Jewish Sources of Late Antiquity* (Jerusalem: Mosad Bialik, 2014), 18–19 [Hebrew].

2. The most important scholarly work on approaches toward alphabetical letters was and still is Franz Dornseiff, *Das Alphabet in Mystik und Magie*, 2nd ed. (Leipzig: Teubner, 1925). Since the second edition of Dornseiff's book, scholars have discovered sources from different cultural contexts that Dornseiff was not acquainted with: the Mandaean sources, discussed by Ethel S. Drower (see below, pp. 22–23); the Samaritan sources, first discussed by Moshe Gaster, *The Samaritans: Their History, Doctrines and Literature* (London: British Academy, 1925): 78–83; Christian sources presented by Brouria Bitton-Ashkelony and Aryeh Kofsky, *The Monastic School of Gaza* (Leiden: Brill, 2006), 109–128; Eliane Ketterer, ed., "*The Alphabet of Rabbi Aqiba*, Version A and Version B: The Name of This Midrash, Its Trends, Its Ideas, and Its Relations with Different Streams in Judaism and Christianity" (Ph.D. diss., Hebrew University, 2005), 221–257 [Hebrew]. For a more general overview, see Weiss, *Letters.* See also Patricia Cox-Miller, "In the Praise of Nonsense," in *Classical Mediterranean Spirituality*, edited by Arthur H. Armstrong (New York: Crossroad, 1986), 481–505; Johanna Drucker, *The Alphabetic Labyrinth: The Letters in History and Imagination* (London: Thames and Hudson, 1995); David Frankfurter, "The Magic of Writing and Writing of Magic: The Power of the Word in Egyptian and Greek Traditions," *Helios* 21 (1994): 189–221; Naomi Janowitz, *Icons of Power: Ritual Practices in Late Antiquity* (University Park, Pa.: Pennsylvania State University Press, 2002).

3. See, e.g., Wilfred G. Lambert, "An Address of Marduk to the Demons," *Archiv für Orientforschung* 17 (1956): 310–321; Jeffrey H. Tigay, "An Early Technique of Aggadic Exegesis," in *History, Historiography, and Interpretation: Studies in Biblical and Cuneiform Literature*, edited by Ḥayim Tadmor et al. (Jerusalem: Magnes Press, 1983), 169–189; Antoine Cavigneaux, "Aux Sources du Midrash: L'Herméneutique Babylonienne," *Aula*

Orientalis 5 (1987): 243–255; Stephen J. Lieberman, "A Mesopotamian Background for the So-Called Aggadic Measures of Biblical Hermeneutics," *Hebrew Union College Annual* 58 (1987): 157–226.

4. See Weiss, *Letters*, 33–35. Recent extensive studies about numbers encoded in biblical poems have been written by Knohl; see Israel Knohl, *The Holy Name* (Or Yehuda: Dvir, 2012) [Hebrew]; Knohl, "Sacred Architecture Dimensions of Biblical Poems," *Vetus Testamentum* 62, no. 2 (2012): 189–197.

5. See, e.g., Dornseiff, *Alphabet in Mystik und Magie*, 1–19; Frankfurter, "Magic of Writing."

6. Benjamin Jowett, ed. and trans., *The Dialogues of Plato in 5 vols.* (New York: Scribner, 1892), *Timaeus* 48b.

7. See, e.g., *Sefer Yeṣirah*, §2, 9, 17, 18.

8. See, e.g., Scholem, *Major Trends*, 77n129. For an alternative approach to the meaning of this phrase, which rejects the Greek connection, see Liebes, *Ars Poetica*, 16–17.

9. Aristotle, "Metaphysics," XIV, 1093a, 1–20, in *The Complete Works of Aristotle*, edited by Jonathan Barnes and translated by William D. Ross (Princeton, N.J.: Princeton University Press, 1985), 2:1727.

10. Plutarch, "Moralia, the E at Delphi," translated by Frank Cole Babbitt (Cambridge, Mass.: Harvard University Press, 1969), 5:194–253. On this source, see Dornseiff, *Alphabet in Mystik und Magie*, 23; Drucker, *Alphabetic Labyrinth*, 64–65.

11. Plutarch, "Moralia, the E at Delphi," 207.

12. On this, see below, pp. 50–52.

13. *Sefer Yeṣirah*, §§39–42, according to Ms. Vat. 299. On the seven plants and *Sefer Yeṣirah*, see Bar-Ilan, *Astrology and Other Sciences*, 118–119.

14. On Irenaeus's approach to alphabetical letters, see, e.g., Dornseiff, *Alphabet in Mystik und Magie*, 126–133; Ketterer, "*The Alphabet of Rabbi Aqiba*," 215–220.

15. On Irenaeus's representation of Marcus, see Niclas Förster, *Marcus Magus: Kult, Lehre und Gemeindeleben einer valentinianischen Gnostikergrouppe—Sammlung der Quellen und Kommentar* (Tübingen: Mohr Siebeck, 1999).

16. On the similarity of this depiction to the ancient mystical Jewish treatise *Sefer Shi'ur Qomah* (Book of divine dimensions), see, e.g., Gershom Scholem, *On the Mystical Shape of the Godhead: Basic Concepts in the Kabbalah*, translated by Joachim Neugroschel (New York: Schocken, 1991), 25–28; Moshe Idel, "The World of Angels in Human Form," in *Studies in Jewish Mysticism Presented to Isaiah Tishby on His Seventy-Fifth Birthday*, edited by Joseph Dan et al., *Jerusalem Studies in Jewish Thought* 3, nos. 1–2 (1984): 2–6 [Hebrew]; Moshe Gaster, *Studies and Texts in Folklore, Magic, Mediaeval Romance, Hebrew Apocrypha, and Samaritan Archaeology* (New York: Ktav, 1971), 3:1330–

1353 [Hebrew]; Janowitz, *Icons of Power*, 45–48; Martin S. Cohen, *The Shi'ur Qomah: Liturgy and Theurgy in Pre-Kabbalistic Jewish Mysticism* (New York: University Press of America, 1983), 23–25; Nathaniel Deutsch, *The Gnostic Imagination: Gnosticism, Mandaeism, and Merkabah Mysticism* (Leiden: Brill, 1995), 90–91; Peter A. Hayman, "Was God a Magician? *Sefer Yesira* and Jewish Magic," *Journal of Jewish Studies* 4 (1989): 231.

17. Saint Irenaeus of Lyon, *Against the Heresies*, translated by Dominic J. Unger (New York: Paulist Press, 1992), §14.3, 61.

18. *Sefer Yeṣirah*, §§32–34.

19. Ethel S. Drower, *The Secret Adam: A Study of Naṣoraean Gnosis* (Oxford: Clarendon Press, 1960), 12–20; cf. Dan Cohn-Sherbok, "The Alphabet in Mandaean and Jewish Gnosticism," *Religion* 11 (1981): 227–234; R. J. Zwi Werblowsky, "Drower, E. S.: *The Secret Adam*," *Journal of Semitic Studies* 8 (1963): 129–133.

20. See Jorunn J. Buckley, ed. and trans., *The Scroll of Exalted Kingship* (New Haven, Conn.: American Oriental Society, 1993), 59. Cf. Nathaniel Deutsch, *Guardian of the Gate: Angelic Vice Regency in Late Antiquity* (Leiden: Brill, 1999), 100.

21. Ethel S. Drower, trans., *Alf Trisar Šuialia: The Thousand and Twelve Questions* (Berlin: Akad, 1960), 110.

22. Ibid., 180–181.

23. Ibid., §14.5, 61–62.

24. Irenaeus, *Against the Heresies*, §14.5, 61–62.

25. On approaches to the vowels in Greek magic, see, e.g., Dornseiff, *Alphabet in Mystik und Magie*, 35–60; Cox-Miller, "Praise of Nonsense"; Frankfurter, "Magic of Writing"; Ernst Ettisch, *The Hebrew Vowels and Consonants as Symbols of Ancient Astronomic Concepts*, translated by Harry Zohn (New York: Branden, 1987), 5–16; Janowitz, *Icons of Power*, 59–61.

26. The fact that the last succession of letters here is composed of twenty-two letters cannot be considered coincidental. On its significance, see below, pp. 45–48.

27. "The Discourse of the Eighth and the Ninth," in *The Nag Hammadi Library in English*, edited by James M. Robinson (Leiden: Brill, 1977), 326. Cf. Cox-Miller, "Praise of Nonsense," 484. In an additional and lengthy discussion appearing in a text called *Marsanes*, the Aeons are described in terms of the consonants as well as the vowel and semivowel letters (*Nag Hammadi*, 466–470).

28. Cox-Miller, "Praise of Nonsense," 484.

29. Translated by Birger A. Pearson, in "Gnosticism and Platonism: With Special Reference to *Marsanes* (NHC 10,1)," *Harvard Theological Review* 77 (1984): 69. Originally published in Nicomachus, apud C. Janus, *Musici Scriptores Graeci* (Leipzig: Teubner, 1895; Hildesheim: Olms, 1962), 276–277.

30. An approach like that of Marcus, in another rare example of a text that does not elevate the vowels over the other letters, is "The Gospel of Truth" (*Nag Hammadi*, 43). See, e.g., David Frankfurter, *Religion in Roman Egypt: Assimilation and Resistance* (Princeton, N.J.: Princeton University Press, 1998), 254–255; idem, "Magic of Writing," 207; Bitton-Ashkelony and Kofsky, *Monastic School of Gaza*, 123. On the possibility that the composition "The Gospel of Truth," mentioned by Irenaeus (§3.11), is the one found in the Nag Hammadi library, see Harold W. Attridge and George W. MacRae's *Introduction to the Translation of the Nag Hammadi Treatise*, 38; see also Guy G. Stroumsa, "A Nameless God: Judaeo-Christian and Gnostic," in *The Image of the Judaeo-Christians in Ancient Jewish and Christian Literature*, edited by Peter J. Tomson et al. (Tübingen: Mohr Siebeck, 2003), 239–241; Elliot R. Wolfson, "Inscribed in the Book of the Living; 'Gospel of Truth' and Jewish Christology," *Journal for the Study of Judaism* 38 (2007): 239–340nn16–17.

31. Irenaeus, *Against the Heresies*, §15.4, 66–67.

32. Ibid., §20.1, 76. On this legend, see also the Gospel of Pseudo-Matthew, in *Apocryphal: Gospels, Acts and Revelations*, edited by Alexander Walker (Edinburgh: Clark, 1911), 44; the Greek versions of the Gospel of Thomas: ibid., 78–92, and the Arabic Gospel of the Infancy of the Saviour: ibid., 122. Cf. Ketterer, "*The Alphabet of Rabbi Aqiba*," 208–215; Bitton-Ashkelony and Kofsky, *Monastic School of Gaza*, 121; Wolfson, "Inscribed," 250–251n55; Brian McNeil, "Jesus and the Alphabet," *Journal of Theological Studies* 27 (1976): 126–128. A similar theme can be found in a few Jewish sources; see, e.g., b. Shabbat 104a; Eli Yassif, *The Tales of Ben Sira in the Middle Ages* (Jerusalem: Magnes Press, 1984), 202ff.

33. See Shmuel Sambursky, "The Term *Gematria*: Source and Meaning," *Tarbiz* 45 (1976): 268–271 [Hebrew]; Stephen Gersh, *From Iamblichus to Eriugena: An Investigation of the Prehistory and Evolution of the Pseudo-Dionysian Tradition* (Leiden: Brill, 1978), 289–304; Janowitz, *Icons of Power*, 57–61.

34. Thomas Taylor, trans., *Commentaries of Proclus on the Timaeus of Plato in Five Books* (London, 1820), 274.10–277.26, 2:140–142.

35. This is the first instance known to us that the Greek *isopsephy* is called "geometric number" (γεωμετρικὸς ἀριθμός); according to Shmuel Sambursky, this is the origin for the later Hebrew term *gematria*. See Sambursky, "The Term *Gematria*."

36. See ibid., 268–271.

37. *Proclus on the Timaeus*, 2:141.

38. On the Samaritan sources, see, e.g., Gaster, *The Samaritans*, 78–83; Jarl E. Fossum, *The Name of God and the Angel of the Lord* (Tübingen: Mohr Siebeck, 1985); Nicolas Séd, "Une Cosmologie Juive du Haut Moyen Age: La Berayta di Maaseh Beresit," *Revue*

des Études Juives 124 (1965): 23–123; 123 (1964): 259–305; Liebes, *Ars Poetica*, 46n56; Ithamar Gruenwald, "Uses and Abuses of Gematria," in *Rabbi Mordechai Breuer Festschrift*, edited by M. Bar-Asher (Jerusalem: Academon, 1992), 2:823–832 [Hebrew]; Tzahi Weiss, "The Perception of the Letters in the Samaritan *Memar Marqah* and in Its Equivalents in Rabbinic Sources and in the Book of Creation," *Jewish Studies* 43 (2006): 89–129 [Hebrew]. Cf. below, pp. 49–50, 56–58.

39. On letter speculations in the Islamic world, see, e.g., Pierre Lory, *La science de lettres en islam* (Paris: Dervy, 2004) and, most recently, Michael Ebstein, *Mysticism and Philosophy in al-Andalus: Ibn Masarra, Ibn al-'Arabī, and the Ismā'īlī Tradition* (Leiden: Brill, 2014), 77–122.

40. For a similar conclusion, see, e.g., Ketterer, "*The Alphabet of Rabbi Aqiba*," 257; Bitton-Ashkelony and Kofsky, *Monastic School of Gaza*, 112. For more on letter speculations in Christian sources, see Dornseiff, *Alphabet in Mystik und Magie*, 28–29; Chen-Melech Merchavia, *The Church Versus Talmudic and Midrashic Literature: 500–1248* (Jerusalem: Mosad Bialik, 1970), 30–31 [Hebrew]; Arsène Darmesteter, "Anglais au XIV Siècle," *Revue des Études Juives* 4 (1882): 259–268; Gideon Bohak, "Greek-Hebrew Gematrias in 3 Baruch and in Revelation," *Journal for the Study of the Pseudepigrapha* 7 (1990): 119–121.

41. Armand Veilleux, trans., *Pachomian Koinonia III: Instructions, Letters and Other Writings of Saint Pachomius and His Disciples*, Kalamazoo, Mich.: Cistercian, 1982), 51–83. On this correspondence, see Dornseiff, *Alphabet in Mystik und Magie*, 72; James E. Goehring, *Ascetics, Society, and the Desert* (Harrisburg, Pa.: Trinity Press International, 1999), 214, 221–224; Philip Rousseau, *Pachomius: The Making of a Community in Fourth-Century Egypt* (Berkeley: University of California Press, 1985), 38; Henry Chadwick, "Pachomios and the Idea of Sanctity," in *The Byzantine Saint: University of Birmingham Fourteenth Spring Symposium of Byzantine Studies*, edited by Sergei Hackel (London: Fellowship of Saint Alban and Saint Sergius, 1981), 24; Bitton-Ashkelony and Kofsky, *Monastic School of Gaza*, 112–113.

42. Pachomian Koinonia, 76.

43. Ibid., letter no. 1, 51.

44. Ibid., letter no. 6, 67–68.

45. Ibid., letters no. 9A and 9B, 72–74.

46. Ibid., letter no. 6, 67–68.

47. See Bitton-Ashkelony and Kofsky, *Monastic School of Gaza*, 109–128; Ketterer, "*The Alphabet of Rabbi Aqiba*," 252.

48. Cordula Bandt, ed. and trans., *Der Traktat "Von Mysterium der Buchstaben"* (Berlin: W. De Gruyter, 2007), hereafter *The Mysteries of the Greek Letters*.

49. On the book and its author, see Bandt, *The Mysteries of the Greek Letters*, 4–8; Adolphe Hebbelynck, ed. and trans., *Les Mystères des Lettres Grecques: D'après un Manuscript Copte-Arabe* (Louvain: Istas, 1902), 5–13; Émile Galtier, "Sur les Mystères des Lettres Grecques," *Bulletin de l'Institut Français d'Archéologie Orientale* 2 (1902): 139–162; Émile Amélineau, "Les Traités Gnostiques d'Oxford (Deuxième Article)," *Revue de l'Histoire des Religions* 21 (1890): 261–294; Dornseiff, *Alphabet in Mystik und Magie*, 73; Drucker, *Alphabetic Labyrinth*, 89–91; Stroumsa, "Zoroastrian Origin," 19; Khalil Samir, "Mysteries of Greek Letters," *Coptic Encyclopedia* (New York: Macmillan, 1991), 6:1749–1750; Liebes, *Ars Poetica*, 230; Elliot R. Wolfson, *Abraham Abulafia—Kabbalist and Prophet: Hermeneutics, Theosophy and Theurgy* (Los Angeles: Cherub Press, 1994), 349n80; Frankfurter, "Magic of Writing," 211.

50. On the historical period of the mysteries of the Greek Letters, see Bandt, *The Mysteries of the Greek Letters*, 8; Hebbelynck, *The Mysteries of the Greek Letters—Coptic*, 5–13; Amélineau, "Traités Gnostiques," 266–276; Bitton-Ashkelony and Kofsky, *Monastic School of Gaza*, 124n75; Samir, "Greek Letters."

51. Bandt, *The Mysteries of the Greek Letters*, §3, 108.

52. Ibid., §4, 112.

53. Ibid., §5, 114.

54. Ibid., §14, 130–132.

55. See, e.g., ibid., §14, 132; §17, 138; §17, 146.

56. See, e.g., ibid., §17, 138–146; §10, 118; §32, 170.

57. See, e.g., ibid., §17, 140; §24, 161.

58. On the approach to alphabetical letters in Syriac sources, see Adam H. Becker, *Fear of God and the Beginning of Wisdom: The School of Nisibis and the Christian Scholastic Culture in Late Antique Mesopotamia* (Philadelphia: University of Pennsylvania Press, 2006), 131; Paz and Weiss, "From Encoding to Decoding"; Tzahi Weiss, "Soft and Hard: More Comments on the Syrian Context of *Sefer Yeṣirah*," *Kabbalah* 26 (2012): 229–242 [Hebrew]; Idem, "Brief Comments on the Syrian Context of *Sefer Yeṣirah*," *Jerusalem Studies in Jewish Thought* 22 (2011): 75–89 [Hebrew]. Cf. also Chap. 3.

59. Artemidorus, *The Interpretation of Dreams*, translated by Robert J. White (Park Ridge, N.J.: Noyes Press, 1975), II §70, 134–138; III §28, 165; III §34, 166–167; IV §24, 196. On the rabbinic literature and Artemidorus, see, e.g., Saul Lieberman, *Hellenism in Jewish Palestine* (New York: P. Feldheim, 1950), 71–72; Haim Weiss, *All Dreams Follow the Mouth: A Reading in the Talmudic Dream Tractate* (Or Yehuda: Dvir, 2011), 186–188 [Hebrew].

60. See T. Weiss, "Perception."

61. Zosimos of Panopolis, *On the Letter Omega*, edited and translated by Howard M. Jackson (Missoula, Mont.: Scholars Press, 1978).

CHAPTER 2

1. Gershom Scholem argued that at a deeper level of meaning, *Sefer Yeṣirah*'s treatment of creation through letters refers to the letters of God's name. See Scholem, *On the Kabbalah and Its Symbolism*, 166–167; idem, *Kabbalah* (Jerusalem: Keter, 1974), 25–26. Urbach, by contrast, interprets all the myths about the creation of the world from letters as referring to all the letters of the alphabet: see Ephraim E. Urbach, *The Sages: Their Concepts and Beliefs* (Jerusalem: Magnes Press, 1975), 20n60.

2. Peter A. Hayman, "*Sefer Yesira* and the Hekhalot Literature," *Jerusalem Studies in Jewish Thought* 6 (1987): 80–82.

3. On the ontological meaning of the written formula of the name of God in Jewish sources in late antiquity, see Weiss, *Letters*, 147–167. On the influence of the Greek vowels on the way in which the name of God was perceived by Jews, see Naomi Janowitz's important conclusion: "The Hebrew name theory and the Greek vowels theory merge when the Hebrew divine name is thought to consist of only vowels" (Janowitz, *Icons of Power*, 60). See also Gideon Bohak, *Ancient Jewish Magic: A History* (Cambridge: Cambridge University Press, 2008), 264–265, 305–307.

4. Josephus Flavius, *The Jewish War* IV–VII, translated by H. St. J. Thackeray, Loeb Classical Library (London: William Heinemann, 1928), 172–173 (5.5.7).

5. On the concept of creation ex nihilo in rabbinic literature, see, e.g., David Winston, "The Book of Wisdom's Theory of Cosmogony," *History of Religions* 11 (1971): 185–202; idem, "Creation Ex Nihilo Revisited: A Reply to Jonathan Goldstein," *Journal of Jewish Studies* 37 (1986): 88–91; Jonathan A. Goldstein, "The Origins of the Doctrine of Creation Ex Nihilo," *Journal of Jewish Studies* 35 (1984): 127–135; Goldstein, "Creation Ex Nihilo: Recantations and Restatements," *Journal of Jewish Studies* 38 (1987): 187–194; Menahem Kister, "Tohu wa-Bohu, Primordial Elements and Creation Ex Nihilo," *Jewish Studies Quarterly* 14 (2007): 229–256. On creation ex nihilo and *Sefer Yeṣirah*, see Peter A. Hayman, "The Doctrine of Creation in *Sefer Yesira*: Some Text Critical Problems," in *Rashi, 1040–1990: Hommage à Ephraïm E. Urbach: congrès européen des études juives*, edited by Gabrielle Sed-Rajna (Paris: Éditions du Cerf, 1993), 219–227.

6. On these sources, see, e.g., Fossum, *Name of God*, 249, 256; Ithamar Gruenwald, *Apocalyptic and Merkavah Mysticism* (Leiden: Brill, 1980), 11; Gershom Scholem, "The Name of God and the Linguistic Theory of the Kabbala," Part I, *Diogenes* 79–80 (1972): 69; Daniel Sperber, "On Sealing the Abysses," *Journal of Semitic Studies* 10 (1966): 170; Hayman, "Was God a Magician?," 228.

7. Jubilees (James H. Charlesworth, ed., *The Old Testament Pseudepigrapha*, vols. 1–2 [Garden City, N.Y.: Doubleday, 1985]) 36:1–7.

8. The Prayer of Manasseh (Charlesworth), 1–3.

9. 1 Enoch (Charlesworth), 69:14–26.

10. Rabbinic sources offer different versions of the basic element that went into the creation of the world, e.g., the Torah (m. Avot 3:14), or the speech of God, e.g., m. Avot 5:1; Genesis Rabbah (Judah Theodor and Hanoch Albeck, eds., *Bereshit Rabbah* [Jerusalem: Wahrmann, 1965]), 17:1; b. Rosh haShanah 32a; b. Megilah 21b. For other accounts of the mythical or moral foundations of the world, see Genesis Rabbah (Theodor-Albeck) 1:1; b. Bava Batra 74b; b. Ḥagiga 12a; b. Pesaḥim 54a. On *ma'aseh bereishit* in rabbinic literature, see, e.g., Urbach, *Sages*, 184–213; Alon Goshen-Gottstein, "Is *Ma'aseh Bereshit* Part of Ancient Jewish Mysticism?," *Journal of Jewish Thought and Philosophy* 4, no. 2 (1995): 185–201; Kister, "*Tohu wa-Bohu*"; Yair Furstenberg, "The Rabbinic Ban on *Ma'aseh Bereshit*: Sources, Contexts, and Concerns," in *Jewish and Christian Cosmogony in Late Antiquity*, edited by Lance Jenott and Sarit Kattan Gribetz (Tübingen: Mohr Siebeck, 2013), 39–63.

11. b. Menaḥot 29b; y. Ḥagiga 77c (786); Genesis Rabbah (Theodor-Albeck) 12:10; Salomon Buber, ed., *Midrasch Tehilim: Schocher tob* (Vilna: Wittwe & Gebrüder Romm, 1891), 62, 114; Meir Friedmann (Ish-Shalom), ed., *Pesikta Rabbati* (Vienna: Josef Kaiser IX, 1880), 21 (109); Salomon Buber, ed., *Midrasch Tanḥuma* (Vilna: Wittwe & Gebrüder Rom, 1885), Wayyiqra 13.

12. b. Sukkah 53a–b; b. Makkot 11a; y. Sanhedrin 29a (1323–1324); Salomon Buber, ed., *Midrash Samuel: Agadische Abhandlung über das Buch Samuel* (Cracow: Fischer, 1893), 26; Pseudo-Jonathan: John W. Etheridge, ed., *The Targums of Onkelos and Jonathan ben Uzziel of the Pentateuch with Fragments of the Jerusalem Targum* (Hoboken, N.J.: Ktav, 1969), Exod. 28:30.

13. Parallels to this midrash, also in the names of R. Abbahu and of R. Yoḥanan, are in y. Ḥagiga 73c (p. 786); *Pesikta Rabbati* (Ish-Shalom), 21; Tanḥuma Genesis (Buber), 17. This midrash was quoted anonymously in *Midrasch Tehilim* (Buber), 62, 114.

14. Harry Freedman and Maurice Simon, eds., *Midrash rabbah*, vols. 1–2 (Genesis) (London: Soncino Press, 1951), 12:10.

15. Genesis Rabbah [English] 39:11.

16. The common translation of the words *ṣur 'olamim* (צור עולמים) from Isa. 26:4 is "an everlasting rock," but here, as well as in other variants of this midrash, the words are interpreted differently: *ṣur* is understood as *yaṣer* (יצר), i.e., created; and *'olamim* is understood literally as the plural of world.

17. Genesis Rabbah [English] 12:10.

18. Tanḥuma Leviticus: John T. Townsend, trans., *Midrash Tanḥuma* (Hoboken, N.J.: Ktav, 1997), Wayyiqra 13, with a few corrections of mine. On the connection be-

tween transgression and the use of the abbreviation of the tetragrammaton, see b. Eruvin 18b; Bernard Mandelbaum, ed., *Pesikta de-Rav Kahana According to an Oxford Manuscript with Variants from All Known Mss. and Genizoth Fragments and Parallel Passages* (New York: Jewish Theological Seminary Press, 1962), 3:16; *Pesikta Rabbati* (Ish-Shalom), 12.

19. See above, pp. 38–39.

20. "And they sealed up the abysses with the seal of the Lord"; J. Rendel Harris, ed., *An Early Christian Psalter* (London: J. Nisbet, 1910), 24:5.

21. On the creation by the ineffable name in Christian and Gnostic sources, see Sperber, "On Sealing the Abysses"; Hayman, "*Sefer Yesira* and the Hekhalot," 75; Hayman, "Was God a Magician?," 227–230.

22. *Shittin* (pl. of *shith*) are the pits by the side of the altar into which the remainder of libations was poured (Jastrow dictionary, p. 1570). According to some traditions, these pits reached the depth of the primordial abyss.

23. b. Sukkah 53a–b; b. Makkot 11a; y. Sanhedrin 29a (1323–1324).

24. y. Sanhedrin 10:2 (Neusner p. 345).

25. Pseudo-Jonathan (Targumim), Exod. 28:30. On this midrash, see, e.g., Sperber, "Sealing the Abysses," 169; Avigdor Shinan, *The Embroidered Targum: The Aggadah in Targum Pseudo-Jonathan to the Pentateuch* (Jerusalem: Magnes Press, 1992), 134–138 [Hebrew]; Naomi Koltun-Fromm, "Rock over Water: Prehistoric Rocks and Primordial Waters from Creation to Salvation in Jerusalem," in *Jewish and Christian Cosmogony in Late Antiquity*, edited by Lance Jenott and Sarit Kattan Gribetz (Tübingen: Mohr Siebeck, 2013), 244.

26. b. Berakhot 55a.

27. Peter Schäfer, ed., *Synopse zur Hekhalot Literatur* (Tübingen: Mohr Siebeck, 1981), §16, 59, 389, 396, 832, 833.

28. Scholem, *Kabbalah and Its Symbolism*, 166–167. Cf. Idel, "According to some Midrashic and Talmudic statements, the world was created by the combination of the letters, apparently the letters of the divine name. This operation was repeated by Bezalel when he created the Tabernacle" (Idel, *Golem*, English edition, 31).

29. Genesis Rabbah (Theodor-Albeck) 1:10; y. Ḥagiga 77c (785).

30. *Letters of R. Akiva*, version A, 14–16.

31. *Letters of R. Akiva*, version B, 27–38.

32. "B. (ב) every glorious thing was magnified in the world, both the opening and closing of it—of what had passed and of what was yet to come. In the beginning, it closed and it opened. It closed what was passed, and it opened what was yet to come" (John Macdonald, ed. and trans., *Memar Marqah: The Teaching of Marqah* [Berlin: Töpelmann,

1963], 2:134, with corrections of mine). Cf. Zeev Ben-Ḥayyim, ed. and trans., *Tībåt Mårqe: A Collection of Samaritan Midrashim* (Jerusalem: Israel Academy of Sciences and Humanities, 1988), 231–233 (173b–174b), hereafter *Memar Marqah*. On this source, see below, pp. 56–58.

33. Ephraim E. Urbach, "Tanḥuma-Yelamdenu Fragments," *Kovetz al-Yad* 6 (1966): 10 [Hebrew].

34. *Letters of R. Akiva*, version A, 16.

35. Urbach, "Tanḥuma," 20. For more on the comparison between this midrash and *Sefer Yeṣirah*, see Scholem, *Kabbalah*, 27. Among the many references to the Torah as the source for the twenty-two letters, see, e.g., b. Sanhedrin 102b; Lamentations Rabbah: Salomon Buber, ed., *Midrasch Echa Rabbati* (Vilna: Wittwe & Gebrüder Romm, 1899), introduction, p. 24.

36. See below, pp. 50–52.

37. On the editing of the Hekhalot literature, see, e.g., Peter Schäfer, "Tradition and Redaction in Hekhalot Literature," *Journal for the Study of Judaism* 14 (1983): 172–181; Klaus Herrmann, "Rewritten Mystical Texts: The Transmission of the Hekhalot Literature in the Middle Ages," *Bulletin of the John Rylands University Library in Manchester* 75 (1993): 97–116; Anneleis Kuyt, "Traces of a Mutual Influence of the *Ḥaside Ashkenaz* and the Hekhalot Literature," in *From Narbonne to Regensburg: Studies in Medieval Hebrew Texts*, edited by N. A. van Uchelen and Irene E. Zwiep (Amsterdam: Juda Palache, 1993), 62–86; Moshe Idel, *Ben: Sonship and Jewish Mysticism* (London: Continuum, 2007), 242–243.

38. Much has been written over the years about the place/s and period/s in which the Hekhalot material was written. For surveys of scholarly attitudes on this subject, see David J. Halperin, *The Faces of the Chariot: Early Jewish Responses to Ezekiel's Vision* (Tübingen: Mohr Siebeck, 1988), 359–363; Michael D. Swartz, *Scholastic Magic, Ritual and Revelation in Early Jewish Mysticism* (Princeton, N.J.: Princeton University Press, 1966), 9–13; Swartz, *Mystical Prayer in Ancient Judaism: An Analysis of Ma'aseh Merkavah* (Tübingen: Mohr Siebeck, 1992), 216–220; Swartz, "Piyut and Heikhalot: Recent Research and Its Implications for the History of Ancient Jewish Liturgy and Mysticism," in *The Experience of Jewish Liturgy: Studies Dedicated to Menahem Schmelzer*, edited by Debra Reed Blank (Leiden: Brill, 2011), 263–282; Ra'anan Boustan, "Rabbinazation and the Making of Early Jewish Mysticism," *Jewish Quarterly Review* 101 (2011): 482–501; Rebecca M. Lesses, *Ritual Practices to Gain Power: Angels, Incantations and Revelation in Early Jewish Mysticism* (Harrisburg, Pa.: Trinity Press International, 1998), 24–55; James R. Davila, *Descenders to the Chariot: The People Behind the Hekhalot Literature* (Leiden: Brill, 2001), 6–24.

39. This is an example of combinations of letters or *nomina barbara* that are prevalent in the Hekhalot literature; these combinations signify names of God or other celestial entities.

40. *Synopsis of the Hekhalot Literature*, §595–596 (O1534).

41. See above, p. 35.

42. *Synopsis of the Hekhalot Literature*, §637 (O1531).

43. Peter Schäfer, ed., *Geniza-Fragmente zur Hekhalot-Literatur: Texts and Studies in Ancient Judaism* (Tübingen: J. C. B. Mohr, 1984), 175: 21-1b (T.–S. K21.95a). For a new reconstruction of this section from the Geniza, see Gideon Bohak, "The Hidden Hekhalot: Toward Reconstructing an Unknown Hekhalot Composition from the Cairo Geniza," *Tarbiz* 82 (2014): 407–446; the lines above are at p. 419:
א[חד] הוא העולם אחד הם ישראל אחד [ה]וא העולם מה[ ]|| שבארץ אחד הוא מי שיברא את העולם אלו
ישראל[בין?]|| האומות. אחד הוא מי שיברא כנגד אות אחת ש[בשמו | קודם שברא העולם כנגד אות
אחת שבשמ[ו . . .

44. On *Seder Rabbah de Bereishit*, see Séd, "Cosmologie Juive"; *Synopsis of the Hekhalot Literature*, iv; Weiss, *Letters*, 94n29.

45. *Synopsis of the Hekhalot Literature*, §832 (M22).

46. Ibid., §78 (V288).

47. The seventeenth- or eighteenth-century Ms. Oxford 556.

48. On the holiness of the Hebrew language versus the holiness of the language of the angels, see John C. Poirier, *The Tongues of Angels: The Concept of Angelic Languages in Classical Jewish and Christian Texts* (Tübingen: Mohr Siebeck, 2010).

49. *Synopsis of the Hekhalot Literature*, §637 (O1531). On the language of purity in the Hekhalot literature, see Ithamar Gruenwald, "Writing, Inscription, and the Ineffable Name: Magic, Spirituality, and Mysticism," in *Massu'ot: Studies in Kabbalistic Literature and Jewish Philosophy in Memory of Prof. Ephraim Gottlieb*, edited by Michal Oron and Amos Goldreich (Jerusalem: Mosad Bialik, 1994), 86 [Hebrew]; Lesses, *Ritual Practices*, 213–215; Poirier, *Tongues of Angels*, 97. On the language of the angels and language of purity, see Poirier, *Tongues of Angels*, 47–109.

50. *Synopsis of the Hekhalot Literature*, §364 (O1534).

51. That the letters in the sequence number twenty-two is according to Ms. Oxford 1531. In the other manuscripts, and in a similar paragraph from the Cairo Geniza (no. 18 in Schäfer's ed.), the count of letters is close to but not precisely twenty-two. Nevertheless, the change in the number of letters is apparently due to scribal errors; it seems likely that in the early versions of this paragraph, the number of the letters was twenty-two.

52. *Synopsis of the Hekhalot Literature*, §364 (O1534).

53. For an interesting instance of the well-known name of forty-two letters that was written by the letters of the ineffable name, see Lawrence Schiffman, "A Forty-Two-Letter Divine Name in the Aramaic Magic Bowls," *Bulletin of the Institute of Jewish Studies* 1 (1973): 97–102.

54. *Nag Hammadi*, 210; cf. Birger A. Pearson, *Gnosticism and Christianity in Roman and Coptic Egypt* (New York: T&T Clark International, 2004), 233.

55. Little has been written on the relationship between *Memar Marqah* and rabbinic midrashim, despite the fact that this kind of comparison can be very fruitful; see, e.g., Fossum, *Name of God*; Séd, "Memar Samaritain"; Mathias Delcor, "La Légende de la mort de Moïse dans le 'Memar Marqah' Comparée à Quelques Traditions Juives," in *New Samaritans Studies: Essays in Honour of G. D. Sixdenier*, edited by Alan D. Crown and Lucy Davey (Sydney: Mandelbaum, 1995), 25–45; Weiss, "Perception."

56. On the historical context of Marqah, see *Memar Marqah*, 14–16; *Memar Marqah—English*,, 2:xvii.

57. *Memar Marqah*, 15ff.

58. See, e.g., ibid., 2:108.

59. Ibid., 4–25.

60. *Memar Marqah -English*, 158. Cf. *Memar Marqah*, 265; 205b–206a. See also the concluding remarks in Fossum, *Name of God*, 87.

61. *Memar Marqah -English*, 139–140. Cf. *Memar Marqah*, 243; 181a–181b. For more on the creation of the world from the letter *he*, see *Memar Marqah*, 276; 207a; ibid., 379; 310a.

62. Accounts of the sealing of the dimensions of the universe with the name of God appear in *Letters of R. Akiva*, version A, 19–20, and in chap. 136 of the *Pistis Sophia* (Carl Schmidt, ed., *Pistis Sophia*, Coptic Gnostic Library [Leiden: Brill, 1978], 353). On the last, see below, p. 53. On *Pistis Sophia*'s resemblance to this section in *Sefer Yeṣirah*, see Fossum, *Name of God*, 248; Hayman, "*Sefer Yesira* and the Hekhalot," 75; Hayman, "Was God a Magician?," 230.

63. *Sefer Yeṣirah*, §15, Ms. Vat. 299.

64. See Hayman's edition of *Sefer Yeṣirah*, 90.

65. See Weiss, *Letters*, 147–168.

66. See Gruenwald, "Some Critical Notes," 511.

67. Ibid., 479. See also Scholem, *Kabbalah and Its Symbolism*, 168–169; Scholem, *Origins of Kabbalah*, 33.

68. On the tetragrammaton and its perceptions, see, e.g., Sean M. McDonough, *YHWH at Patmos: Rev 1:4 in Its Hellenistic and Early Jewish Setting* (Tübingen: Mohr Siebeck, 1999); Weiss, *Letters*, 147–167; and, most recently, in the extensive and compre-

hensive work of Robert Wilkinson, *Tetragrammaton: Western Christians and the Hebrew Name of God: From the Beginnings to the Seventeenth Century* (Leiden: Brill, 2015).

69. For a survey of the bibliography on the pronunciation of the tetragrammaton, see Weiss, *Letters*, 148n3.

70. See, e.g., George Howard, "The Tetragram and the New Testament," *Journal of Biblical Literature* 96 (1977): 63–83; Weiss, *Letters*, 149–154; Wilkinson, *Tetragrammaton*, 45ff.

71. *Pistis Sophia*, chap. 136, p. 353. And see above, pp. 50–51.

CHAPTER 3

1. *Sefer Yeṣirah*, §19, Ms. Vat. 299.

2. *Memar Marqah—English*, 2:134, with a few corrections of mine. Cf. *Memar Marqah*, 231–233 (173b–174b).

3. On the book and its author, see *The Mysteries of the Greek Letters*, 4–8*; The Mysteries of the Greek Letters-Coptic*, 5–13; Galtier, "Sur les Mystères des Lettres Grecques"; Amélineau, "Traités Gnostiques"; Dornseiff, *Alphabet in Mystik und Magie*, 73; Drucker, *Alphabetic Labyrinth*, 89–91 ;Stroumsa, "Zoroastrian Origin," 19; Samir, "Greek Letters"; Liebes, *Ars Poetica*, 230; Wolfson, *Abulafia*, 349n80; Frankfurter, "Magic of Writing," 211.

4. Jubilees 2:2–15. On the numbers twenty-two and thirty-two in *Sefer Yeṣirah*, the Book of Jubilees, and *Memar Marqah*, see Séd, "Memar Samaritain"; Weiss, "Perception." A late, interesting adaptation of the second chapter of the Book of Jubilees is in Adolf Jellinek, ed., "Midrash Tadshé" in *Beit haMidrash* (Jerusalem: Wahrmann, 1938), sec. 3, 169. For more on this matter, see Guy Darshan, "Twenty-Four or Twenty-Two Books of the Bible and the Homeric Corpus," *Tarbiz* 77 (2007): 5–22 [Hebrew].

5. *The Mysteries of the Greek Letters*, §3, 108–110. This and the following sources from *The Mysteries of the Greek Letters* were translated into English from Greek by my dear friend Yakir Paz, and I would like to thank him for all his help.

6. There is a lengthy discussion of a different subgroup of fourteen letters in *The Mysteries of the Greek Letters*, §14, 130–132.

7. Ibid., §4, 112.

8. Ibid., §5, 114.

9. Ibid., §17, 142.

10. On this myth and its roots, see Louis Ginzberg, *Of Halakhah and Aggadah: Research and Essays* (Tel Aviv: Dvir, 1960), 205–219 [Hebrew].

11. There are many sources for the legend about Cadmus and the alphabet. A classical source is Herodotus, who wrote: "These Phoenicians who came with Cadmus [and of whom the Gephyraeans were a part] brought with them to Hellas, among many other kinds of learning, the alphabet, which had been unknown before this, I think, to the Greeks. As time went on, the sound and the form of the letters were changed"; Alfred D. Godley, trans., *Herodotus: The Histories*, Loeb Classical Library 117 (Cambridge, Mass.: Heinemann, 1920), 5:58. For more on Cadmus and the alphabet, see, e.g., Dornseiff, *Alphabet in Mystik und Magie*, 5–10; Frankfurter, "Magic of Writing," 195–196; David Diringer, *The Alphabet: A Key to the History of Mankind* (London: Hutchinson's Scientific and Technical Publications, 1948), 450–453.

12. *The Mysteries of the Greek Letters* §19, 148.

13. Ibid., §17, 140.

14. Ibid., §32, 170.

15. Eusebius of Caesarea, *Preparation for the Gospel*, translated by Edwin H. Gifford (Eugene, Ore.: Wipf and Stock, 2002), 506–507.

16. Ibid., §X4.

17. Ibid., §X5.

18. Milka Rubin, "The Language of Creation or the Primordial Language: A Case of Cultural Polemics in Antiquity," *Journal of Jewish Studies* 49 (1998): 321–328; James Kugel, *Traditions of the Bible: A Guide to the Bible as It Was at the Start of the Common Era*, rev. ed. (Cambridge Mass.: Harvard University Press, 1998), 236. On Syriac as the first language, see Ri Su-Min, *Le Caverne des trésors: Les deux recensions Syriaques* (Louvain: E. Peeters, 1987), 70–72; Jacques-M. Vosté, ed., and Ceslas Van den Eynde, trans., *Commentaire d'Iso'dad de Merv sur l'Ancien Testament* (Louvain: Secr. du Corpus, 1955), 146–148; Kathleen E. McVey, trans., *Ephrem the Syrian: Hymns* (New York: Paulist Press, 1989), 126–127.

19. On Syriac treatment of the letters of the alphabet, see Ketterer, "*The Alphabet of Rabbi Aqiba*," 253–257; Paz and Weiss, "From Encoding to Decoding," 45–65.

20. On the authenticity of the hymn's attribution to Ephrem, see Edmund Beck, ed. and trans., *Des Heiligen Ephraem des Syrers Hymnen de Nativitate* (Louvain: Secr. du Corpus, 1959), 29.

21. Elliot R. Wolfson, *Along the Path: Studies in Kabbalistic Myth, Symbolism, and Hermeneutics* (Albany, N.Y.: SUNY, 1995), 65n17.

22. Ketterer, "*The Alphabet of Rabbi Aqiba*," 256n194.

23. Nicolas Séd, "Notes sur l'homélie no. 34 de Narsaï," *L'Orient Syrien* 10 (1965): 511–524. On this *mêmrâ*, see also Robin Anne Darling, "Narsai of Nisibis: On the Expression, 'In the Beginning' and Concerning the Existence of God," in *Biblical*

Interpretation, edited by Joseph Wilson Trigg (Wilmington, Del.: Michael Glazier, 1988), 203–220.

24. Ephrem, *Hymnen de Nativitate*, 139. More sources describing the six half-dimensions are mentioned by Liebes, *Ars Poetica*, 212.

25. *Sefer Yeṣirah*, §7, Ms. Vat. 299.

26. Following Shlomo Pines and Guy Stroumsa, Yehuda Liebes demonstrates the structural resemblance between different sources describing the six half-dimensions, with God (or *Shabbat*) at their center (Liebes, *Ars Poetica*, 212).

27. Trans. according to Darling, "Narsai of Nisibis," 205, with an alteration of mine.

28. *Sefer Yeṣirah*, §20, Ms. Vat. 299.

29. Ibid., §40, Ms. Vat. 299.

30. Becker, *Fear of God*, 131.

31. Ibid., 5–6.

32. Adam H. Becker, ed. and trans., *Sources for the Study of the School of Nisibis* (Liverpool: Liverpool University Press, 2008), 118–119. Cf. Addaï Scher, trans., *Cause de la Fondation des Écoles* (Turnhout: Éditions Brepols, 1981), 349/1–13.

33. On the unique terminology of *Sefer Yeṣirah*, see Allony, "Zunz, Krauss, and Scholem," 65.

34. *Sefer Yeṣirah*, §19, Ms. Vat. 299.

35. On the number thirty-two in other sources of late antiquity and the early Middle Ages, see Séd, "Memar Samaritain," 159–184.

36. On the Syriac translation of Dionysius Thrax, see Adelbertus Merx, *Historia artis grammaticae apud Syros* (Leipzig: Brockhaus, 1889), Syriac sec., pp. 49ff. English trans.: Thomas Davidson, trans., *The Grammar of Dionysios Thrax* (St. Louis, 1874). On the possibility that an early scholion of Dionysius Thrax influenced *Sefer Yeṣirah*, see Liebes, "The Seven Double Letters."

37. *Dionysios Thrax*, §7, 6.

38. Pines, "Points of Similarity," 113. Pines based his argument on Merx, *Historia: Artis Grammaticae*, 30–31. Cf. Refael Talmon, "Jacob of Edessa the Grammarian," in *Jacob of Edessa and the Syriac Culture of His Day*, edited by Bas ter Haar Romeny (Leiden: Brill, 2008), 168–169.

39. *Sefer Yeṣirah*, §19, Ms. Vat. 299.

40. See Judah B. Segal, "Qussaya and Rukkaka: A Historical Introduction," *Journal of Semitic Studies* 34 (1989): 83–91.

41. Moshe Zvi Segal, *Basics of Hebrew Phonetics* (Jerusalem: Ha-sefer, 1928), 99–100 [Hebrew]; Paul E. Kahle, *The Cairo Geniza*, 2nd ed. (Oxford: Blackwell, 1959), 182–184;

Wilhelm Bacher, *Die Anfänge der hebräische Grammatik* (Leipzig: Brockhaus, 1985), 22; Morag, "Sarah-Sarai," 140; Bar-Ilan, *Astrology and Other Sciences*, 116–117n171.

42. Bacher, *Anfänge der hebräische Grammatik*; cf. Kahle, *Cairo Geniza*, 184.

43. J. Segal, "Qussaya and Rukkaka," 484n6.

44. Talmon, "Jacob of Edessa," 173.

45. J. Segal, "Qussaya and Rukkaka," 484.

46. Morag, "Sarah-Sarai," 140.

47. Bar-Ilan, *Astrology and Other Sciences*, 116–117n17. Cf. Liebes, "The Seven Double Letters," 243n22 and idem, "Response," 144.

48. πνεῦμα δασύ, rough breathing.

49. πνεῦμα ψιλόν, smooth breathing.

50. On whether the letters *BGD KFT* had actually pronounced allophones, see Kahle, *Cairo Geniza*, 179–184; Yechezkel E. Kutscher, "Studies in North-Western Semantics," *Journal of Semitic Studies* 10 (1965): 25–34; Naftali H. Tur-Sinai, *The Language and the Book*, 3 vols. (Jerusalem: Mosad Bialik, 1954), 1:164–174.

51. On this matter, see Kahle, *Cairo Geniza*, 182–184.

52. *Sefer Yeṣirah*, §19, Ms. Parma 2784.14.

53. See, e.g., Epstein, *Jewish Antiquities*, 184.

54. Pines, "Points of Similarity," 113.

55. On the Jewish communities in north Mesopotamia, see Judah B. Segal, "The Jews of North Mesopotamia Before the Rise of Islam," in *Studies in the Bible Presented to Professor M. H. Segal by His Colleagues and Students*, edited by Joshua M. Grintz and Jacob Liver (Jerusalem: Kiryat Sefer, 1964), *32–*63. On the ninth-century Jewish thinker who created in Nisibis under the influence of Syriac Christianity, see Sarah Stroumsa, *Dāwūd al-Muqammaṣ' Twenty Chapters: A Parallel Judeo-Arabic Edition Transliterated into Arabic Characters, with a Parallel English Translation, Notes, and Introduction* (Provo, Utah: Brigham Young University Press, 2017), xv–xvi.

56. On the Hekhalot literature and its scholarship, see Chap. 2, nn. 38–39.

57. On the differences between *Sefer Yeṣirah* and the Hekhalot literature, see Hayman, "*Sefer Yesira* and the Hekhalot."

58. In the words of Peter Hayman: "There is little on the surface which is Jewish in our 'earliest recoverable text' of SY" (*Sefer Yetsirah* [Hayman], 34). Cf. Gruenwald, "Some Critical Notes," 477; Wasserstrom, "*Sefer Yesira* and Early Islam," 19; Pines, "Points of Similarity," 113; Bar-Ilan, *Astrology and Other Sciences*, 217–218.

59. Pines suggested that they were Jewish-Christian. I did not find any justification for this suggestion (Pines, "Points of Similarity," 113). For more on this matter, see Meroz, "Interreligious Polemic."

60. An interesting treatise that was written in a fluent Hebrew and could possibly have been composed at the same period is *The Hebrew Book of Medications* (*Sefer Refout*), which was attributed to Asaf. This is a layered treatise that is considered to be a great literary mystery in its own right and was recently compared to *Sefer Yeṣirah* by Meir Bar-Ilan (Bar-Ilan, *Astrology and Other Sciences*, 225–233). Bar-Ilan's study, which points to a few similarities between these two compositions, is interesting but unequivocal and problematic from a philological point of view. As is well known, *Sefer Asaf* is a layered composition, and the similarities that Bar-Ilan found between the book and *Sefer Yeṣirah* pertain, in all probability, to a later layer of the book. It should be recalled that one of the earliest Jewish sages, if not the earliest one, who used *Sefer Asaf* was the tenth-century Shabbetai Donnolo, the Italian physician who was also one of the three early commentators of *Sefer Yeṣirah*. It does not seem to be a coincidence that the similarities that Bar-Ilan found between the compositions are related to the subjects that were of interest to Donnolo: the human organs and the zodiacs. It would be reasonable to assume that the sections from *Sefer Asaf* that Bar-Ilan compares to *Sefer Yeṣirah* are just quotations of *Sefer Yeṣirah* in *Sefer Asaf* that were inserted into it by Shabbetai Donnolo or one of his disciples. Another extremely problematic matter in Bar-Ilan's argument relates to the origin of these two compositions. Bar-Ilan asserts that *Sefer Asaf* is of Palestinian origin and therefore concludes that *Sefer Yeṣirah* is a Palestinian composition as well. Nevertheless, most of *Sefer Asaf*'s scholars have not connected it to Palestine. It is not the best method to learn about an enigmatic treatise such as *Sefer Yeṣirah* by comparing it in a very preliminary way with another and no less enigmatic composition such as *Sefer Asaf*. For a scholarly survey on the philological problems of *Sefer Asaf*, its early manuscripts, and the place of Shabbetai Donnolo in its history of acceptance, see, e.g., Aviv Melzer, "Asaph the Physician—the Man and His Book: A Historical Philological Study of the Medical Treatise *The Book of Drugs*" (Ph.D. diss., University of Wisconsin Madison, 1972), 34–67; Elinor Lieber, "An Ongoing Mystery: The So-Called Book of Medicines Attributed to Asaf the Sage," *Bulletin of Judaeo-Greek Studies* 8 (1991): 18–25; *Shabbatai Donnolo's Sefer Ḥakhmoni: Introduction, Critical Text, and Annotated English Translation*, edited by Piergabriele Mancuso (Leiden: Brill, 2010), 8.

61. Ezra Fleischer, "On the Antiquity of *Sefer Yeṣirah*: The Qilirian Testimony Revisited," *Tarbiz* 71 (2002): 424 [Hebrew]. The same argument has been used by Allony. See Allony, "Zunz, Krauss, and Scholem," 42–43.

62. See n. 58 above.

CHAPTER 4

1. Solomon Joachim Halberstam, ed., *Commentar zum Sepher Jezira von R. Jehuda b. Barsilai* (Berlin: Meqize nirdamim, 1885), 257 [Hebrew], hereafter Yehudah Barzillai.

2. Nehemya Allony, "Saadya's Works," in *Studies in Medieval Philology and Literature: Collected Papers*, edited by Yosef Tobi et al. (Jerusalem: Mekhon Ben Zevi, 1986), 1:347 [Hebrew].

3. *Saadya* (Kafiḥ), 99.

4. *Shabbatai Donnolo's Sefer Ḥakhmoni* (ed. Mancuso), 352; Shabbetai Donnolo's commentary, though based on the long version of *Sefer Yeṣirah*, is not identical to Ms. Vat. 299. On Donnolo's commentary, see Wolfson, "Shabbetai Donnolo"; *Sefer Yeṣirah* (Hayman), 31.

5. Words and letters that were probably omitted, being taken as implied, appear in square brackets; others that should be omitted are in parentheses. A similar, though not identical, suggestion for this version of the paragraph was made by Allony ("Saadya's Works," 347).

6. *Sefer Yeṣirah*, §56, Ms. TS K21/56, with a few changes of mine.

7. For a similar interpretation of holy names, see *Letters of R. Akiva*, version A, 33.

8. *Sefer Yeṣirah*, §1.

9. *Sefer Yeṣirah* (Hayman), 171; cf. Hayman, "*Sefer Yesira* and the Hekhalot," 79–80.

10. See Haim S. Horovitz and Israel A. Rabin, eds., *Mekhilta d'Rabbi Ismael* (Jerusalem: Bamberger & Wahrmann, 1960), Masekhta d'Shira 1, 120.

11. See, e.g., Genesis Rabbah (Theodor-Albeck), vol. 1, 5.8; ibid., vol. 1, 47.3, 460; Tanḥuma Bereishit (Buber), Lekh lekha 25, 80; Chaim M. Horovitz, ed., *Pirkei d'Rabbi Eliezer* (Jerusalem: Makor, 1972), chap. 3.

12. See *Avoth de-Rabbi Nathan: Solomon Schechter Edition with References to Parallels in the Two Versions and to the Addenda in the Schechter Edition*, Prolegomenon by Menahem Kister (New York: Jewish Theological Seminary Press, 1997) [Hebrew], version A, chap. 34, p. 52a; version B, chap. 43, p. 61a.

13. Hyman G. Enelow, ed., *The Mishnah of Rabbi Eliezer, or, the Midrash of Thirty-Two Hermeneutic Rules* (New York: Bloch, 1931), 11.11, 209.

14. See b. Yevamot 21a; b. Bava Batra 88b.

15. Yehudah Barzillai (Halberstam), 257.

16. Tzahi Weiss, "'God of Israel—a Prince Before God': On the Meanings and the Origins of a Jewish Tradition from the Early Middle Ages," *Jewish Studies* 52 (2017): 129–142 [Hebrew].

17. On this motif in Jewish sources of late antiquity and its development in later treatises, see Wolfson, *Along the Path*, 4–9; Jonathan Z. Smith, *Map Is Not Territory:*

Studies in the History of Religions (Leiden: Brill, 1978), 24–66; Idel, *Ben: Sonship*, 25–26; Fossum, *Name of God*, 188–189, 313–317; Yair Lorberbaum, *The Image of God: Halakhah and Aggadah* (Jerusalem: Schocken, 2004), 324–327 [Hebrew]; Ronnie Goldstein, "A New Look at Deuteronomy 32:8–9 and 43 in the Light of Akkadian Sources," *Tarbiz* 79 (2010): 5–22 [Hebrew]; Shraga Bar-On and Yakir Paz, "The Lord's Allotment Is His People: The Myth of the Election of Israel by Casting of Lots and the Gnostic-Christian-Pagan-Jewish Polemic," *Tarbiz* 79 (2010): 23–62 [Hebrew].

18. Gen. 33:20.

19. b. Megilah 18a, trans. Wolfson, *Along the Path*, 6.

20. Karl E. Grözinger, "The Names of God and the Celestial Powers: Their Function and Meaning in the Hekhalot Literature," *Jerusalem Studies in Jewish Thought* 6 (1987): 54.

21. On seder Rabbah deBereishit, see *Synopsis for the Hekhalot Literature*, §§428–467, 518–540, 714–727, 743–820, 832–853, and also p. vii of the introduction to the Synopsis. A different edition was edited by Séd, "Cosmologie Juive"; Séd's introduction to this treatise was published a year earlier.

22. *Synopsis for the Hekhalot Literature* §832, 280, according to Ms. Oxford 1531. Although R. Shabbetai Donnolo understood that the sentence: "[Yh] two names Yhwh four names" is associated with rabbinic midrashim about the creation of the world from the letters *yod* and *he*, he was not familiar with the terminology of the Hekhalot literature, where letters are names and names are letters. In explaining this sentence, he pointed to different combinations of letters in the ineffable name, which construct names. According to Donnolo, the meaning of the words "[Yh] two names" is that one can divide the tetragrammaton into two names—"Yh" (יה) and "Wh" (וה)—and the meaning of the words "Yhwh four names" is that there are four possible combinations of the pairs *yod* and *he, and vav and he*; in Donnolo's words: "Trust in the Lord forever and ever, for in Y-h the Lord you have an everlasting Rock [צור עולמים] [Isa. 26:4]. . . . [T]wo worlds and not one: this World and the World to Come. This verse teaches you that with Y-h (יה) the Lord, the everlasting Rock, with the name of Y-h (יה), he formed the two worlds, for there are two names: Y-h (יה) and H-y (הי). With the first name, he formed this world, and with the second name, [he formed] the World to Come. Yhwh (יהוה): Yh (יה), Wh (וה). Four names: Yh(יה), Hy(הי), Wh(וה), Hw(הו)" (*Donnolo*, 352).

23. We have indications of an unknown commentary from a short excerpt quoted once by Yehudah Barzillai (Yehudah Barzillai (Halberstam), 179) and at least three times by Elazar of Worms (Elazar of Worms, *Commentary on Sefer Yeṣirah* [Przemysl: Ḥ. A. Zupniḳ ṿe-H. Ḳnoller, 1883], 3a). See also Gad Freudenthal, "'The Air Blessed Be He,' in *Sefer ha-Maskil*," *Da'at* 32 (1994): 226 [Hebrew]. A careful comparison between the

quotation in Yehudah Barzillai's commentary and those in the writings of Elazar of Worms demonstrates that the latter did not take this paragraph from the Yehudah Barzillai's version but from another source.

24. Georges Vajda, ed., "R. Elḥanan ben Yakar of London's First Commentary of *Sefer Yeṣirah*," *Kobetz al Yad* 6, no. 1 (1966): 156 [Hebrew].

25. For a bibliographical survey of references to Agobard's description, see Reuven Bonfil, "The Cultural and Religious Traditions of French Jewry in the Ninth Century," in *Studies in Jewish Mysticism Presented to Isaiah Tishby on His Seventy-Fifth Birthday*, edited by Joseph Dan and Joseph Hacker, *Jerusalem Studies in Jewish Thought* 3, nos. 1–2 (1986): 328n2 [Hebrew]. Important discussions on Agobard and the Jews can also be found in Merchavia, *Church Versus Talmudic*, 71–84; Jeremy Cohen, *Living Letters of the Law: Ideas of the Jew in Medieval Christianity* (Los Angeles: University of California Press, 1999), 123–146; Anna Beht Langenwalter, "Agobard of Lyon: An Exploration of Carolingian Jewish-Christian Relations" (Ph.D. diss., University of Toronto, 2001).

26. Translation from Cohen, *Living Letters*, 129.

27. In her dissertation on *Letters of R. Akiva*, versions A and B (Ketterer "*The Alphabet of Rabbi Aqiba*," 86), Eliane Ketterer emphasizes that Agobard's claims refer to *Letters of R. Akiva*, version B. Her assertion seems implausible; she herself mentions the great differences between *Letters of R. Akiva*, version B, and Agobard's description (ibid., 95)—most important, that in *Letters of R. Akiva*, version B, the twenty-two Hebrew letters do not have any role in the heavenly realm or in the created world.

28. *Sefer Yeṣirah*, §41, Ms. Vat. 299.

29. On the origins of the belief in the evil thoughts of God, see Moshe Idel, "The Evil Thought of the Deity," *Tarbiz* 49 (1980): 356–364 [Hebrew].

30. Ben-Shammai, "Saadya's Goal," 9. We hear a similar resonance with nonphilosophical commentaries on *Sefer Yeṣirah* in the introduction to Dunash Ibn Tamim's commentary: "Nous avons vu que la plupart de nos coreligionnaires s'étaient trompés à son sujet et s'étaient montrés incapables d'en comprendre les mystères par suite de la profondeur de ses allégories . . . que ne saurait résoudre, interpréter et comprendre que celui qui est verse dans les philosophie" (Georges Vajda, ed., *Le Commentaire sur le "Livre de la Création" de Dūnaš ben Tāmīm de Kairouan (Xe siècle)*, rev. ed., edited by Paul B. Fenton [Paris: Peeters, 2002], 38). On another critical approach of the tenth century to Saadya's commentary to *Sefer Yeṣirah*, see Moshe Zucker, ed. and trans., *A Critique Against the Writings of R. Saadya Gaon, by R. Mubashshir Halevi* (New York: P. Feldheim, 1955), 15–16, 68–70 [Hebrew]. Cf. Segol, *Word and Image*, 26–27.

CHAPTER 5

1. See Dan, "Three Phases." Cf. recent scholarship: Langermann, "Hebrew Scientific Literature"; Wasserstrom, "Further Thoughts"; Fleischer, "Antiquity of *Sefer Yeṣirah*," 424; *Donnolo*, 46n21.

2. Yehuda Liebes, "Rabbi Solomon Ibn Gabirol's Use of the *Sefer Yeṣirah* and a Commentary on the Poem 'I Love Thee,'" *Jerusalem Studies in Jewish Thought* 6 (1987): 73–123 [Hebrew]. On Rabbi Solomon Ibn Gabirol's approach to *Sefer Yeṣirah*, see also Israel Levin, *Mystical Trends in the Poetry of Solomon Ibn Gabirol* (Lod: Habermann Institute for Literary Research, 1986), 65–91 [Hebrew]; Jacques E. Schlanger, "Sur le rôle du "tout" dans la Création selon Ibn Gabirol," *Revue des Études Juives* 124 (1965): 125–135.

3. Wolfson, "Shabbetai Donnolo"; Segol, *Word and Image*, 33–34. On letter combinations in Donnolo's interpretation of *Sefer Yeṣirah*, see Moshe Idel, *Language, Torah, and Hermeneutics in Abraham Abulafia* (Jerusalem: Schocken, 1994), 28 [Hebrew].

4. Herrmann, "Feuer aus Wasser."

5. Daniel Abrams, "A History of the Unique Cherub: A Review Essay of Joseph Dan, *The Unique Cherub: A School of Mystics and Esoterics in Medieval Germany*," *Jewish Quarterly Review* 90, nos. 3–4 (2000): 400.

6. Herrmann, "An Unknown Commentary on the *Book of Creation*."

7. Allony, "Saadya's Works," 347.

8. Ithamar Gruenwald, "A Preliminary Critical Edition of *Sefer Yeṣirah*," *Israel Oriental Studies* 1 (1971): 135 [Hebrew]; *Sefer Yeṣira* (Hayman), 12.

9. Benjamin Richler, Malachi beit-Arié, and Nurit Pasternak, *Hebrew Manuscripts in the Vatican Library: Catalog* (Vatican: Biblioteca Apostolica Vaticana, 2008), 238–239.

10. This source, with minor alterations, can be found in Ms. BN Héb. 763 fol. 29r–29v copied in 1284; Ms. Parma 2784 (De Rossi 1390), fol. 92v–93r copied in 1286; and in Ms. BL 752 fol. 26r–26v from the fourteenth century. A short version of this midrash can be found in Pesikta Ḥadata: Adolph Jellinek, ed., *Bet haMidrash*, 3rd ed. (Jerusalem: Wahrmann 1967), 6:36–37.

11. See Yehuda Liebes, *Elisha's Sin*, 2nd ed. (Jerusalem: Academon, 1990), 131–137 [Hebrew].

12. Ms. Vat. ebr. 299/4, Italian square script, catalog no. in the Institute of Microfilmed Hebrew Manuscripts: 8701. For the Hebrew version, see Appendix 3.

13. The Hebrew verb ישא also means "to take."

14. On this motif in the early *piyyut*, see Joseph Yahalom, "*Shi'ur Qomah* in a Misidentified Qalirian Poem for Pentecost," *Kabbalah: Journal for the Study of Jewish Mystical*

Texts 32 (2014): 93–133. On the image of the Torah as female, see, e.g., Elliot R. Wolfson, "Female Imaging of the Torah: From Literary Metaphor to Religious Symbol," in *From Ancient Israel to Modern Judaism—Intellect in Quest of Understanding: Essays in Honor of Marvin Fox*, edited by Jacob Neusner, Ernest S. Frerichs, and Nahum M. Sarna (Atlanta: Scholars Press, 1989), 2:271–307.

15. The Hebrew word בדים means "liars" and was understood in this way by most medieval Jewish commentators. It can also be understood as "single": בדד, which can also be written as בד, as in the biblical phrase בד בבד (Exod. 30:34). It seems that in the talmudic midrash attributed to R. Yosi Ben R. Ḥanina, it was read this way.

16. Jer. 50:36.

17. b. Berakhot 63b; b. Ta'anit 7a; b. Makot 10a.

18. See Scholem, *Kabbalah and Its Symbolism*, 175; Liebes, *Elisha's Sin*, 131–137; Moshe Idel, *Golem: Magical and Mystical Jewish Traditions of the Artificial Anthropoid*, translated by Azan Meir-Levi (Jerusalem: Schocken, 1996), 271–275 [Hebrew], hereafter *Golem*, Hebrew edition; Idel, "Golems and God: Mimesis and Confrontation," in *Mythen der Kreativität: Das Schöpferische zwischen Innovation und Hybris*, edited by Oliver Krüger et al. (Frankfurt am Main: Lembeck, 2003), 235–237; Dan, *Mysticism and Esotericism*, 4:373.

19. Scholem, *Kabbalah and Its Symbolism*, 175–182; Idel, *Golem*, Hebrew edition, 271–275; Idel, "Golems and God," 235–243.

20. Scholem discusses this source and notes that Barzillai's version is the earliest testimony to its existence (Scholem, *Kabbalah and Its Symbolism*, 175). Liebes also quotes the midrash from Barzillai's version, applying corrections and adding the first part from Ms. Vat. 299 and Ms. BL 752, without referring to the date of these manuscripts (Liebes, *Elisha's Sin*, 131–137). The Hebrew version of Idel's book about the Golem has a special appendix on this midrash. Idel bases his edition on two manuscripts from the thirteenth century and not on Ms. Vat. 299, which he mistakenly dates to the fourteenth century. Following Scholem and Liebes, Idel argues that the date of the midrash is not later than the twelfth century, based on its citation in Barzillai's commentary to *Yeṣirah* (Idel, *Golem*, Hebrew edition, 271–275; cf. his English article "Golems and God," 235–237).

21. Now Ms. Heb. 24°6990, at the University and National Library in Jerusalem.

22. Dan, *Jewish Mysticism and Esotericism*, 4:373.

23. Now Ms. Heb. 24°6990, at the University and National Library in Jerusalem.

24. In the introduction to his edition of tales from the Middle Ages about Ben Sira, Eli Yassif argues, based on studies by Scholem and Dan, that our midrash about *Sefer Yeṣirah* and Ben Sira was written long after the other medieval tales of Ben Sira, which were probably written around the end of the ninth century (Yassif, *Tales of Ben*

Sira, 33). Nevertheless, Yassif's claim should also be reexamined, along with the arguments of Scholem, Dan, and others regarding the dating of this midrash. On Ben Sira and Jeremiah in stories from the Middle Ages, see Yassif, *Tales of Ben Sira*, 32–36. On the relation of Ben Sira to Jeremiah, on the one hand, and to Uziel and Yosef, on the other, as an important criterion in distinguishing between the *Tales of Ben Sira* and *The Alphabet of Ben Sira*, see ibid., 158.

25. Ms. Vat. 299 fol. 71r–73v.

26. In *Gematria*, Sira (סירא) and Abu Aharon (אבו אהרון) can both stand for the number 271.

27. Israel Weinstock, "Discovered Legacy of Mystic Writings Left by abu-Aharon of Baghdad," *Tarbiz* 32 (1963): 157–158 [Hebrew].

28. b. Sanhedrin 65b; cf. 67b.

29. The scribe repeated words in at least three places (lines 16, 19, 30).

30. See Pirkei de Rabbi Eliezer, chap. 3: "R. Eliezer ben Hyrḳanos opened: 'Who can utter the mighty acts of the Lord, or shew forth all his praise?' (Ps. 102:2). Is there any man who can utter the mighty acts of the Holy One, blessed be he, or who can shew forth all his praise? Not even the ministering angels are able to narrate [the Divine praise]. But to investigate a part of his mighty deeds with reference to what he has done, and what he will do in the future, so that his name should be exalted among his creatures, whom he has created from one end of the world to the other, as it is said: 'One generation to another shall laud thy work' (Ps. 145:4). Before the world was created, the Holy one, blessed be he, with his name alone existed, and the thought arose in him to create the world. He began to trace [the foundations of] the world before himself, but it would not stand. They told a parable, To what is the matter like? To a king who wishes to build a palace for himself. If he had not traced in the earth its foundations, its exits, and its entrances, he does not begin to build. Likewise the Holy One, blessed be he, was tracing [the palace of] the world before himself, but it did not remain standing until he created repentance'" (Gerald Friedlander, trans., *Pirḳê de Rabbi Eliezer* [New York: Hermon, 1970], 9–10).

31. On the period in which Pirkei de R. Eliezer was written, see Dina Stein, *Maxims, Magic, Myth: A Folkloristic Perspective on Pirkei deRabbi Eliezer* (Jerusalem: Magnes Press, 2005), 2 [Hebrew]; Rachel Adelman, *The Return of the Repressed: Pirqe de-Rabbi Eliezer and the Pseudepigrapha* (Leiden: Brill, 2009), 3–42.

32. Dan mentions this in many of his works about ancient Jewish mysticism and *Sefer Yeṣirah*, e.g., Dan, *Jewish Mysticism*, 60ff. See also Peter A. Hayman, "Some Observations on *Sefer Yeṣira*: Its Use of Scripture," *Journal of Jewish Studies* 35 (1984): 168–184; Gruenwald, "Some Critical Notes," 477.

33. Genesis Rabbah (Theodor-Albeck) 1:1.

34. In his introduction to his commentary to *Sefer Yeṣirah*, Donnolo writes: "Let us begin the commentary on the beginning of the work of the Creation and on the book of formation of the world (ספר יצירת העולם) that the Holy one—blessed be he—transmitted to our father Abraham—peace be upon him, as it is written: The Lord created me at the beginning of his course [Prov. 8:22] (יהוה קנני ראשית דרכו). . . . I was with him as a confidant, a source of delight every day [Prov. 8:30] (ואהיה אצלו אמון ואהיה שעשועים יום יום)" (Donnolo, 279). The depiction of *Sefer Yeṣirah* as the book of formation of the world (ספר יצירת העולם) as well as Donnolo's use of these verses from Proverbs on which the midrash in Genesis Rabbah based on does not look coincidental; it seems clear that Donnolo based its argument on that midrash.

35. *Saadya* (Kafiḥ), 33, 142. In the introduction to his commentary to *Sefer Yeṣirah*, Dunash Ibn Tamim wrote similarly: "Nous avons lu jadis un livre de provenance rabbanite attributé à Abraham" (*Dūnaš ben Tamim*, 38).

36. On Barzillai's commentary to *Sefer Yeṣirah*, see Joseph Dan, "The Commentary of R. Yehuda ben Barzillai Barceloni to *Sefer Yeṣirah*: Its Character and Trends," in *Ma'asu'ot: Studies in Kabbalistic Literature and Jewish Philosophy in Memory of Prof. Ephraim Gottlieb*, edited by Michal Oron and Amos Goldreich (Jerusalem: Mosad Bialik, 1994), 99–119 [Hebrew]; Elliot R. Wolfson, *Through a Speculum That Shines: Vision and Imagination in Medieval Jewish Mysticism* (Princeton, N.J.: Princeton University Press, 1994), 148–160.

37. Yehudah Barzillai (Halberstam), 100. On this source, see also Dan, "The Commentary of R. Yehuda ben Barzillai Barceloni to *Sefer Yeṣirah*," 116.

38. Based on b. Avodah Zarah 14b.

39. Yehudah Barzillai (Halberstam), 100.

40. Ibid., 187.

41. On the motivations of *Sefer Yeṣirah*'s early commentators, see Jospe, "Philosophical Commentaries," 370–388.

42. See Avraham Shoshana, ed., *The Book of Job with the Commentaries of Rashi, Rabbenu Jacob b. Meir Tam and Disciple of Rashi* (Jerusalem: Makhon Ofek, 1999) [Hebrew], 28:23; ibid., 28:27; b. Berakhot 55a; b. Shabbat 104a; b. Ḥagiga 13a; b. Sanhedrin 65b; ibid. 67b; b. Menaḥot 29b; Salomon Buber, ed., *Siddur Raschi: Ritualwerk R. Salomo ben Isaak Zugeschrieben* (Berlin: Meqize nirdamim, 1911), §178, §514. On Rashi's awareness of Jewish mystical lore and treatises, see Joseph Dan, "Rashi and the Merkavah," in *Rashi, 1040–1990: Hommage à Ephraïm E. Urbach: congrès européen des études juives*, edited by Gabrielle Sed-Rajna (Paris: Éditions du Cerf, 1993), 259–264. Unlike Dan, who argues in a very preliminary way that Rashi was not acquainted with the Merkavah cor-

pus, Kanarfogel has recently demonstrated in a detailed study that Rashi was indeed familiar with some important mystical traditions, including those of the Divine Names, the Merkavah, and *Sefer Yeṣirah*: Ephraim Kanarfogel, "Rashi's Awareness of Jewish Mystical Literature and Traditions," in *Raschi und sein Erbe*, edited by Daniel Krochmalkin et al. (Heidelberg: Heidelberg Universitätsverlag Winter, 2007), 23–34. On Rashi's adherence to lesser-known views of *Sefer Yeṣirah*, see *Siddur Raschi*, 82, §178; 256–257, §514. See also in the important work of Ben-Shachar on the commentary to *Sefer Yeṣirah* that was attributed to Saadya: Na'ama Ben-Shachar, *Commentary to Sefer Yeṣirah Attributed to R. Saadya Gaon* (Los Angeles: Cherub Press, 2015), 42–44, 211 [Hebrew].

43. b. Ḥagiga 13a.

44. Scholem, *Kabbalah and Its Symbolis*, 169n1; Idel, *Golem*, English edition, xviii; 30–31. For an alternative point of view, see Liebes, *Ars Poetica*, 63–64.

45. Idel, *Golem*, English edition, Idid 14.

46. Shoshana, ed., *Job with Commentaries*, 173.

47. Genesis Rabbah 1:1.

48. On Rashi's interpretation of Job 28 and his view of mystical traditions in *Sefer Yeṣirah*, see Sara Japhet, *The Commentary of Rabbi Samuel Ben Meir (Rashbam) on the Book of Job* (Jerusalem: Magnes Press, 2000), 154–157 [Hebrew].

49. I would like to thank Moshe Idel for drawing my attention to this *piyyut* commentary.

50. The meaning of the words *tseruf ilumekha* (צרוף עילומך) is not clear. I think that it refers, as the commentator saw, to combining (*tseruf*) the letters of God's ineffability (*ilumekha*), i.e., his ineffable name.

51. The form *yeṣirat* (יצירת) instead of *yeṣirah* (יצירה) is probably the result of a scribal error.

52. Oxford, Bodleian Library Ms. Opp. 171 (Neubauer 1207), 124v.

53. In late antique and early medieval Jewish sources, the word צפיה describes a mystical vision of the heavenly realm. See Eliezer Ben-Yehuda, *A Complete Dictionary of Ancient and Modern Hebrew*, edited by Naftali Herz Tur-Sinai (Jerusalem: Ben-Yehuda, 1951), 11:5593 [Hebrew]. On this sense of the word, Gershom Scholem wrote: "In the Hebrew of the oldest esoteric texts from the Talmudic period, the verb *tsafah* always has this meaning of a profound contemplative vision" (*Kabbalah and Its Symbolism*, 170n2). Cf. Idel, "Golems and God," 237. On the word צפיה in the conjunction of *Sefer Yeṣirah* and the Hekhalot literature, see Hayman, "*Sefer Yesira* and the Hekhalot," 74.

54. *Sefer Yeṣirah*, §64, Ms. Vat. 299: הדין ספר אותיות דאברהם אבינו דמתקרי הלכות יצירה. כל דצפי ביה לית שיעור לחוכמתיה.

55. *Sefer Yeṣirah*, §64.

56. Yehudah Barzillai (Halberstam), 100. The popularity of this version is also made clear later in Barzillai's writings, where he rejects views attributing *Sefer Yeṣirah* to Abraham. Thus Barzillai does not base his argument on the last part of *Sefer Yeṣirah*, which reads: "When Abraham our father came, and looked, and saw, and investigated, and understood, and carved, and combined, and hewed, and pondered, and succeeded" (*Sefer Yeṣirah*, §61, Ms. Vat. 299) but rather on the aforementioned version of כל דיצפיה ביה ("whoever contemplates it"). Barzillai argues: "It is possible that because of this the people of this generation wrote: 'This is the book of the letters of Abraham our father,' and not because it is necessarily known that it was handed down to us from him [Abraham], [and later] from one sage to another" (Yehudah Barzillai (Halberstam), 101).

57. On צפיה, see above, n. 53.

58. See Scholem, *Kabbalah and Its Symbolism*, 169–170; Idel, *Golem*, English edition, 14–15; Peter Schäfer, "The Magic of the Golem: The Early Development of the Golem Legend," *Journal of Jewish Studies* 46 (1995): 257; Liebes, *Ars Poetica*, 65–71.

59. On Abraham as God's son, see Idel, *Ben: Sonship*, 133–134.

60. *Sefer Yeṣirah*, §61, Ms. Parma 2784.14, with a few changes of mine.

61. I agree with Scholem's argument that the description of the creation of the world in the introduction to *Sefer Yeṣirah*, as in this short quotation, is "purely contemplative" (Scholem, *Kabbalah and Its Symbolism*, 178), as opposed to Idel's view of it as practical magic (Idel, *Golem*, English edition, 20).

62. *Sefer Yeṣirah*, §64, Ms. Vat. 299.

63. See above, nn. 2–6.

64. On Jewish mysticism in the period between the geonic period and the end of the twelfth century, see, e.g., Ithamar Gruenwald, "Jewish Mysticism's Transition from *Sefer Yeṣirah* to the *Bahir*," *Jerusalem Studies in Jewish Thought* 6 (1987): 15–54 [Hebrew]; Ronit Meroz, "The Middle Eastern Origins of the Kabbalah," *Journal for the Study of Sephardic and Mizrahi Jewry* 1 (2007): 39–56; Klaus Herrmann, "Jewish Mysticism in the Geonic Period: The Prayer of Rav Hamnuna Sava," in *Jewish Studies Between the Disciplines: Papers in Honor of Peter Schäfer on the Occasion of His 60th Birthday*, edited by Klaus Herrmann et al. (Leiden: Brill, 2003), 187–217; Rina Drory, *The Emergence of Jewish-Arabic Literary Contacts at the Beginning of the Tenth Century* (Tel Aviv: Hakibbutz Hameuchad, 1988), 25–28 [Hebrew]; Arthur Green, *Keter: The Crown of God in Early Jewish Mysticism* (Princeton, N.J.: Princeton University Press, 1997); Reimund Leicht and Joseph Yahalom, "*Sefer Zeh Sefer Toledot Adam*: An Unknown Esoteric Midrash on Genesis 5:1 from the Geonic Period," *Ginzei Qedem: Genizah Research Annual* 4 (2008): 9–82; Wolfson, *Speculum That Shines*; Wolfson, "The Theosophy of Shabbetai Donnolo"; Moshe

Idel, *Kabbalah: New Perspectives* (New Haven, Conn.: Yale University Press, 1988); Idel, *Ben: Sonship*; Michael Fishbane, *Biblical Myth and Rabbinic Mythmaking* (Oxford: Oxford University Press, 2003), 3–13; Fishbane, *Exegetical Imagination: On Jewish Thought and Theology* (Cambridge, Mass.: Harvard University Press, 1998), 22–40.

EPILOGUE

1. See, e.g., Langermann, "Hebrew Scientific Literature"; Wasserstrom, "*Sefer Yesira* and Early Islam"; Wasserstrom, "Further Thoughts"; Herrmann, *Sefer Jeẓira*, 184–204.

2. The role and the influence of Syriac sources on the Arabic renaissance is a complicated issue; see the survey study, Hidemi Takahashi, "Syriac as the Intermediary in Scientific Graeco-Arabica: Some Historical and Philological Observations," *Intellectual History of the Islamicate World* 3 (2015): 66–97. See also Dimitri Gustas, *Greek Thought, Arabic Culture: The Graeco-Arabic Translation Movement in Baghdad and Early 'Abbāsid Society* (New York: Routledge, 1998).

3. See Appendix 1.

4. See Meroz, "Interreligious Polemic."

APPENDIX 1

I would like to thank my dear friend Michael Ebstein for his assistance in writing this appendix. Needless to say, all mistakes are mine alone.

1. Wasserstrom, "*Sefer Yesira* and Early Islam"; idem, "Further Thoughts"; Langermann, "Hebrew Scientific Literature."

2. Even Wasserstrom, in his first article, said that the Syriac possibility should be seriously examined (Wasserstrom, "*Sefer Yesira* and Early Islam," 15).

3. See above, pp. Introduction nn1–6.

4. *Sefer Yeṣirah*, §§31–34, Ms. Vat. 299.

5. This element is named throughout the discussion about the letters A-M-Š in *Sefer Yeṣirah*, both as *awir* and *ruaḥ*. See, in Appendix 2, §§23–36.

6. Louis Massignon, *Salmân Pâk et les prémices spirituelle de l'Islam iranien* (Tours: Arrault et cie, 1934), 394.

7. Paul Kraus, *Jābir Ibn Ḥayyān: Contribution à l'Histoire des Idées Scientifiques dans l'Islam* (Cairo: Institut français d'archéologie orientale du Caire Institut d'Egypte, 1942), 2:227–270, esp. 266–269.

8. Henry Corbin, *Avicenna and the Visionary Recital*, translated by Willard R. Trask (Dallas: Spring, 1980), 276.

9. Allony, "Zunz, Krauss, and Scholem," 55.

10. Wasserstrom, "*Sefer Yesira* and Early Islam"; idem, "Further Thoughts."

11. Cf. Kraus: "Dans le judaïsme, c'est Aaron qui prend la place de 'Alī aux côtés de Moïse (=Mūsā=mīm). Ce fait ne suffit-il pas pour expliquer la raison qui aurait amené les gnostiques juifs à remplacer le 'Ayn par le Alif, première consonne du nom hébreu de Aaron?" (Kraus, *Jābir Ibn Ḥayyān*, 267n6). Cf. Wasserstrom, "*Sefer Yesira* and Early Islam," 3.

12. Liebes, *Ars Poetica*, 234–235.

13. See, e.g., Donald R. Hill, "The Literature of Arabic Alchemy," in *Religion, Learning and Science in the Abbasid Period*, edited by Michael J. L. Young et al. (Cambridge: Cambridge University Press, 1990), 333–334.

14. Jābir Ibn Ḥāyyan, *Texte choisis*, edited by Paul Kraus (Paris: G. P. Maisonneuve, 1935), 1:115–125.

15. See Heinz Halm, *Kosmologie und Heilslehre der frühen Ismāʿīlīya: Eine Studie zur islamischen Gnosis* (Wiesbaden: Steiner in Komm, 1978), 161; Michael Brett, "The Mīm, the 'Ayn and the Making of Ismāʿīlism," *Bulletin of the School of Oriental and African Studies* 54 (1994): 25–39.

16. Wasserstrom, "*Sefer Yesira* and Early Islam."

17. See Meir M. Bar-Asher and Aryeh Kofsky, *The Nuṣayrī 'Alawī Religion: An Enquiry into Its Theology and Liturgy* (Leiden: Brill, 2002), 191.

18. On the Islamic science of letters, its origins, and development, see Lory, *La science de lettres*, 41ff., and, most recently, Ebstein, *Mysticism and Philosophy*, 77–122.

19. See Chapter 3, n58.

APPENDIX 2

1. This paragraph is missing from Ms. Vatican 299 and was added according to the Saadya recension of the Cairo Geniza (T.S. K21/56).

APPENDIX 3

1. It seems that עצש"ט is a miscopy of מצש"ט since ע and מ might look similar. מצש"ט in the AṬBḤ letter exchange method is סירא. On the AṬBḤ method, see Paz and

Weiss, "From Encoding to Decoding." I would like to thank Yakir Paz for suggesting this interpretation to me.

2. Ps. 106:2.

3. Gen. 18:17.

4. Instead of אל.

5. Jer. 50:36.

6. b. Berakhot 63b; b. Ta'anit 7a; b. Makot 10a.

7. The word was omitted in Ms. Vat. 299. I added it, according to Ms. Parma 2784.

8. Eccles. 4:9.

9. Jer. 10:10.

10. From this point on, the last two lines were copied again on the next page by the same scribe.

Bibliography

PRIMARY SOURCES

Albeck, Hanoch, ed. *Midrash Berešit Rabbati: Ex libro R. Mosis Haddaršan*. Jerusalem: Meqize nirdamim, 1940.

Apocryphal: Gospels, Acts and Revelations. Edited by Alexander Walker. Edinburgh: Clark, 1911.

Aristotle. "Metaphysics." In *The Complete Works of Aristotle*, edited by Jonathan Barnes and translated by William D. Ross, vol. 2. Princeton, N.J.: Princeton University Press.

Artemidorus. *The Interpretation of Dreams*. Translated by Robert J. White. Park Ridge, N.J.: Noyes Press, 1975.

Avoth de-Rabbi Nathan: Solomon Schechter Edition with References to Parallels in the Two Versions and to the Addenda in the Schechter Edition. Prolegomenon by Menahem Kister. New York: Jewish Theological Seminary Press, 1997.

Bandt, Cordula, ed. and trans. *Der Traktat "Von Mysterium der Buchstaben."* Berlin: W. De Gruyter, 2007.

Beck, Edmund, ed. and trans. *Des Heiligen Ephraem des Syrers Hymnen de Nativitate*. Louvain: Secr. du Corpus, 1959.

Becker, Adam H., ed. and trans. *Sources for the Study of the School of Nisibis*. Liverpool: Liverpool University Press, 2008.

Ben-Ḥayyim, Zeev, ed. and trans. *Tībåt Mårqe: A Collection of Samaritan Midrashim*. Jerusalem: Israel Academy of Sciences and Humanities, 1988.

Buber, Salomon, ed. *Midrasch Echa Rabbati*. Vilna: Wittwe & Gebrüder Romm, 1899.

———. *Midrasch Tanḥuma*. Vilna: Wittwe & Gebrüder Rom, 1885.

———. *Midrasch Tehilim: Schocher tob*. Vilna: Wittwe & Gebrüder Romm, 1891.

———. *Midrash Samuel: Agadische Abhandlung über das Buch Samuel*. Cracow: Fischer, 1893.

———. *Siddur Raschi: Ritualwerk R. Salomo ben Isaak Zugeschrieben*. Berlin: Meqize nirdamim, 1911 [Hebrew].

Buckley, Jorunn Jacobsen, ed. and trans. *The Scroll of Exalted Kingship*. New Haven, Conn.: American Oriental Society, 1993.

Charlesworth, James H., ed. *The Old Testament Pseudepigrapha*. Vols. 1–2. Garden City, N.Y.: Doubleday, 1985.

Cohen, Martin S. *The Shi'ur Qomah: Liturgy and Theurgy in Pre-Kabbalistic Jewish Mysticism*. New York: University Press of America, 1983.

Davidson Thomas, trans. *The Grammar of Dionysios Thrax*. St. Louis, 1874.

Drower, Ethel S., trans. *Alf Trisar Šuialia: The Thousand and Twelve Questions*. Berlin: Akad, 1960.

Dunansky, Shimshon, ed. *Shir haShirim Rabbah*. Tel Aviv: Dvir, 1980.

Elazar of Worms. *Commentary on Sefer Yeṣirah*. Przemysl: Ḥ. A. Zupniḳ ṿe-H. Ḳnoller, 1883.

Enelow, Hyman G., ed. *The Mishnah of Rabbi Eliezer, or, the Midrash of Thirty-Two Hermeneutic Rules*. New York: Bloch, 1931.

Etheridge, John W., ed. *The Targums of Onkelos and Jonathan ben Uzziel of the Pentateuch with Fragments of the Jerusalem Targum*. Hoboken, N.J.: Ktav, 1969.

Eusebius of Caesarea. *Preparation for the Gospel*. Translated by Edwin Hamilton Gifford. Eugene, Ore.: Wipf and Stock, 2002.

Freedman, Harry, and Maurice Simon, eds. *Midrash rabbah*. Vols. 1–2 (Genesis). London: Soncino Press, 1951.

Friedlander, Gerald, trans. *Pirḳê de Rabbi Eliezer*. New York: Hermon, 1970.

Friedmann (Ish-Shalom), Meir, ed. *Pesikta Rabbati*. Vienna: Josef Kaiser IX, 1880.

Godley, Alfred D., trans. *Herodotus*. Loeb Classical Library. Cambridge, Mass.: Heinemann, 1920.

Halberstam, Solomon Joachim, ed. *Commentar zum Sepher Jezira von R. Jehuda b. Barsilai*. Berlin: Meqize nirdamim, 1885.

Harris, J. Rendel, ed. *An Early Christian Psalter*. London: J. Nisbet, 1910.

Hayman, Peter A., ed. *Sefer Yesira: Edition, Translation and Text-Critical Commentary*. Tübingen: Mohr Siebeck, 2004.

Hebbelynck, Adolphe, ed. and trans. *Les Mystères des Lettres Grecques: D'après un Manuscript Copte-Arabe*. Louvain: Istas, 1902.

Horovitz, Chaim M., ed. *Pirkei d'Rabbi Eliezer*. Jerusalem: Makor, 1972. Originally published in Michael Higger, "Pirkei Rabbi Eliezer," *Horeb* 8 (1946): 82–119; 9 (1947): 94–166; 10 (1948): 185–294.

Horovitz, Haim S., and Israel A. Rabin, eds. *Mekhilta d'Rabbi Ismael*. Jerusalem: Bamberger & Wahrmann, 1960. Repr. of Frankfurt, 1928–1931.

Ibn Ḥāyyan, Jābir. *Textes choisis*. Edited by Paul Kraus. Vol. 1: *Textes Choisis*. Paris: G. P. Maisonneuve, 1935.

Irenaeus of Lyons, Saint. *Against the Heresies*. Translated by Dominic J. Unger. Vols. 1–3. New York: Paulist Press, 1992.

Jellinek, Adolf, ed. *Bet haMidrash*. 3rd ed. Vols. 1–6. Jerusalem: Wahrmann, 1967.

Josephus Flavius. *The Jewish War*, IV–VII. Translated by H. St. J. Thackeray. Loeb Classical Library. London: William Heinemann, 1928.

Jowett, Benjamin, ed. and trans. *The Dialogues of Plato in 5 vols*. New York: Scribner, 1892.

Kafiḥ, Joseph, ed. and trans. *The Commentary of Saadya Gaon on* Sefer Yeṣirah. Jerusalem: Ha-Va'ad le-Hotsaat Sifre Rasag, 1972.

Ketterer, Eliane, ed. "*The Alphabet of Rabbi Aqiba: Version A and Version B:* The Name of This Midrash, Its Trends, Its Ideas, and Its Relations with Different Streams in Judaism and Christianity." Ph.D. diss., Hebrew University, 2005 [Hebrew].

Labourt, Jérôme, ed. and trans. *Saint Jérôme Lettres*, 1–3. Paris: Les belles lettres, 1951.

Lieberman, Saul, ed. *Deuteronomy Rabbah*. 3rd rev. ed. Jerusalem: Wahrmann, 1974.

Macdonald, John, ed. and trans. *Memar Marqah: The Teaching of Marqah*. Vols. 1–2. Berlin: Töpelmann, 1963.

Mandelbaum, Bernard, ed. *Pesikta de-Rav Kahana According to an Oxford Manuscript with Variants from All Known Mss. and Genizoth Fragments and Parallel Passages*. New York: Jewish Thelogical Seminary Press, 1962.

Margulies, Mordechai, ed. *Midrash Wayyikra Rabbah*. Jerusalem: Wahrmann, 1972.

McVey, Kathleen E., trans. *Ephrem the Syrian*: *Hymns*, New York: Paulist Press, 1989.

Nicomachus apud C. Janus. "Musici Scriptores Graeci." In "Gnosticism and Platonism, with Special Reference to *Marsanes* (NHC 10,1)," translated by Birger A. Pearson. *Harvard Theological Review* 77 (1984): 69. Originally published in Nicomachus apud C. Janus, *Musici Scriptores Graeci*, 276–277 (Leipzig: Teubner, 1895; Hildesheim: Olms, 1962).

Numbers Rabbah. Jerusalem: H. Vagshal, 2001.

Plutarch. "Moralia, the E at Delphi." Translated by Frank Cole Babbitt. Loeb Classical Library 306, Vol 5. 194–253. Cambridge, Mass.: Harvard University Press, 1969.

Robinson, James M., ed. *The Nag Hammadi Library in English*. Translated by members of the Coptic Gnostic Library Project. Leiden: Brill, 1977.

Schäfer, Peter, ed. *Geniza-Fragmente zur Hekhalot-Literatur*. Texts and Studies in Ancient Judaism. Tübingen: J. C. B. Mohr, 1984.

———. *Synopse zur Hekhalot Literatur.* Tübingen: Mohr Siebeck, 1981.

Scher, Addaï, trans. *Cause de la Fondation des Écoles.* Turnhout: Éditions Brepols, 1981.

Schmidt, Carl, ed. *Pistis Sophia.* Translated by Violet MacDermot. Nag Hammadi Studies 9. Coptic Gnostic Library. Leiden: Brill, 1978.

Shabbatai Donnolo's Sefer Ḥakhmoni: Introduction, Critical Text, and Annotated English Translation. Edited by Piergabriele Mancuso. Leiden: Brill, 2010.

Shinan, Avigdor, ed. *Midrash Shemot Rabbah: Chapters I–XIV: A Critical Edition Based on a Jerusalem Manuscript with Variants, Commentary, and Introduction.* Jerusalem: Dvir, 1984.

Shoshana, Avraham, ed. *The Book of Job with the Commentaries of Rashi, Rabbenu Jacob b. Meir Tam and Disciple of Rashi.* Jerusalem: Makhon Ofek—Sifriyat Fridberg, 1999 [Hebrew].

Su-Min, Ri. *Le Caverne des Trésors: Les deux recensions syriaques.* Louvain: E. Peeters, 1987.

Taylor, Thomas, trans. *Commentaries of Proclus on the Timaeus of Plato in Five Books.* London, 1820.

Theodor, Judah, and Hanoch Albeck, eds. *Bereishit Rabbah.* Jerusalem: Wahrmann, 1965.

Townsend, John T., trans. *Midrash Tanḥuma.* Hoboken, N.J.: Ktav, 1997.

Vajda, Georges, ed. "R. Elḥanan ben Yakar of London's First Commentary of *Sefer Yeṣirah.*" *Kobetz al Yad* 6, no. 1 (1966): 147–197 [Hebrew].

———. *Le Commentaire sur le "Livre de la Création" de Dūnaš ben Tāmīm de Kairouan (Xe siècle).* Edited by Paul B. Fenton. Rev. ed. Collection de la Revue des Études Juives. Paris: Peeters, 2002.

Veilleux, Armand, trans. *Pachomian Koinonia III: Instructions, Letters and Other Writings of Saint Pachomius and His Disciples.* Kalamazoo, Mich.: Cistercian, 1982.

Vosté, Jacques-M., and Ceslas Van den Eynde, eds. and trans. *Commentaire d'Iso'dad de Merv sur l'Ancien Testament.* Louvain: Secr. du Corpus, 1955.

Zosimos of Panopolis. *On the Letter Omega.* Edited and translated by Howard M. Jackson. Missoula, Mont.: Scholars, 1978.

Zucker, Moshe, ed. and trans. *A Critique Against the Writings of R. Saadya Gaon, by R. Mubashshir Halevi.* New York: P. Feldheim, 1955 [Hebrew].

SECONDARY SOURCES

Abrams, Daniel. "A History of the Unique Cherub: A Review Essay of Joseph Dan, *The Unique Cherub: A School of Mystics and Esoterics in Medieval Germany.*" *Jewish Quarterly Review* 90, nos. 3–4 (2000): 394–404.

———. *Kabbalistic Manuscripts and Textual Theory*. Jerusalem: Cherub Press, 2010.

Adelman, Rachel. *The Return of the Repressed: Pirqe de-Rabbi Eliezer and the Pseudepigrapha*. Leiden: Brill, 2009.

Allony, Nehemya. "Saadya's Works." In *Studies in Medieval Philology and Literature: Collected Papers*. Prepared for publication by Yosef Tobi and Robert Attal; editorial advice, S. Morag. Vol. 1. Jerusalem: Mekhon Ben Zevi, 1986 [Hebrew].

———. "Zunz, Krauss, and Scholem Teach Their Theories of *Sefer Yeṣirah*." *Sinai* 74 (1974): 42–66 [Hebrew].

Amélineau, Émile. "Les Traités Gnostiques d'Oxford (Deuxième Article)." *Revue de l'Histoire des Religions* 21 (1890): 261–294.

Bacher, Wilhelm. *Die Anfänge der hebräische Grammatik*. Leipzig: Brockhaus, 1895.

Baeck, Leo. "Zum *Sepher Jezira*." In *Aus drei Jahrtausende: Wissenschaftliche Untersuchungen und Abhandlungen zur Geschichte des jüdischen Glaubens*, 382–397. Berlin: Schocken, 1938.

Bar-Asher Siegal, Michal. *Early Christian Monastic Literature and the Babylonian Talmud*. New York: Cambridge University Press, 2013.

Bar-Asher, Meir M., and Aryeh Kofsky. *The Nuṣayrī 'Alawī Religion: An Enquiry into Its Theology and Liturgy*. Leiden: Brill 2002.

Bar-Ilan, Meir. *Astrology and Other Sciences Among the Jews of Israel in the Roman-Hellenistic and Byzantine Periods*. Jerusalem: Mosad Bialik, 2010 [Hebrew].

Bar-On, Shraga, and Yakir Paz. "The Lord's Allotment Is His People: The Myth of the Election of Israel by Casting of Lots and the Gnostic-Christian-Pagan-Jewish Polemic." *Tarbiz* 79 (2010): 23–62 [Hebrew].

Becker, Adam H. *Fear of God and the Beginning of Wisdom: The School of Nisibis and the Christian Scholastic Culture in Late Antique Mesopotamia*. Philadelphia: University of Pennsylvania Press, 2006.

———. "The Comparative Study of 'Scholasticism' in Late Antique Mesopotamia: Rabbis and East Syrians." *AJS Review* 34 (2010): 91–113.

Ben-Shachar, Na'ama. *Commentary to Sefer Yeṣirah Attributed to R. Saadya Gaon*. Los Angeles: Cherub Press, 2015 [Hebrew].

Ben-Shammai, Haggai. "Saadya's Goal in His Commentary on *Sefer Yezira*." In *A Straight Pass: Studies in Medieval Philosophy and Culture: Essays in Honor of Arthur Hyman*, edited by Ruth Link-Salinger, 1–9. Washington, D.C.: Catholic University of America Press, 1988.

Ben-Yehuda, Eliezer. *A Complete Dictionary of Ancient and Modern Hebrew*. Edited by Naftali Herz Tur-Sinai. Vol. 11. Jerusalem: Ben-Yehuda, 1951 [Hebrew].

Bitton-Ashkelony, Brouria, and Aryeh Kofsky. *The Monastic School of Gaza*. Leiden: Brill, 2006.

Bohak, Gideon. *Ancient Jewish Magic: A History*. Cambridge: Cambridge University Press, 2008.

———. "Greek-Hebrew Gematrias in 3 Baruch and in Revelation." *Journal for the Study of the Pseudepigrapha* 7 (1990): 119–121.

———. "The Hidden Hekhalot: Toward Reconstructing an Unknown Hekhalot Composition from the Cairo Geniza." *Tarbiz* 82 (2014): 407–446.

Bonfil, Reuven. "The Cultural and Religious Traditions of French Jewry in the Ninth Century." In *Studies in Jewish Mysticism Presented to Isaiah Tishby on His Seventy-Fifth Birthday*, edited by Joseph Dan and Joseph Hacker. *Jerusalem Studies in Jewish Thought* 3, nos. 1–2 (1986): 327–348 [Hebrew].

Boyarin, Daniel. *Socrates and the Fat Rabbis*. Chicago: University of Chicago Press, 2009.

Brett, Michael. "The Mīm, the 'Ayn and the Making of Ismā'īlism." *Bulletin of the School of Oriental and African Studies* 54 (1994): 25–39.

Boustan, Ra'anan. "Rabbinazation and the Making of Early Jewish Mysticism." *Jewish Quarterly Review* 101 (2011): 482–501.

Cavigneaux, Antoine. "Aux Sources du Midrash: L'Herméneutique Babylonienne." *Aula Orientalis* 5 (1987): 243–255.

Chadwick, Henry. "Pachomios and the Idea of Sanctity." In *The Byzantine Saint: University of Birmingham Fourteenth Spring Symposium of Byzantine Studies*, edited by Sergei Hackel, 11–24. London: Fellowship of Saint Alban and Saint Sergius, 1981.

Cohen, Jeremy. *Living Letters of the Law: Ideas of the Jew in Medieval Christianity*. Los Angeles: University of California Press, 1999.

Cohn-Sherbok, Dan. "The Alphabet in Mandaean and Jewish Gnosticism." *Religion* 11 (1981): 227–234.

Corbin, Henry. *Avicenna and the Visionary Recital*. Translated by Willard R. Trask. Dallas: Spring Publications, 1980.

Cox-Miller, Patricia. "In the Praise of Nonsense." In *Classical Mediterranean Spirituality*, edited by Arthur H. Armstrong, 481–505. New York: Crossroad, 1986.

Dan, Joseph. "The Commentary of R. Yehuda ben Barzillai Barceloni to *Sefer Yeṣirah*: Its Character and Trends." In *Ma'asu'ot: Studies in Kabbalistic Literature and Jewish Philosophy in Memory of Prof. Ephraim Gottlieb*, edited by Michal Oron and Amos Goldreich, 99–119. Jerusalem: Mosad Bialik, 1994 [Hebrew].

———. *History of Jewish Mysticism and Esotericism*. Vols. I–II. Jerusalem: Zalman Shazar Center for Jewish History, 2009–2016 [Hebrew].

———. *Jewish Mysticism: Studies in Jewish Mysticism in Late Antiquity*. Vol. 1. Northvale, N.J.: Jason Aronson, 1998.

———. "Rashi and the Merkavah." In *Rashi, 1040–1990: Hommage à Ephraïm E. Urbach: congrès européen des études juives*, edited by Gabrielle Sed-Rajna, 259–264. Paris: Éditions du Cerf, 1993.

———. "Three Phases of the History of the *Sefer Yezira*." *Frankfurter Judaistische Beiträge* 21 (1994): 7–29.

Darling, Robin Anne. "Narsai of Nisibis: On the Expression 'In the Beginning' and Concerning the Existence of God." In *Biblical Interpretation*, edited by Joseph Wilson Trigg, 203–220. Wilmington, Del.: Michael Glazier, 1988.

Darmesteter, Arsène. "Anglais au XIV Siècle." *Revue des Études Juives* 4 (1882): 259–268.

Darshan, Guy. "Twenty-Four or Twenty-Two Books of the Bible and the Homeric Corpus." *Tarbiz* 77 (2007): 5–22 [Hebrew].

Davila, James R. *Descenders to the Chariot: The People Behind the Hekhalot Literature*. Leiden: Brill, 2001.

Delcor, Mathias. "La Légende de la Mort de Moïse dans le 'Memar Marqah' Comparée à Quelques Traditions Juives." In *New Samaritans Studies: Essays in Honour of G. D. Sixdenier*, edited by Alan D. Crown and Lucy Davey, 25–45. Sydney: Mandelbaum, 1995.

Deutsch, Nathaniel. *The Gnostic Imagination: Gnosticism, Mandaeism, and Merkabah Mysticism*. Leiden: Brill, 1995.

———. *Guardian of the Gate: Angelic Vice Regency in Late Antiquity*. Leiden: Brill, 1999.

Diringer, David. *The Alphabet: A Key to the History of Mankind*. London: Hutchinson's Scientific and Technical Publications, 1948.

Dornseiff, Franz. *Das Alphabet in Mystik und Magie*. 2nd ed. Leipzig: Teubner, 1925.

Drory, Rina. *The Emergence of Jewish-Arabic Literary Contacts at the Beginning of the Tenth Century*. Tel Aviv: Hakibbutz Hameuchad, 1988 [Hebrew].

Drower, Ethel S. *The Secret Adam: A Study of Naṣoraean Gnosis*. Oxford: Clarendon Press, 1960.

Drucker, Johanna. *The Alphabetic Labyrinth: The Letters in History and Imagination*. London: Thames and Hudson, 1995.

Ebstein, Michael. *Mysticism and Philosophy in al-Andalus: Ibn Masarra, Ibn al-ʿArabī, and the Ismāʿīlī Tradition*. Leiden: Brill, 2014.

Epstein, Abraham. *Of the Jewish Antiquities: Studies and Monographs*. Edited by Abraham M. Haberman. Jerusalem: Mosad Harav Kook, 1957 [Hebrew].

Ettisch, Ernst. *The Hebrew Vowels and Consonants as Symbols of Ancient Astronomic Concepts*. Translated by Harry Zohn. New York: Branden, 1987.

Fishbane, Michael. *Biblical Myth and Rabbinic Mythmaking*. Oxford: Oxford University Press, 2003.

———. *Exegetical Imagination: On Jewish Thought and Theology*. Cambridge, Mass.: Harvard University Press, 1998.

Fleischer, Ezra. "On the Antiquity of *Sefer Yeṣirah*: The Qilirian Testimony Revisited." *Tarbiz* 71 (2002): 405–432 [Hebrew].

Förster, Niclas. *Marcus Magus: Kult, Lehre und Gemeindeleben einer valentinianischen Gnostikergrouppe—Sammlung der Quellen und Kommentar*. Tübingen: Mohr Siebeck, 1999.

Fossum, Jarl E. *The Name of God and the Angel of the Lord*. Tübingen: Mohr Siebeck, 1985.

Frankfurter, David. "The Magic of Writing and Writing of Magic: The Power of the Word in Egyptian and Greek Traditions." *Helios* 21 (1994): 189–221.

———. *Religion in Roman Egypt: Assimilation and Resistance*. Princeton, N.J.: Princeton University Press, 1998.

Freudenthal, Gad. "'The Air Blessed Be He,' in *Sefer ha-Maskil*." *Da'at* 32 (1994): 187–234 [Hebrew].

Furstenberg, Yair. "The Rabbinic Ban on *Ma'aseh Bereshit*: Sources, Contexts, and Concerns." In *Jewish and Christian Cosmogony in Late Antiquity*, edited by Lance Jenott and Sarit Kattan Gribetz, 39–63. Tübingen: Mohr Siebeck, 2013.

Gafni, Isaiah. "Nestorian Literature as a Source for the History of the Babylonian Yeshivot." *Tarbiz* 51 (1982): 567–576 [Hebrew].

Galtier, Émile. "Sur les Mystères des Lettres Grecques." *Bulletin de l'Institut Français d'Archéologie Orientale* 2 (1902): 139–162.

Gaster, Moshe. *The Samaritans: Their History, Doctrines and Literature*. London: British Academy, 1925.

———. *Studies and Texts in Folklore, Magic, Mediaeval Romance, Hebrew Apocrypha, and Samaritan Archaeology*. 3 vols. New York: Ktav, 1971 [Hebrew].

Gersh, Stephen. *From Iamblichus to Eriugena: An Investigation of the Prehistory and Evolution of the Pseudo-Dionysian Tradition*. Leiden: Brill, 1978.

Ginzberg, Louis. *Of Halakhah and Aggadah: Research and Essays*. Tel Aviv: Dvir, 1960 [Hebrew].

Goehring, James E. *Ascetics, Society, and the Desert*. Harrisburg, Pa.: Trinity Press International, 1999.

Goldstein, Jonathan A. "Creation Ex Nihilo: Recantations and Restatements." *Journal of Jewish Studies* 38 (1987): 187–194.

———. "The Origins of the Doctrine of Creation Ex Nihilo." *Journal of Jewish Studies* 35 (1984): 127–135.

Goldstein, Ronnie. "A New Look at Deuteronomy 32:8–9 and 43 in the Light of Akkadian Sources." *Tarbiz* 79 (2010): 5–22 [Hebrew].

Goshen-Gottstein, Alon. "Is *Ma'aseh Bereshit* Part of Ancient Jewish Mysticism?." *Journal of Jewish Thought and Philosophy* 4, no. 2 (1995): 185–201.

Green, Arthur. *Keter: The Crown of God in Early Jewish Mysticism*. Princeton, N.J.: Princeton University Press, 1997.

Grözinger, Karl E. "The Names of God and the Celestial Powers: Their Function and Meaning in the Hekhalot Literature." *Jerusalem Studies in Jewish Thought* 6 (1987): 53–70.

Gruenwald, Ithamar. *Apocalyptic and Merkavah Mysticism*. Leiden: Brill, 1980.

———. "Jewish Mysticism's Transition from *Sefer Yeṣirah* to the *Bahir*." *Jerusalem Studies in Jewish Thought* 6 (1987): 15–54 [Hebrew].

———. "A Preliminary Critical Edition of *Sefer Yeṣirah*." *Israel Oriental Studies* 1 (1971): 132–177 [Hebrew].

———. "Some Critical Notes on the First Part of *Sefer Yeṣirah*." *Revue des Études Juives* 82 (1973): 475–512.

———. "Uses and Abuses of Gematria." In *Rabbi Mordechai Breuer Festschrift*, edited by M. Bar-Asher, 2:823–832. Jerusalem: Academon, 1992 [Hebrew].

———. "Writing, Inscription, and the Ineffable Name: Magic, Spirituality, and Mysticism." In *Massu'ot: Studies in Kabbalistic Literature and Jewish Philosophy in Memory of Prof. Ephraim Gottlieb*, edited by Michal Oron and Amos Goldreich, 75–98. Jerusalem: Mosad Bialik, 1994 [Hebrew].

Gustas, Dimitri. *Greek Thought, Arabic Culture: The Graeco-Arabic Translation Movement in Baghdad and Early 'Abbāsid Society (2nd–4th/ 8th–10th centuries)*. New York: Routledge, 1998.

Halm, Heinz. *Kosmologie und Heilslehre der frühen Ismā'īlīya: Eine Studie zur islamischen Gnosis*. Wiesbaden: Steiner in Komm, 1978.

Halperin, David J. *The Faces of the Chariot: Early Jewish Responses to Ezekiel's Vision*. Tübingen: Mohr Siebeck, 1988.

Hayman, Peter A. "The Doctrine of Creation in *Sefer Yesira*: Some Text Critical Problems." In *Rashi, 1040–1990: Hommage à Ephraïm E. Urbach: congrès européen des études juives*, edited by Gabrielle Sed-Rajna, 219–227. Paris: Éditions du Cerf, 1993.

———. "The Original Text of *Sefer Yeṣirah* or the 'Earliest Recoverable Text.'" In *Reflection and Refraction: Studies in Biblical Historiography in Honour of A. Graeme Auld*, edited by Robert Rezetko et al., 175–186. Leiden: Brill, 2007.

———. "*Sefer Yesira* and the Hekhalot Literature." *Jerusalem Studies in Jewish Thought* 6 (1987): 71–85.

———. "Some Observations on *Sefer Yeṣira*: Its Use of Scripture." *Journal of Jewish Studies* 35 (1984): 168–184.

———. "Was God a Magician? *Sefer Yesira* and Jewish Magic." *Journal of Jewish Studies* 4 (1989): 225–237.

Herrmann, Klaus. "Feuer aus Wasser zum Fortleben eines unbekannten *Sefer Yesira*-Kommentars in der Hekhalot-Literatur." *Frankfurter Judaistische Beiträge* 20 (1993): 43–95.

———. "Jewish Mysticism in the Geonic Period: The Prayer of Rav Hamnuna Sava." In *Jewish Studies Between the Disciplines: Papers in Honor of Peter Schäfer on the Occasion of His 60th Birthday*, edited by Klaus Herrmann, Margarete Schlüter, and Giuseppe Veltri, 187–217. Leiden: Brill, 2003.

———. "Rewritten Mystical Texts: The Transmission of the Hekhalot Literature in the Middle Ages." *Bulletin of the John Rylands University Library in Manchester* 75 (1993): 97–116.

———. *Sefer Jeẓira: Buch der Schöpfung*. Frankfurt am Main: Verlag der Weltreligionen, 2008.

———. "An Unknown Commentary on the *Book of Creation* (*Sefer Yeṣirah*) from the Cairo Genizah and Its Re-Creation Among the *Ḥaside Ashkenaz*." In *Creation and Re-Creation in Jewish Thought*, edited by Rachel Elior and Peter Schäfer, 103–112. Tübingen: Mohr Siebeck, 2005.

Hill, Donald R. "The Literature of Arabic Alchemy." In *Religion, Learning and Science in the Abbasid Period*, edited by Michael J. L. Young, John Derek Latham, and Robert Bertram Serjeant, 333–334. Cambridge: Cambridge University Press, 1990.

Howard, George. "The Tetragram and the New Testament." *Journal of Biblical Literature* 96 (1977): 63–83.

Idel, Moshe. *Ben: Sonship and Jewish Mysticism*. London: Continuum, 2007.

———. "The Evil Thought of the Deity." *Tarbiz* 49 (1980): 356–364 [Hebrew].

———. *Golem: Jewish Magical and Mystical Traditions on the Artificial Anthropoid*. Albany, N.Y.: SUNY, 1990.

———. *Golem: Magical and Mystical Jewish Traditions of the Artificial Anthropoid*. Translated by Azan Meir-Levi. Jerusalem: Schocken, 1996 [Hebrew].

———. "Golems and God: Mimesis and Confrontation." In *Mythen der Kreativität: Das Schöpferische zwischen Innovation und Hybris*, edited by Oliver Krüger, Refika Sarıönder, and Annette Deschner, 224–268. Frankfurt am Main: Lembeck, 2003.

———. *Kabbalah: New Perspectives*. New Haven, Conn.: Yale University Press, 1988.

———. *Language, Torah, and Hermeneutics in Abraham Abulafia*. Jerusalem: Schocken, 1994 [Hebrew].

———. "The World of Angels in Human Form." In *Studies in Jewish Mysticism Presented to Isaiah Tishby on His Seventy-Fifth Birthday*, edited by Joseph Dan and Joseph Hacker. *Jerusalem Studies in Jewish Thought* 3, nos. 1–2 (1984): 1–66 [Hebrew].

Janowitz, Naomi. *Icons of Power: Ritual Practices in Late Antiquity*. University Park: Pennsylvania State University Press, 2002.

Japhet, Sara. *The Commentary of Rabbi Samuel Ben Meir (Rashbam) on the Book of Job*. Jerusalem: Magnes Press, 2000 [Hebrew].

Jospe, Raphael. "Early Philosophical Commentaries on the *Sefer Yezirah*: Some Comments." *Revue des Études Juives* 149 (1990): 369–415.

Kahle, Paul E. *The Cairo Geniza*. 2nd ed. Oxford: Blackwell, 1959.

Kanarfogel, Ephraim. "Rashi's Awareness of Jewish Mystical Literature and Traditions." In *Raschi und sein Erbe*, edited by Daniel Krochmalkin, Hanna Lis, and Ronen Reichman, 23–34. Heidelberg: Heidelberg Universitätsverlag Winter, 2007.

Ketterer, Eliane. "*The Alphabet of Rabbi Aqiba*, Version A and Version B: The Name of This Midrash, Its Trends, Its Ideas, and Its Relations with Different Streams in Judaism and Christianity." Ph.D. diss., Hebrew University, 2005 [Hebrew].

Khan, Geoffrey. "The Pronunciation of *Reš* in the Tiberian Tradition of Biblical Hebrew," *Hebrew Union College Annual* 66 (1995): 67–80

Kister, Menahem. "*Tohu wa-Bohu*, Primordial Elements and Creation Ex Nihilo." *Jewish Studies Quarterly* 14 (2007): 229–256.

Knohl, Israel. *The Holy Name*. Or Yehuda: Dvir, 2012 [Hebrew].

———. "Sacred Architecture Dimensions of Biblical Poems." *Vetus Testamentum* 62, no. 2 (2012): 189–197.

Koltun-Fromm, Naomi. "Rock over Water: Prehistoric Rocks and Primordial Waters from Creation to Salvation in Jerusalem." In *Jewish and Christian Cosmogony in Late Antiquity*, edited by Lance Jenott and Sarit Kattan Gribetz, 240–254. Tübingen: Mohr Siebeck, 2013.

Kraus, Paul. *Jābir ibn Ḥayyān: Contribution à l'Histoire des Idées Scientifiques dans l'Islam*. Cairo: Institut français d'archéologie orientale du Caire Institut d'Egypte, 1942.

Kugel, James. *Traditions of the Bible: A Guide to the Bible as It Was at the Start of the Common Era*. Rev. ed. Cambridge, Mass.: Harvard University Press, 1998.

Kutscher, Yechezkel E. "Studies in North-Western Semantics." *Journal of Semitic Studies* 10 (1965): 25–34.

Kuyt, Anneleis. "Traces of a Mutual Influence of the *Ḥaside Ashkenaz* and the Hekhalot Literature." In *From Narbonne to Regensburg: Studies in Medieval Hebrew Texts*, edited by N. A. van Uchelen and Irene E. Zwiep, 62–86. Amsterdam: Juda Palache, 1993.

Lambert, Wilfred G. "An Address of Marduk to the Demons." *Archiv für Orientforschung* 17 (1956): 310–321.

Langenwalter, Anna Beht. "Agobard of Lyon: An Exploration of Carolingian Jewish-Christian Relations." Ph.D. diss., University of Toronto, 2001.

Langermann, Y. Tzvi. "On the Beginning of Hebrew Scientific Literature and on Studying History Through *Maqbilot*." *Aleph* 2 (2002): 169–176.

———. "A New Redaction of *Sefer Yeṣirah*?." *Kabbalah* 2 (1997): 49–63.

Leicht, Reimund, and Joseph Yahalom. "*Sefer Zeh Sefer Toledot Adam*: An Unknown Esoteric Midrash on Genesis 5:1 from the Geonic Period." *Ginzei Qedem: Genizah Research Annual* 4 (2008): 9–82.

Lesses, Rebecca M. *Ritual Practices to Gain Power: Angels, Incantations and Revelation in Early Jewish Mysticism*. Harrisburg, Pa.: Trinity Press International, 1998.

Levin, Israel. *Mystical Trends in the Poetry of Solomon Ibn Gabirol*. Lod: Habermann Institute for Literary Research, 1986 [Hebrew].

Lieber, Elinor. "An Ongoing Mystery: The So-Called Book of Medicines, Attributed to Asaf the Sage." *Bulletin of Judaeo-Greek Studies* 8 (1991): 18–25.

Lieberman, Saul. *Hellenism in Jewish Palestine: Studies in the Literary Transmission Belief and Manners of Palestine in the I Century BCE–IV Century CE*. New York: P. Feldheim, 1950.

Lieberman, Stephen J. "A Mesopotamian Background for the So-Called Aggadic Measures of Biblical Hermeneutics?." *Hebrew Union College Annual* 58 (1987): 157–226.

Liebes, Yehuda. *Ars Poetica in "Sefer Yeṣirah."* Jerusalem: Schocken, 2000 [Hebrew].

———. *Elisha's Sin*. 2nd ed. Jerusalem: Academon, 1990 [Hebrew].

———. "Rabbi Solomon Ibn Gabirol's Use of the *Sefer Yeṣirah* and a Commentary on the Poem 'I Love Thee.'" *Jerusalem Studies in Jewish Thought* 6 (1987): 73–123 [Hebrew].

———. "Response to Shlomo Morag's Arguments." *Tarbiz* 63 (1994): 143–144 [Hebrew].

———. "The Seven Double Letters *BGD KFRT*: On the Double *RESH* and the Background of *Sefer Yeṣirah*." *Tarbiz* 61 (1992): 237–247 [Hebrew].

Lorberbaum, Yair. *The Image of God: Halakhah and Aggadah*. Jerusalem: Schocken, 2004 [Hebrew].

Lory, Pierre. *La science de lettres en islam*. Paris: Dervy, 2004.

Massignon, Louis. *Salmân Pâk et les prémices spirituelle de l'Islam iranien*. Tours: Arrault et cie, 1934.

McDonough, Sean M. *YHWH at Patmos: Rev 1:4 in Its Hellenistic and Early Jewish Setting*. Tübingen: Mohr Siebeck, 1999.

McNeil, Brian. "Jesus and the Alphabet." *Journal of Theological Studies* 27 (1976): 126–128.

Melzer, Aviv. "Asaph the Physician: The Man and His Book: A Historical Philological Study of the Medical Treatise *The Book of Drugs*." Ph.D. diss., University of Wisconsin, Madison, 1972.

Merchavia, Chen-Melech. *The Church Versus Talmudic and Midrashic Literature: 500–1248*. Jerusalem: Mosad Bialik, 1970 [Hebrew].

Meroz, Ronit. "Between *Sefer Yezirah* and Wisdom Literature: Three Binitarian Approaches in *Sefer Yezirah*." *Journal for the Study of Religions and Ideologies* 18 (2007): 101–142.

———. "Interreligious Polemic, Messianism, and Revelation in the Short Recension of *Sefer Yeṣirah*." *Da'at* 81–82 (2016): 1–37 [Hebrew].

———. "The Middle Eastern Origins of the Kabbalah." *Journal for the Study of Sephardic and Mizrahi Jewry* 1 (2007): 39–56.

Merx, Adelbertus *Historia artis grammaticae apud Syros*. Leipzig: Brockhaus, 1889.

Morag, Shlomo. "The Seven Double Letters BGD KFRT." *Proceedings of Israeli Society for Biblical Research* 8 (1960): 207–242 [Hebrew].

———. "On the Seven Double Letters BGD KPRT and the Names Sarah-Sarai, Avram-Avraham." *Tarbiz* 63 (1994): 135–142 [Hebrew].

Paz, Yakir, and Tzahi Weiss. "From Encoding to Decoding: The AṬBḤ of R. Ḥiyya in Light of a Syriac, Greek, and Coptic Cipher." *Journal of Near Eastern Studies* 74 (2015): 45–65.

Pearson, Birger A. *Gnosticism and Christianity in Roman and Coptic Egypt*. New York: T&T Clark International, 2004.

Pines, Shlomo. "Points of Similarity Between the Exposition of the Doctrine of the *Sefirot* in the *Sefer Yezira* and a Text of the Pseudo-Clementine Homilies." *Proceedings of Israel Academy of Science and Humanities* 7, no. 3 (1989): 63–142.

Poirier, John C. *The Tongues of Angels: The Concept of Angelic Languages in Classical Jewish and Christian Texts*. Tübingen: Mohr Siebeck, 2010.

Richler, Benjamin, Malachi beit-Arié, and Nurit Pasternak. *Hebrew Manuscripts in the Vatican Library: Catalog*. Vatican: Biblioteca Apostolica Vaticana, 2008.

Rousseau, Philip. *Pachomius: The Making of a Community in Fourth-Century Egypt*. Berkeley: University of California Press, 1985.

Rubin, Milka. "The Language of Creation or the Primordial Language: A Case of Cultural Polemics in Antiquity." *Journal of Jewish Studies* 49 (1998): 306–333.

Sambursky, Shmuel. "The Term *Gematria*: Source and Meaning." *Tarbiz* 45 (1976): 268–271 [Hebrew].

Samir, Khalil. "Mysteries of Greek Letters." *Coptic Encyclopedia*, 6:1749–1750. New York: Macmillan, 1991.

Schäfer, Peter. "The Magic of the Golem: The Early Development of the Golem Legend." *Journal of Jewish Studies* 46 (1995): 249–261.

———. "Tradition and Redaction in Hekhalot Literature." *Journal for the Study of Judaism* 14 (1983): 172–181.

Schiffman, Lawrence, "A Forty-Two-Letter Divine Name in the Aramaic Magic Bowls." *Bulletin of the Institute of Jewish Studies* 1 (1973): 97–102.

Schlanger, Jacques E. "Sur le rôle du 'tout' dans la création selon Ibn Gabirol." *Revue des Études Juives* 124 (1965): 125–135.

Scholem, Gershom. *Kabbalah*. Jerusalem: Keter, 1974.

———. *Major Trends in Jewish Mysticism*. 3rd rev. ed. New York: Schocken, 1995.

———. "The Name of God and the Linguistic Theory of the Kabbala—Part I." *Diogenes* 79 (1972): 59–80.

———. "The Name of God and the Linguistic Theory of the Kabbala—Part II." *Diogenes* 80 (1973): 164–194.

———. *On the Kabbalah and Its Symbolism*. Translated by Ralph Manheim. New York: Schocken, 1965.

———. *On the Mystical Shape of the Godhead: Basic Concepts in the Kabbalah*. Translated by Joachim Neugroschel. New York: Schocken, 1991.

———. *The Origins of the Kabbalah and the Book Bahir: Lectures of Gershom Scholem*. Edited by Rivka Schatz. Jerusalem: Academon, 1962 [Hebrew].

Séd, Nicolas. "Une Cosmologie Juive du Haut Moyen Age: La Berayta di Maaseh Beresit: Le Texte, le Manuscrits et le Diagrammes." *Revue des Études Juives* 124 (1965): 23–123; 123 (1964): 259–305.

———. "Le Memar Samaritain, le *Sefer Yesira* et les 32 Sentiers de la Sagesse." *Revue de l'Histoire des Religions* 170 (1966): 159–184.

———. "Notes sur l'homélie no. 34 de Narsaï." *L'Orient Syrien* 10 (1965): 511–524.

Segal, Judah B. "The Jews of North Mesopotamia Before the Rise of Islam." In *Studies in the Bible Presented to Professor M. H. Segal by His Colleagues and Students*, edited by Joshua M. Grintz and Jacob Liver. Jerusalem: Kiryat Sefer, 1964, *32–*63.

———. "Qussaya and Rukkaka: A Historical Introduction." *Journal of Semitic Studies* 34 (1989): 83–91.

Segal, Moshe Zvi. *Basics of Hebrew Phonetics*. Jerusalem: Ha-sefer, 1928 [Hebrew].

Segol, Marla. *Word and Image in Medieval Kabbalah: The Text, Commentaries and Diagrams of Sefer Yetsirah*. New York: Palgrave Macmillan, 2012.

Shinan, Avigdor. *The Embroidered Targum: The Aggadah in Targum Pseudo-Jonathan to the Pentateuch*. Jerusalem: Magnes Press, 1992 [Hebrew].

Smith, Jonathan Z. *Map Is Not Territory: Studies in the History of Religions*. Leiden: Brill, 1978.

Sperber, Daniel. "On Sealing the Abysses." *Journal of Semitic Studies* 10 (1966): 168–174.

Stein, Dina. *Maxims, Magic, Myth: A Folkloristic Perspective on Pirkei deRabbi Eliezer*. Jerusalem: Magnes Press, 2005 [Hebrew].

Stroumsa, Guy G. "The Mystery of the Greek Letters: A Byzantine Kabbalah?." *Historia Religionum* 6 (2014): 35–44.

———. "A Nameless God: Judaeo-Christian and Gnostic." In *The Image of the Judaeo-Christians in Ancient Jewish and Christian Literature*, edited by Peter J. Tomson and Doris Lambers-Petry, 231–243. Tübingen: Mohr Siebeck, 2003.

———. "A Zoroastrian Origin to the *Sefirot*?." *Irano-Judaica* 3 (1994): 17–33.

Stroumsa, Sarah. *Dāwūd al-Muqammaṣ' Twenty Chapters: A Parallel Judeo-Arabic Edition Transliterated into Arabic Characters, with a Parallel English Translation, Notes, and Introduction*. Provo, Utah: Brigham Young University Press, 2017.

Swartz, Michael D. *Mystical Prayer in Ancient Judaism: An Analysis of Ma'aseh Merkavah*. Tübingen: Mohr Siebeck, 1992.

———. "Piyut and Heikhalot: Recent Research and Its Implications for the History of Ancient Jewish Liturgy and Mysticism." In *The Experience of Jewish Liturgy: Studies Dedicated to Menahem Schmelzer*, edited by Debra Reed Blank, 263–282. Leiden: Brill, 2011.

———. *Scholastic Magic, Ritual and Revelation in Early Jewish Mysticism*. Princeton, N.J.: Princeton University Press, 1966.

Takahashi, Hidemi. "Syriac as the Intermediary in Scientific Graeco-Arabica: Some Historical and Philological Observations." *Intellectual History of the Islamicate World* 3 (2015): 66–97.

Talmon, Refael. "Jacob of Edessa the Grammarian." In *Jacob of Edessa and the Syriac Culture of His Day*, edited by Bas ter Haar Romeny, 159–188. Leiden: Brill, 2008.

Tigay, Jeffrey H. "An Early Technique of Aggadic Exegesis." In *History, Historiography, and Interpretation: Studies in Biblical and Cuneiform Literature*, edited by Ḥayim Tadmor et al., 169–189. Jerusalem: Magnes Press, 1983.

Tur-Sinai, Naftali H. *The Language and the Book*. 3 vols. Jerusalem: Mosad Bialik, 1954 [Hebrew].

Urbach, Ephraim E. *The Sages: Their Concepts and Beliefs*. Jerusalem: Magnes Press, 1975.

———. "Tanḥuma-Yelamdenu Fragments." *Kovetz Al-Yad* 6 (1966): 1–54 [Hebrew].

Vidas, Moulie. "Greek Wisdom in Babylonia." In *Envisioning Judaism: Studies in Honor of Peter Schäfer on the Occasion of His Seventieth Birthday*, edited by Ra'anan S. Boustan et al., 287–305. Tübingen: Mohr Siebeck, 2013.

Wasserstrom, Steven M. "Further Thoughts on the Origins of *Sefer Yeṣirah*." *Aleph* 2 (2002): 201–221.

———. "*Sefer Yesira* and Early Islam: A Reappraisal." *Journal of Jewish Thought and Philosophy* 3 (1993): 1–30.

Weinstock, Israel. "A Clarification of the Version of *Sefer Yeṣirah*." In *Temirin*, edited by Israel Weinstock, 1: 9–61. Jerusalem: Mosad Harav Kook, 1972.

———. "Discovered Legacy of Mystic Writings Left by abu-Aharon of Baghdad." *Tarbiz* 32 (1963): 153–159 [Hebrew].

Weiss, Haim. *All Dreams Follow the Mouth: A Reading in the Talmudic Dream Tractate*. Or Yehuda: Dvir- Kineret-Zmora-Bitan 2011 [Hebrew].

Weiss, Tzahi. "Brief Comments on the Syrian Context of *Sefer Yeṣirah*." *Jerusalem Studies in Jewish Thought* 22 (2011): 75–89 [Hebrew].

———. "God of Israel—a Prince Before God: On the Meanings and the Origins of a Jewish Tradition from the Early Middle Ages." *Jewish Studies* 52 (2017): 129–142 [Hebrew].

———. *Letters by Which Heaven and Earth Were Created: The Origins and the Meanings of the Perceptions of Alphabetic Letters as Independent Units in Jewish Sources of Late Antiquity*. Jerusalem: Mosad Bialik, 2014 [Hebrew].

———. "The Perception of the Letters in the Samaritan *Memar Marqah* and in Its Equivalents in Rabbinic Sources and in the Book of Creation." *Jewish Studies* 43 (2006): 89–129 [Hebrew].

———. "The Reception of *Sefer Yeṣirah* and Jewish Mysticism in the Early Middle Ages." *Jewish Quarterly Review* 103, no. 1 (2013): 26–46.

———. "Soft and Hard: More Comments on the Syrian Context of *Sefer Yeṣirah*." *Kabbalah* 26 (2012): 229–242 [Hebrew].

Werblowsky, Zwi R. J. "Drower, E. S.: *The Secret Adam*." *Journal of Semitic Studies* 8 (1963): 129–133.

Wilkinson, Robert. *Tetragrammaton: Western Christians and the Hebrew Name of God: From the Beginnings to the Seventeenth Century*. Leiden: Brill, 2015.

Winston, David. "The Book of Wisdom's Theory of Cosmogony." *History of Religions* 11 (1971): 185–202.

———. "Creation Ex Nihilo Revisited: A Reply to Jonathan Goldstein." *Journal of Jewish Studies* 37 (1986): 88–91.

Wolfson, Elliot R. *Abraham Abulafia—Kabbalist and Prophet: Hermeneutics, Theosophy and Theurgy*. Los Angeles: Cherub Press, 1994.

———. *Along the Path: Studies in Kabbalistic Myth, Symbolism, and Hermeneutics*. Albany, N.Y.: SUNY, 1995.

———. "Female Imaging of the Torah: From Literary Metaphor to Religious Symbol." In *From Ancient Israel to Modern Judaism: Intellect in Quest of Understanding: Essays in Honor of Marvin Fox*, vol. 2, edited by Jacob Neusner, Ernest S. Frerichs, and Nahum M. Sarna, 271–307. Atlanta: Scholars Press, 1989.

———. "Inscribed in the Book of the Living: 'Gospel of Truth' and Jewish Christology.'" *Journal for the Study of Judaism* 38 (2007): 234–271.

———. "Jewish Mysticism: A Philosophical Overview." In *History of Jewish Philosophy*, vol. 2, edited by Daniel H. Frank and Oliver Leaman, 450–498. London: Routledge, 1997.

———. "The Theosophy of Shabbetai Donnolo, with Special Emphasis on the Doctrine of *Sefirot* in His *SY Ḥakhmoni*." *Jewish History* 6 (1992): 281–316.

———. *Through a Speculum That Shines: Vision and Imagination in Medieval Jewish Mysticism*. Princeton, N.J.: Princeton University Press, 1994.

Yahalom, Joseph. "*Shi'ur Qomah* in a Misidentified Qalirian Poem for Pentecost." *Kabbalah: Journal for the Study of Jewish Mystical Texts* 32 (2014): 93–133.

Yassif, Eli. *The Tales of Ben Sira in the Middle Ages: A Critical Text and Literary Studies*. Jerusalem: Magnes Press, 1984 [Hebrew].

Index

Acknowledgments

This book brings together previous studies of mine written in the past few years, mostly in Hebrew with new material. It took me a while to understand that out of my research into the meanings of the Hebrew alphabet and, subsequently, *Sefer Yeṣirah*, a portrait of unknown Jewish contexts was coalescing. I would like to thank the readers of my previous works and their publishers for all their questions and remarks. Chapters 1 and 2 of this book comprise some material from my Hebrew book *Otiot shenivreu bahen shamaaim veareṣ* (*Letters by Which Heaven and Earth Were Created*). Chapter 3 combines two Hebrew papers, with additional material that I came across after their publication. One paper, "Brief Comments on the Syrian Context of *Sefer Yeṣirah*," was published in *Jerusalem Studies in Jewish Thought*; the other, "Soft and Hard," in *Kabbalah*. Chapters 4 and 5 further develop "The Reception of *Sefer Yeṣirah* and Jewish Mysticism in the Early Middle Ages," published in the *Jewish Quarterly Review*.

Many friends and colleagues over the years have helped me evolve arguments about the context of *Sefer Yeṣirah*, and I would like to take this opportunity to thank them all: Daniel Abrams, Adam Afterman, Brouria Bitton-Ashkelony, Gideon Bohak, Jonathan Garb, Michael Ebstein, Michael Fagenblat, Michael Fishbane, Uri Gabbay, Yuval Harari, Klaus Herrmann, Moshe Idel, Yehuda Liebes, Ronit Meroz, Sara Offenberg, Dina Stein, Guy Stroumsa, Haim Weiss, and Elliot Wolfson. My thanks are also extended to Mark Joseph and Zvi Kunshtat for their assistance in editing the book and to David Luljak for preparing the index. I would like also to thank my academic home, the Open University of Israel, which gave me the necessary academic and financial support to write this book. A deep sense of gratitude goes to the University of Pennsylvania Press: to the editor Jerome E. Singerman, to the anonymous readers of the book, and to the editorial board of the Divinations series: Virginia Burrus, Derek Krueger, and, especially, Daniel Boyarin, who worked with me very closely on the manuscript and encouraged me to improve it. I owe a special debt of gratitude to Yakir Paz and Bella Fuchs: without their consistent help, none of this could have happened. Last but not least, thanks to my wife, Judith, and to our three inquisitive daughters: Miriam, Sarah, and Rachel—the beloved voices in my life.